PENTECOSTALISM AS A CHRISTIAN MYSTICAL TRADITION

Pentecostalism as a Christian Mystical Tradition

Daniel Castelo

WILLIAM B. EERDMANS PUBLISHING COMPANY
GRAND RAPIDS, MICHIGAN

Wm. B. Eerdmans Publishing Co.
2140 Oak Industrial Drive N.E., Grand Rapids, Michigan 49505
www.eerdmans.com

ISBN 978-0-8028-6956-2

Library of Congress Cataloging-in-Publication Data

Names: Castelo, Daniel, 1978– author.
Title: Pentecostalism as a Christian mystical tradition / Daniel Castelo.
Description: Grand Rapids : Eerdmans Publishing Co., 2017. |
    Includes bibliographical references and index.
Identifiers: LCCN 2016049800 | ISBN 9780802869562 (pbk. : alk. paper)
Subjects: LCSH: Pentecostalism. | Mysticism—Christianity.
Classification: LCC BR1644 .C386 2017 | DDC 270.8/2—dc23
    LC record available at https://lccn.loc.gov/2016049800

To Kimberly

Contents

Foreword

The link between Methodism, mysticism, and Pentecostalism may well be Phoebe Palmer, mother of the nineteenth-century Holiness Movement. Palmer, a lifelong Methodist, repeatedly used the phrase "baptism of the Holy Ghost" to indicate the experience of sanctification. This phrase came to be associated with Pentecostals after other Holiness denominations distanced themselves from Pentecostalism over time.

By "baptism of the Holy Ghost" Palmer referred not to ecstatic phenomena such as speaking in tongues but to a radically transformative encounter with the Holy Spirit, one that resulted in an outward life of holiness and social action. Baptism of the Spirit meant "purity and power," not strange phenomena. In her prayer for the dedication of the Garrett Biblical Institute in 1869, for example, Palmer said this:

> May this school of the prophets ever be a praise on the earth not only for literary advantages and soundness of creed, but for richness of divine unction; or in other words, for the reception of the full baptism of the Holy Ghost, on the part of all who, in coming time, shall be trained within these walls for the holy ministry. Surely, a holy work demands, first of all, a holy heart.[1]

Unfortunately, because John Wesley, the founder of Methodism, eschewed all mysticism because of his mistrust of apophatic spirituality, until the end of the twentieth century Methodism lacked the interpre-

---

1. Phoebe Palmer, *Selected Writings*, ed. Thomas C. Oden, Classics of Western Spirituality Series (New York: Paulist, 1988), 299. For an in-depth study of Palmer's mystical theology see Elaine A. Heath, *Naked Faith: The Mystical Theology of Phoebe Palmer*, Princeton Theological Monograph Series 8 (Eugene, OR: Pickwick Publications, 2009).

tive framework of mystical theology. For this reason Palmer's classically apophatic mysticism came to be misconstrued as a kind of naïve biblical fundamentalism that was caricatured or dismissed by subsequent interpreters. Though she was Methodism's own first-order mystic whose life and work were as significant as those of Catherine of Siena, Thérèse of Lisieux, and other Catholic mystics, Palmer's contributions as a mystic were largely forgotten until recently. When I discovered Palmer during my graduate education, I recognized her apophatic mysticism and devoted significant attention to a recovery of her voice. In particular it is important to note the link between Christian mysticism and social action that formed Palmer's spirituality and that are found in robust Pentecostalism.

One of the reasons I find Palmer's work compelling is that her understanding of baptism of the Holy Spirit is a necessary component of the life of missional engagement. During Palmer's lifetime she was a powerful social activist who inspired many others to work for women's rights, the abolition of slavery, immigrant resettlement support, and much more. That is to say, Palmer is an exemplar of the kind of Pentecostal mysticism that impacts the world beyond the church, tackling many forms of injustice.

A recovery of the grammar and theological framework of Christian mysticism for Pentecostalism includes the contributions of Phoebe Palmer, from whose spiritual descendants Pentecostalism in North America emerged. William J. Seymour, the pastor under whose leadership the Azusa Street Revival took place, was a Methodist Episcopal pastor influenced by the Holiness movement with its egalitarian emphases. Most of the resistance to Seymour's Pentecostalism and the Azusa Street Revival was because of the "scandalous" gender and racial reconciliation that were part of the movement.

I am very grateful for Daniel Castelo's work in this volume, which locates Pentecostalism, including the Azusa Street Revival, firmly within the ancient streams of Christian mysticism. With careful scholarship and attention to the history of marginalization of Pentecostalism in modern scholarship until quite recently, Castelo provides a compelling and necessary corrective. This book is essential reading for anyone who wishes to understand Christian mysticism in Protestant traditions, in Methodist traditions, and in the church universal.

Elaine A. Heath
Dean of the Divinity School and
Professor of Missional and Pastoral Theology
Duke Divinity School

Acknowledgments

This work assumes that the most theologically fruitful approach to Pentecostal beliefs and practices is through the language of spirituality and mysticism and that this approach can generate a number of possibilities within the contemporary realm of theological epistemology, especially when contrasted to many of the traditions loosely labeled "evangelical." The thrust of such proposals relies on insights and arguments culled over years of discussion and thought. I am grateful to the many people and events that have had a role in shaping me with regard to these themes so that this book could come to be.

In particular, I thank the community of the Pentecostal Theological Seminary for mentoring and shaping me in significant ways. I could not have written this text apart from the formative experiences I had there under the tutelage of some very capable and accessible professors. I also express my gratitude to my colleagues at Seattle Pacific University, including Margaret Diddams, director of the Center for Scholarship and Faculty Development, and Provost Jeff Van Duzer for awarding me a faculty research grant for the summer of 2014, which helped significantly in the completion of this manuscript. Also, I want to thank our theological librarian, Steve Perisho, who tirelessly and expeditiously supports my work by securing materials from a variety of libraries for me.

In 2011 I was named a winner of the John Templeton Award for Theological Promise; as part of that award, I received funds to pursue lectures at institutions that would host me. I thank the John Templeton Foundation for this kind of support for young scholars, as well as Michael Welker (longtime supporter of the award) and Larry Hurtado for their gentle probings and supportive conversations regarding the project when it was presented at the University of Heidelberg. Although the prize has changed patronage and name (it is now known as the Manfred Lautenschlaeger Award for Theological Promise), for years the Templeton Foundation helped young scholars like myself make contacts and form relationships that otherwise would not have been possible. In my case, I was able to travel to the United Kingdom in 2012 and lecture on the topic of this book at three institutions. I wish to thank my hosts for their hospitality and encouragement: Oliver Davies of King's College London, William Atkinson of London School of Theology, and Mark McIntosh of Durham University (now of Loyola University Chicago). I appreciate very much their support and the conversations they had with me; I continue to have fond memories of these visits.

I also wish to mention Michael Thomson, acquisitions editor at Eerdmans, who repeatedly has shown me that he believes in my work. He has done an exceptional job in hearing out a number of ideas I have, and he has been instrumental in helping with this project in particular.

I dedicate this work to the person most directly responsible for encouraging and supporting me in the years of this book's gestation—my wife, Kimberly Gwen. We have grown together over the years in wonderful ways; she has helped me become a better person and scholar. She embodies the Spirit of Pentecost like no other person I know. Thank you, Kimberly, for displaying through your life, witness, care, and love much of what I stumblingly explore in this book.

Seattle, Washington
2016

Introduction

Some days simply stand out more than others. I remember, as if it were yesterday, going to the academic dean's office when I was a seminary student to pick up a take-home exam for an intensive course I had just finished. The course itself was related to the theological roots of Pentecostalism, and my professor had been Donald Dayton, the eminent theologian and historian of the Holiness and Pentecostal movements. Perhaps out of a mixture of anxiety and curiosity, I snuck a peek at the exam once I had obtained it and walked out of the office. The first question was jolting: "Is Pentecostalism a Protestant movement?" My typical student response was, "We didn't talk about that in class! That's not a fair question!" But that question has been prominent throughout my reflections on Pentecostalism. It represents a line of inquiry that has taken on a life of its own. At that time, it shook me, and—as this book demonstrates—it continues to do so today. Not a bad exam question after all!

When prompted by the question, I remember quite vividly that I had competing thoughts. I am a Mexican-American who was born and spent my early years in Mexico. During my youth there, if one was not Roman Catholic and yet a self-identified Christian, one was then included in a catch-all category of being one of *los evangélicos* ("the evangelicals"). By default, all in this latter—presumably Protestant—category were deemed "other than" or maybe even "anti-Catholic." In my experience, non-Catholic Mexican Christians tend to bond together as the "other" category in a predominantly Catholic context and culture. Therefore, growing up as a Mexican Pentecostal, I assumed the identity of being *un evangélico*. On the basis of such a background, it made sense to me to conflate Pentecostalism with "evangelicalism," since the latter term was so vague and underdetermined in the Mexican context. For these broader cultural reasons, Mexican Pentecostals could be said to be evangelicals.

But as I pondered the question further and began to ruminate on what I took to be typical Protestant approaches and themes as I understood and experienced them as a young adult (I was living then in the American context), I came to conclude that the label was not entirely suitable. Of course Pentecostalism, as I had experienced it, did have a number of characteristics that one could loosely label Protestant, more specifically, evangelical. These included the way the authority of the Bible was often presented and the expressed need for a "conversion experience" so that one could be deemed saved. And yet as close as these two worlds were, they were nevertheless markedly distinct in my mind. Intuitively, experientially, and practically, I knew that Pentecostalism just did not fit much of the evangelical ethos as I understood and saw it on display in a number of fellowships and movements on the American scene. To be sure, connection points were available, but to me they nevertheless represented two different worlds. And once I brought this realization to the fore of my consciousness, Pentecostalism started to have for me an increasingly strained relationship with that largely indeterminate behemoth known in the Anglophone world as evangelicalism. After these many years, I think, but cannot be certain, that I answered the question on the exam in the negative—that Pentecostalism is *not* a Protestant tradition, because some of the most distinctive features that make Pentecostalism what it is are often not allowed at the Protestant table, whether it be the fundamentalist, the liberal, or the broadly evangelical sectors of that tradition. This intuition was further confirmed to me in conversation with another professor of mine, Stanley Hauerwas, who once mentioned in passing during my doctoral training, "Your tradition is more akin to Roman Catholicism than Protestantism." With my Mexican past, I found this comment startling, but it simply was one further prompt leading me to explore the character of Pentecostalism in light of other Christian options.

The goal of the present work is to flesh out the thought that Pentecostalism on a number of scores is decisively *not* a Protestant tradition generally and *not* part of an amalgam known as evangelicalism particularly. I realize that readers could have very important reasons for rejecting this thesis. For instance, Pentecostalism did not emerge out of a historical and theological vacuum. Many of its dominant characteristics early and subsequently in its history were decisively of the evangelical variety. We cannot romanticize the shape and developments of early Pentecostal identity so as to construct a stable, independent edifice that we can say was only subsequently compromised through accretions and capitulations to the evangelical fold. On the basis of these contextualizing observations, many would say that Pentecostalism is simply an offshoot or at least loosely part of the evangelical camp. In terms of the present, significant dimensions of power, influence, relevance, and credibility all seem to support the thesis that Pentecostalism is best understood as simply an evangelical subtradition. For instance, Pentecostals are now power brokers and leaders in many contexts: they have occupied high government offices in the United States and abroad, they have been presidents of evangelical institutions of higher education, they were early and significant stakeholders in such groups as the National Association of Evangelicals, they are prominent in the media and entertainment industries, and more. As a result, Pentecostals contribute to and benefit from a larger collective deemed "evangelicalism" in such ways as building coalitions, sharing resources, gaining respectability, and influencing the culture at large.

Even with these important realities, I wish to argue that quite a bit is potentially lost with subsuming Pentecostal identity wholly and completely within the larger evangelical fold. Despite comments to the contrary, Pentecostalism never was in its early forms simply "evangelicalism with tongues." Historians and other researchers of the movement have often wished to preserve the distinction on a number of fronts, and both Pentecostals and non-Pentecostals stand to benefit from efforts toward this end. The stakes are quite high in this discussion for the perpetuation of a working sense of Pentecostalism's unique character.

For Pentecostals themselves, what is at stake is the degree to which they are part of a self-conscious tradition, one that monitors and adjudicates continuity and development within its fold so as to perpetuate itself faithfully across time. This process is not necessarily intuitive for traditions on the whole, but it is especially not the case for Pentecostals, since they pride themselves as being "people of the Spirit" who are on the move rather than focused on the past. Forgoing purchase of the land upon which the Azusa Street revival took place because church leaders were "not interested in relics" is representative and symptomatic of this assumed modus operandi. And yet, Pentecostal identity spans now several generations, and significant transitions have occurred within such an expanse. Without the active work of "tradition negotiation," these transitions can potentially be not so much developments but impediments to what Pentecostals have typically valued about themselves, especially if there is not an ongoing, healthy awareness of what Pentecostalism is and its role within God's economy. Understandably, one need not and should not seek to repristinate Pentecostalism in its earlier forms, for changes across time are inevitable and in some sense necessary. One should not romanticize the past. But my concern here is whether Pentecostals have done enough to wrestle with the status of the changes they have undergone across the decades and whether those among their ranks have some working sense of what is distinctive about their tradition, especially when compared to alternative accounts of the Christian life. Given the repeated charges of Pentecostalism's "inferiority complex" and its desire for cultural respectability,[1] one could argue that some of the transitions Pentecostalism has undergone (ones that at times have seemed to align Pentecostalism more closely with the evangelical ethos) were undertaken more out of expediency and immediate advantage than purposeful and measured deliberation.[2] At stake in these matters is thus the degree to which Pentecostals understand and stay true to who they are across time.

For non-Pentecostals, this matter is of significant ecumenical concern and interest. Pentecostalism has a rich and complicated story to tell and life to enact. Its particularities, characteristics, idiosyncrasies, and eccentricities all constitute a gift to the wider church and world. The beauty of ecumenism is on display when specific Christian groups can give robust testimonies of how God works in their midst, but when a particular group cannot render faithfully and effectively their witness, something of the triune God's work is lost to the consciousness of the whole. In their case, if Pentecostals have difficulty articulating and maintaining their unique identity, the stakes for the church catholic are significant. They and other Spirit-movements can be dismissed, misunderstood, or resisted in the wake of this ignorance gap. Lamentably, Pentecostalism can continue in such a situation to be understood as just "evangelicalism with tongues" or (worse) a movement deviant from Christian orthodoxy.

What exactly, then, is Pentecostalism if it is not an evangelical movement per se? The categorization that I hope proves convincing to Pentecostals and non-Pentecostals alike is that Pentecostalism is best framed as

1. The classic expression here is that of Cheryl Bridges Johns, "The Adolescence of Pentecostalism: In Search of a Legitimate Sectarian Identity," *Pneuma* 17, no. 1 (1995): 3–17.

2. This point coincides with the "pragmatic" angle argued by Grant Wacker in *Heaven Below: Early Pentecostals and American Culture* (Cambridge, MA: Harvard University Press, 2001).

a modern instantiation of the mystical stream of Christianity recognizable throughout its history. In other words, Pentecostalism is best understood as *a mystical tradition of the church catholic*. The claim may not be self-evident to readers because of a number of reservations and objections on a host of matters, but I would say that this way of casting Pentecostalism is the most faithful way to preserve its traditional impulses, concerns, priorities, and overall ethos—features that continue to be present in its most vital contemporary forms. These mystical features have been prominent at different stages of the church's history, but sadly, Protestantism generally and evangelicalism particularly have often avoided or dismissed these as part of the gospel witness. The uneasy relationship at times between Pentecostals and Protestants can sometimes be the result of the latter's inability or refusal to account for the mystical dimensions of Christianity. In fact, the reservations evangelicals typically express toward Pentecostalism could also apply to other Spirit-driven constituencies and movements—ones that demonstrate mystical characteristics.

This work therefore looks internally to processes within the negotiation of Pentecostal identity but also outwardly in the sense of claiming the language of mysticism in a theological context in which the mystical continues to be held at bay or with suspicion. Academic theology in the modern West has taken a number of twists and turns, but the divide between theology and spirituality is a legacy that more often than not obfuscates a working understanding of the Christian life. Whereas Christianity is in many ways declining in the trans-Atlantic North, it is flourishing in the global South, and these developments may well represent at least a partial indictment of some of the most troubling features coming out of the modernization of the West, one of these being the splintering and dissolution of theological knowledge. As a case in point, those in the global South are often able to speak of God out of a more confident posture than their Northern counterparts. Sadly, the latter, in a manner further indicative of their malaise, might deem the former as naive and simplistic; the former constituency, however, may very well claim to be the future of Christianity on this planet, asserting that the latter have lost their theological and spiritual bearings.[3] Again, a potential strategy for moving forward in the

---

3. According to Philip Jenkins, "These newer [Pentecostal and independent] churches preach deep personal faith and communal orthodoxy, mysticism, and puritanism, all founded on clear scriptural authority. They preach messages that, to a Westerner, appear simplistically charismatic, visionary, and apocalyptic. . . . For better or worse, the dominant churches of the future could have much in common with those

midst of such a North-South impasse is for both sides to recognize the mystical character of Christian embodiment. A vast array of interconnections can be made among Christianity's many forms once the language of mysticism is viable for contemporary usage.

These claims represent the burden of the arguments that follow. Before proceeding, however, a few clarifying and contextualizing remarks are in order. The forms of Pentecostalism I know best experientially are the Mexican, Latino, and Latin American varieties. The form of Pentecostalism that I largely explore here, however, will be the Anglo-American forms, since much of what I wish to state regarding Pentecostalism requires the resources of the Pentecostal academy (as chapter 1 will show), which to this day is largely an English-driven constituency (although this sector is multiform itself, given Canadian, Australian, and British voices alongside American ones). I realize that this kind of circumscription is problematic, given that so much of contemporary Pentecostalism's most vibrant forms are located outside of this context, and these developments have captured the imagination of many in the academy. For my part, I do not pretend to be able to speak or account for the whole. Many have noted that such a task is simply impossible, given the diversity of Pentecostalism's many expressions,[4] and I tend to agree with such an assessment, since I find it more intellectually compelling to speak of a particular arrangement than to generalize to a global whole. There are many Pentecostalisms, not just one, and this recognition is true not only in global terms but in North American ones as well.[5] My goal is to weave together a number of strands within the American context so as to probe, assess, critique, and work from such an amalgam. Whatever implications these efforts can have on other contexts are best left to their respective representatives and researchers.

Since I have focused on a certain localization of Pentecostalism, it is appropriate to similarly limit the category "evangelicalism." The framing of the latter term is also important, given its wide uses and applications. In

---

of medieval or early modern European times" (*The Next Christendom: The Coming of Global Christianity*, rev. and exp. ed. [Oxford: Oxford University Press, 2007], 8).

4. A helpful rendering of the complexity can be found in Allan H. Anderson, *An Introduction to Pentecostalism*, 2nd ed. (Cambridge: Cambridge University Press, 2014), 1–7.

5. For a dismantling of the assumed unity in the latter context, see Douglas Jacobsen, *Thinking in the Spirit: Theologies of the Early Pentecostal Movement* (Bloomington: Indiana University Press, 2003), 10–11.

chapter 3 I consider more extensively the forms of evangelicalism I have in mind. Encouragingly, certain evangelical scholars have recently shown a greater affinity with some of the sympathies and claims demonstrated in the present book. I fully acknowledge the challenge of accounting for something called evangelicalism, and I realize that many self-identified evangelicals will not agree with some or even most of the ways I define the conglomerate here; therefore, I wish to be forthcoming by admitting that I have consciously and purposefully elected to focus on only one of evangelicalism's particular strands. In my opinion, this strand is an important one; it tends to be loud and self-affirming by claiming to hold the evangelical line, and it is perpetuated through a number of venues, channels, and institutions. I am the first to admit, however, that the voices and movements surveyed here do not represent the whole story of what evangelicalism has been, is, and can be in the future.

Additionally, much is also at stake in how one defines "mysticism" and its cognates. I consider this definition particularly in chapter 2, but a few comments here are also in order. Bernard McGinn notes incisively that the term "mystical theology" preceded "mysticism" by over a millennium. The former, pointing to the *theoria* and *praxis* undergirding the pursuit of a particular kind of life, has a wider orbit than the latter. A bit later, McGinn alludes to another sobering reality: "First-person accounts are rare in the first millennium of Christian mysticism."[6] That is, what many today find to be typical of mystical experience was not the case during Christianity's first thousand years. In terms of these and other topics, McGinn contextualizes the way one can come to understand and pursue the study of mysticism within Christianity. A goal of the present study is to qualify and nuance the language of mysticism in the direction of mystical theology. Put another way, I am convinced that we need to reclaim the language of mysticism as it applies specifically to the Christian theological task. I believe mystical theology merits a place at the table of the various theologies under discussion in the Christian academy today, in part so as to give continuity and coherence to theological knowledge.

Also, "mysticism" and "spirituality" are strongly linked terms in what follows, but for me they are not entirely synonymous. I take "mysticism" to be directly related to the encounter with the God of Christian confession, with "spirituality" considering such an encounter within its wider orbit,

6. Bernard McGinn, *The Foundations of Mysticism: Origins to the Fifth Century* (New York: Crossroad, 1991), xiv.

including the activities and practices that anticipate both the encounter itself and the outcomes and obligations stemming from it. Within this arrangement, Christian mysticism is a subtheme within the broader domain of Christian spirituality.

Readers on occasion may come to believe that the vision sustained in this book is artificial, anachronistic, or interpolative. I am quite sure some readers will suspect that my assessment of Pentecostalism's theological character is mine and only mine. In response to this judgment, let me offer two sets of remarks. First, this work is in many ways a constructive effort. I am not a historian, and what follows will most likely not satisfy a historian's eye and sensibilities. Some might label my use of source materials, whether Pentecostal (chap. 4) or from the broader Christian tradition (chap. 5), as eclectic or strategic. Why suffer this risk? I do so because I believe that past voices can be resources for a tradition facing contemporary challenges. The goal with this reliance on the past is not strictly to hear these voices in their original contexts. The purpose, rather, is to hear these witnesses so that they can speak into the present and offer some direction to those of us looking for aid.

I am convinced that Pentecostalism has been unhelpfully saddled with mutually contradictory epistemologies and theological methodologies across its reflective history, each often claimed exclusively by its espousers as "the Pentecostal option." Making headway in such a confusing situation involves contextualizing and gaining perspective for the proposals on hand and doing so in conversation with broader and deeper resources. Such is the rationale for thinking of Pentecostalism as a mystical tradition. If the God Pentecostals worship and witness at work in their settings is the true God of Christian confession, then we need to move beyond the epistemological and theological constraints of the late nineteenth and early twentieth centuries and focus on the totality of self-disclosure by this One who is the same yesterday, today, and forever. As for the suitability and applicability of the language of mysticism itself for such a purpose, I prefer to appeal to a kind of reasoning I believe is at work in Athanasius for the relevance of the word *homoousios*, despite its nonexistence in the biblical testimony: *verbum non est, sed res ubique* ("the word is not there, but the reality is everywhere"). In what follows, I argue for such an understanding, namely, that we view the Pentecostal movement as a Christian mystical tradition.

Finally, I wish the present study as a whole to strengthen the body of Christ; I strive to identify with and contribute to the church catholic. I attempt to give a workable account of a narrative tradition, one that identifies and substantiates in a complex yet meaningful way what it means to be Christian across space and time. A number of complications (historical, theological, sociological, cultural, political) are introduced when one speaks of "the church" or "the church catholic," but I also believe that quite a bit is lost if we cannot do so. Given their thought forms, speech acts, and practices, Pentecostals are thoroughly part of a wider orbit, a larger story of God's people peregrinating alongside this self-disclosing God. This journeying has taken place in a wide assortment of contexts, including Jerusalem, as recorded in Acts 2; the Abbey of St. Victor, Paris; a prison cell in Toledo, Spain; and a dilapidated building at 320 Azusa Street, Los Angeles. This is a meaningful story—and a compelling and beautiful one at that—because it has the triune God at the center—the One who satisfies and fans eternal desire.

CHAPTER 1

The Challenge of Method

This work necessarily operates within the domains of theological method and epistemology. Several proposals on this front exist in Pentecostal theology, as a recent comparative study has shown.[1] For the purposes of this book, however, I will highlight the approach that views Pentecostalism as a spirituality, since this orientation addresses features of Pentecostal life not available otherwise in theological speech. These features are partly captured in the following comments by Walter Hollenweger, who notes that the strength of Pentecostals "does not lie in what they conceptualize but in what happens to the participants in their liturgies. Their contribution is strongest on the level of spirituality and lived liturgy and not on the level of interpreting spirituality, liturgy, and theology."[2] Pentecostals have been prone to prioritize the enactment and dynamics of faith over paying attention to its conceptualization or rationalization (although they do this kind of work as well, a reality not always known or acknowledged by observers). This kind of privileging could very well set up the theological task in a distinct way. Should theological methodology be affected as a result of this prioritization? And if so, how? This chapter engages these crucial questions.

We begin by considering the pioneering work that granted spirituality a central role in Pentecostal theologizing, and we also consider challenges

---

1. Christopher A. Stephenson, *Types of Pentecostal Theology: Method, System, Spirit* (Oxford: Oxford University Press, 2013).

2. Walter Hollenweger, "Pentecostals and the Charismatic Movement," in *The Study of Spirituality*, ed. Cheslyn Jones, Geoffrey Wainwright, and Edward Yarnold (Oxford: Oxford University Press, 1986), 553–54.

that continue to be at the forefront of such an approach. Despite growing awareness of the need for somehow including spirituality in theological efforts, the matter continues to create confusion and maybe even frustration, for there is no consensus on precisely how to do so methodologically.

Daring to Conceive of Pentecostalism as a Spirituality within the Academy

In many ways, the publication of Steven J. Land's *Pentecostal Spirituality* was a watershed moment for Pentecostal studies.[3] The book was the inaugural volume of the series "Journal of Pentecostal Theology Supplement," which originated with the beginning of the *Journal of Pentecostal Theology*. Both endeavors arose in the early 1990s out of conversations John Christopher Thomas and Rickie Moore were having with Sheffield Academic Press. Upon reflecting on the details of these developments, Thomas notes that the 1990 meeting of the Society for Pentecostal Studies was especially important, for at the time, it appeared that Pentecostal scholarship had reached a critical mass. When pinpointing how to move forward with the series in particular, Thomas and Moore were in agreement. Thomas later reflected about this moment, "We knew immediately what the first volume should be, Steve Land's soon to be completed Emory University PhD dissertation on Pentecostal Spirituality, a work that in large part would chart the course for a variety of constructive engagements in the area of Pentecostal Theology."[4]

This intuition of the importance of Land's work was appropriate, for Land was calling for a revisioning of North American Pentecostalism, not so much from explicitly historical, sociological, psychological or other nontheological perspectives, but from the ethos of Pentecostals themselves as known through an inductive theological methodology. Land focused on the testimonies and practices of early American Pentecostals during the first decade of the movement, a time that in his mind (and following the lead of Walter Hollenweger) marks the heart of Pentecos-

---

3. Steven J. Land, *Pentecostal Spirituality: A Passion for the Kingdom*, Journal of Pentecostal Theology Supplement 1 (Sheffield: Sheffield Academic Press, 1993). This book has been reprinted through CPT Press (2010).

4. John Christopher Thomas, "Editorial," *Journal of Pentecostal Theology* 18, no. 1 (2009): 2–3.

talism.[5] When Land read the testimonies and happenings of these early Pentecostals, he began to search for appropriate categories to describe what he was finding, ones that could bear the constructive direction he was interested in pursuing. The master category that came to the fore for him was "spirituality." According to Land, the term is useful because it can account for, among other things, Pentecostalism's "height" (praise, worship, prayer to God) and its "depth" (convictions, passions, dispositions). Land's reasoning was as follows: since the focus of Pentecostal life is communal worship, what Pentecostals believe can be properly considered only in conjunction with their practices and dispositions. Land's approach is thus distinctive in that it emphasizes this multidimensional quality both analytically and constructively.

Talk of "spirituality" has garnered quite a bit of popularity as of late, both within and outside of Christian circles, but only relatively recently has it been deemed a serious theological category meriting scrutiny within formal academic settings.[6] The long-standing divide between the church and academy, forged over centuries in western Europe, has continued to plague formal theological efforts, and within such a setting, "spirituality" cannot help but sound privatistic, pietistic, and excessively churchy. For some who assume these conclusions, serious theology needs to avoid the bias and lack of sophistication that can come with talk of people's faith journeys, worship practices, and deep, life-orienting commitments. The way to preserve this division has often been through the demarcation of methodological and epistemological boundaries so that the subject matter of theology is determined at the outset in a way that makes it academically respectable. As a result, "spirituality" is often cast as something beyond the bounds of legitimate academic scrutiny.

To Land's credit, he believed that approaching Pentecostalism through a theological lens required a methodological approach that was germane to, and reflective of, the Pentecostal ethos itself. Otherwise, to systematize Pentecostal faith along some conceptual and organizational apparatus could involve missing some of its most important distinctives, since such a

---

5. Hollenweger, "Pentecostals and the Charismatic Movement," 551.

6. The term will be considered more extensively in chapter 2, but it is interesting to note here how recently the word has been used in English to designate what it does today. Whereas it was a term used for reproach in French during the seventeenth century, in English it gained its emphasis on prayerful piety in the eighteenth and especially the nineteenth centuries. See the preface to Jones, Wainwright, and Yarnold, *The Study of Spirituality*, xxiv–xxvi.

process would necessarily involve abstracting and possibly even divorcing Pentecostal beliefs from the life-giving features native to their originating environments. Again, Hollenweger is helpful here in addressing the point directly: "It is, however, difficult to introduce this kind of spirituality into the ecumenical discussion because—if reduced to concepts and propositions—it loses its very essence."[7] Therefore, testimonies, sermons, altar activity, and similar happenings were deemed by Land as necessarily relevant on their own terms when he was accounting for the Pentecostal movement's theological ethos.

As a result of noting Land's methodological orientation, however, one senses a significant tension within the field of theology itself that can be highlighted by asking, Who establishes methodological privilege in the theological task? As an academic writing a book that had its origins as a PhD dissertation, Land might have been tempted to present his work more in line with a kind of methodological orientation that was "more suitable" to contemporary theology, particularly the kind that exhibits properties associated with the qualifier "systematic." Despite such pressures, Land wrote his book with a different methodological self-understanding. As a Pentecostal formed by the academy, he pursued Pentecostal theology *in a self-consciously Pentecostal way*. Given his creativity (and fortitude!), Land is to be credited with a methodological breakthrough in Pentecostal theologizing.

Land could write as he did in part because of the influence of his *Doktorvater*, Don Saliers. During his long career, Saliers has shown the dynamics and possibilities of the intersection between theology and spirituality, a research program partly informed by his Wesleyan identity, as well as his formation as a musician.[8] In *Pentecostal Spirituality*, Land draws from Saliers's orienting concerns by quoting extensively Saliers's treatment of Karl Barth's reflections on prayer and its primacy for theological work.[9] Among other things, this primacy is grounded in the "I-Thou" encounter between the pray-er and the One prayed to. Hollenweger describes the dynamic as follows: "It is impossible for Christians submerged in this spirituality (at any rate in the Third World) to speak about God without speaking to God, thus reintroducing or reinforcing a Catholic and Eastern Orthodox

7. Hollenweger, "Pentecostals and the Charismatic Movement," 553.

8. See, for instance, Don Saliers, *Worship as Theology: Foretaste of Glory Divine* (Nashville: Abingdon, 1994).

9. These reflections can be found in Karl Barth, *Prayer*, 50th ann. ed. (Louisville: Westminster John Knox, 2002).

principle into the theological discourse."[10] Under such a depiction, theologizing is a provisional activity of accounting for the God of Christian confession that is ultimately rendered to God as an act of worship itself.[11] As *Pentecostal Spirituality* details, Land found such a model especially appealing for rendering the theological form and increasing the productivity of Pentecostal theology. Rather than a bifurcation mandated by academic strictures, the spirituality-theology divide could be understood within this framework as a genuine interface in which there was mutual conditioning and influence.

Land's approach, although helpful in conveying a number of dimensions inherent to the thinking and experience of early Pentecostals, nevertheless creates a number of challenges, ones that critics would no doubt be inclined to raise as challenges to its viability. For instance, Land wishes "to emphasize the importance of the Holy Spirit as a starting point for a distinctive Pentecostal approach to theology as spirituality,"[12] yet pneumatology as a whole is a challenging field to secure epistemically. If the Holy Spirit is a "starting point," how can such an origin be identified and communicated in a way that is useful for theological construction? Yes, a so-called theology of the Nicene Creed's third article appears to be especially congenial to Pentecostal sensibilities,[13] but there are perils to avoid from a number of sides with such a self-identified program, including those that would reflect significant privatization, interiority, and subjectivity. Additionally, the integrationist impulse that Land pursues between Pentecostal beliefs and practices is difficult to maintain, given that it operates out of the grounds of experience and specific events. How can such conditions and their associated practices be accounted for in theological efforts, given that the latter is typically done separately from the former?[14]

10. Hollenweger, "Pentecostals and the Charismatic Movement," 553.

11. Land, *Pentecostal Spirituality*, 36–37.

12. Land, *Pentecostal Spirituality*, 39.

13. This work is gradually being undertaken by a number of scholars. One is D. Lyle Dabney; see in particular his essays "Otherwise Engaged in the Spirit: A First Theology for a Twenty-First Century," in *The Future of Theology: Essays in Honor of Jürgen Moltmann*, ed. Miroslav Volf, Carmen Krieg, and Thomas Kucharz (Grand Rapids: Eerdmans, 1996), 154–63, and "Why Should the Last Be First? The Priority of Pneumatology in Recent Theological Discussion," in *Advents of the Spirit: An Introduction to the Current Study of Pneumatology*, ed. Bradford E. Hinze and D. Lyle Dabney (Milwaukee, WI: Marquette University Press, 2001), 240–61. Amos Yong has also pursued such an agenda in many of his works.

14. Again, proposals are available to answer such queries, but they are counter-

Finally, motivations, dispositions, and affections are internal features of individual selves that arise from some implicit psychology. With this last theme there are also anthropological and moral commitments to be considered.[15] On all these scores, debates abound. Land's approach is thus burdened with a number of challenges, and so it makes perfect sense why theology does not typically pursue its work within the domain associated with "spirituality" in general. Rather than principally being a discursive and analytic form of activity, Land's approach welcomes pneumatological and praxis-oriented, this-worldly elements of life as central to the theological task, ones that systematic theology typically has difficulty accommodating, since the latter tends to abstraction and decontextualization. In the midst of these factors, one may be led to ask: How can one press forward in articulating a theology in terms of spirituality, given that the approach itself stands in tension with so many of the ways theology has often been pursued?

Before moving too quickly to answer this question generally, perhaps one strategy would be to keep our gaze at a local level, that is, to consider this challenge in terms of the particular case of Pentecostalism—how it has had difficulties accounting for itself theologically and how this situation is symptomatic of the long-standing divide between spirituality and theology. As will be shown below, Pentecostals have repeatedly tried to account for something that can be labeled "Pentecostal theology," but they have struggled mightily before such a task largely because of the fragmented nature of the contemporary theological enterprise out of which they have pursued such work. Pentecostal scholars often have had some intuited sense of what Pentecostalism is generally and experientially, but

---

ing long-standing disciplinary divides. One thinks, for instance, of Reinhard Hütter's depiction of theology as a church practice, as well as the sundry accounts that derive from Alasdair MacIntyre's general account of "practices." See Reinhard Hütter, *Suffering Divine Things: Theology as Church Practice* (Grand Rapids: Eerdmans, 2000); James J. Buckley and David S. Yeago, eds., *Knowing the Triune God: The Work of the Spirit in the Practices of the Church* (Grand Rapids: Eerdmans, 2001); and Miroslav Volf and Dorothy Bass, eds., *Practicing Theology: Beliefs and Practices in Christian Life* (Grand Rapids: Eerdmans, 2002).

15. Land largely works from a Wesleyan account of such matters, which is in keeping with the formation he received at Emory University's Candler School of Theology, a United Methodist seminary. Land was also influenced at Emory by Theodore Runyon and Roberta Bondi. Together, these scholars helped Land see the central role that narrative and the affections play in the Christian life. Both themes are operative in *Pentecostal Spirituality*.

they have been ill served by the academy in finding categories and methods that can help them account for and articulate what they know at a tacit and visceral level about their tradition.

The Scandal of Pentecostal Theology

One occasion that prompted methodological concerns of this kind to come to the fore was the engagement by certain Pentecostal scholars with Mark Noll's *The Scandal of the Evangelical Mind* (1994). Noll's volume spurred a number of discussions related to the intersection of faith and the academy. In short, Noll laments the way evangelicalism has emerged within the American scene as largely anti-intellectual and indifferent to the fostering of a Christian "life of the mind," the latter being understood as "the effort to think like a Christian—to think within a specifically Christian framework—across the whole spectrum of modern learning." In addition to citing the limits of the American university system that have contributed to this "scandal," Noll writes a scathing critique of a number of religious movements that he categorizes under the rubric "fundamentalism." According to Noll, fundamentalism contributed to the scandal through developments associated with Holiness, Pentecostal, and dispensationalist Christians. With regard to the first group, Noll mentions that the language Holiness adherents promoted was one that "bespoke a growing concern to experience the realities of Christian spirituality,"[16] especially through terms associated with sanctification and pneumatology.[17] As for Pentecostalism, he mentions that, whereas the fourfold gospel (depicting Jesus as Savior, Spirit-baptizer, Healer, and soon-coming King) was a key cluster of themes for Pentecostalism's early forms, "its central feature remained the belief that the person of the Holy Spirit could be experienced—verbally, physically, spiritually—in this latter day."[18]

Noll principally decries dispensationalism in terms of the attention he gives in his overall critique of fundamentalism; nevertheless, the lumping of Pentecostal and Holiness movements together with dispensationalism was lacking in nuance and even a bit unfair, a point he has since acknowl-

16. Mark A. Noll, *The Scandal of the Evangelical Mind* (Grand Rapids: Eerdmans, 1994), 7, 116.

17. From their end, Holiness scholars responded to Noll's work in *Wesleyan Theological Journal* 32.1 (1997).

18. Noll, *The Scandal of the Evangelical Mind*, 116.

edged to some degree.[19] More to the point of this chapter, it is clear that part of what Noll finds "innovative" (which for him is not a compliment) about these movements is their particular emphasis on pneumatology, religious experience, and the like. Noll explicitly claims he does not oppose the merits of spirituality per se, but he is keen to emphasize how certain related forms (including those features of Pentecostal life as he narrates them) have contributed to the problem he wishes to expose within Protestant scholarship.

Noll's work struck a nerve, partly because he was on to an uncomfortable point overall, namely, that an emphasis on "spiritual" things in modern forms of American revivalist culture has historically had the potential to weaken concern for the "natural." If reality is framed dualistically—which is often a feature of modernity shared by Pentecostals and their allies and critics of various stripes—then inevitably one feature will be emphasized to the neglect of the other. An otherworldliness as highlighted by revivalist culture could overshadow regard for matters of this-worldly concern, which in this case would not be so much "sinful pleasures" as it would be regard for the creaturely—and so intellectual—realms.

Given Noll's sweeping and to some degree biting analysis, Pentecostal scholars responded directly to his work. Two of these responses were from Cheryl Bridges Johns and James K. A. Smith.[20] Johns's critique is essentially that Noll perpetuates modern assumptions about knowledge—that he utilizes "one historically conditioned form of mind to criticize another historically conditioned mind,"[21] and such an approach necessarily marginalizes groups like Pentecostals (and by implication topics like spirituality and pneumatology), since they do not fit the standard paradigm at work that Noll assumes and that makes his critique possible. Johns's alternative reading is that Pentecostalism inhabits the postmodern space more adequately than the modern because the former allows for a kind of particularity that a generic proposal like "to think like a Christian" (Noll's

19. See Mark A. Noll, *Jesus Christ and the Life of the Mind* (Grand Rapids: Eerdmans, 2011), 151–52.

20. Cheryl Bridges Johns, "Partners in Scandal: Wesleyan and Pentecostal Scholarship," *Pneuma* 21 (1999): 183–97, and James K. A. Smith, "Scandalizing Theology: A Pentecostal Response to Noll's Scandal," *Pneuma* 19 (1997): 225–38. Johns's paper was originally presented at the 1998 Annual Meeting of the Society for Pentecostal Studies but was not published until 1999. Yong's response (to be cited below) responds to Johns's paper yet was published in 1998.

21. Johns, "Partners in Scandal," 188.

slogan) does not. She finds that phrases used by those whom Noll criticizes are actually intellectually respectable (including "letting go and letting God," as well as "laying all on the altar") in that they speak overtly against the presumption and hubris of modern thought-forms. With this kind of challenge, Johns interestingly welcomes deconstructionists as partners for Pentecostals struggling to resist evangelical portrayals of the "Christian mind" that are modern at their core.

For his part, Smith argues in an earlier article that Pentecostalism became fundamentalist only later in its life and did so in dire tension with its roots.[22] For Smith, Pentecostalism is best understood not as anti-intellectual but as anti-intellectualist.[23] Pentecostals have a critical tradition that has marked their movement from the beginning,[24] yet their instincts betray the belief that a theory is not necessary for the recognition of intelligibility and coherence. Smith believes that Noll collapses faith and theology in his integrationist model, with the former being absorbed into the latter in a way that the theology in question continues to depend on features of the "evangelical enlightenment" stemming from Old Princeton and other nineteenth-century influences. Smith also recognizes that there has never been a single evangelical theology; rather, we have multiple evangelical theologies, given the complexity surrounding the conglomerate that is evangelicalism on the American scene. For Smith, what Noll disparages about these "theologically innovating" movements suggests something of Noll's implicit and specific theological-methodological orientation. Smith

22. In the same year of this article, Smith pursued this line of argument in more detail in "The Closing of the Book: Pentecostals, Evangelicals, and the Sacred Writings," *Journal of Pentecostal Theology* 5, no. 11 (1997): 49–71.

23. This concern stems partly from the need early Pentecostals saw to be humble before God, even in their thinking. In the first issue of Azusa's *Apostolic Faith* newsletter, Brother S. J. Mead communicated the sentiment as follows: "My soul groans out this morning for the Holy Spirit to have perfect control of His temple. We often hinder the blessed wooing and power of His love by cross currents of our human mind and thought. May God help us to be little in our own eyes, not over anxious to serve much, but to love Him with all our heart, mind, and strength" (*Apostolic Faith* 1.1 [1906]: 3).

24. Smith repeatedly has mentioned the work of Walter Hollenweger, which gives voice to the Pentecostal "critical" tradition; see Hollenweger, "The Critical Tradition of Pentecostalism," *Journal of Pentecostal Theology* 1 (1992): 7–17. In his summary, Hollenweger states that Pentecostals "try to articulate a theology which expresses, in a true biblical way, God's interest and love in *this* world without giving up the conviction that God is always beyond our experiences of God and that the Spirit of God is not identical with how we experience him (or her)" (9). On this last point, Hollenweger sounds very close to the Christian mystical tradition, particularly its apophatic forms.

claims that it is not at all clear from the pages of *Scandal* what Noll believes theology is or should be,[25] only that theology properly understood (1) should not advocate for an otherworldliness (a kind of supernaturalism) that in turn would neglect an attentiveness to a this-worldly reality (i.e., a kind of naturalism) and (2) should have the capacity to integrate and interact with other academic disciplines. According to Smith, on both scores it seems that Noll comes exceedingly close to defining and intellectualizing theology as a kind of foundationalist-modernist theory that in turn can define the conditions for coherence and intelligibility (presumably) necessarily required in the engagement with all other forms of knowledge. For their part, Pentecostals do not usually assume such a paradigm; they are inclined to think that the theoretical "will always be exceeded by the experience of faith."[26] No wonder, then, that they cannot help but be deemed as innovative on the basis of Noll's grounding and all-encompassing account.

These pieces by Johns and Smith occasioned a response by Amos Yong.[27] As a self-identified Pentecostal systematic theologian, Yong felt compelled to engage Johns and Smith. His main charge was not so much related to what Johns and Smith were saying about Noll's work (their main target) but the side claims they were making about Pentecostalism itself and their implications for the theological task more generally as these could be understood by the Pentecostal fold as a whole. Yong agrees with much of what Smith and Johns declare about Noll's project, but he has more difficulty with the kinds of inferences Pentecostals in particular could draw from what they say about Pentecostalism in response to Noll. Yong worries that Johns's argument could backfire—that her opening the door for deconstruction would in turn potentially leave the matter open

25. Noll's *Jesus Christ and the Life of the Mind*, his sequel to *Scandal*, is telling, for there he chooses a christological idiom to specify more deeply his theological orientation. It seems that Noll believes that such an idiom can help secure the discursive and public appeal of theology in a way that a pneumatological idiom cannot.

26. Smith, "Scandalizing Theology," 236. Smith has gone on to give more substantial treatments of these matters; see his *Speech and Theology: Language and the Logic of Incarnation* (London: Routledge, 2002) and *Thinking in Tongues: Pentecostal Contributions to Christian Philosophy* (Grand Rapids: Eerdmans, 2010). Smith transparently relies on various postmodern philosophical alternatives, including the early Heidegger. But again, as with Hollenweger previously, so with Smith now: one perceives a resonance with the Christian mystical traditions, particularly those of the apophatic variety.

27. Amos Yong, "Whither Systematic Theology? A Systematician Chimes In on a Scandalous Conversation," *Pneuma* 20 (1998): 85–93.

for the questioning of all metanarratives, including a scriptural one. A postmodern sensibility can lead to the conclusion that all metanarratives are totalizing.[28] If followed through to these implications, postmodern reasoning would subvert Pentecostalism itself. For Yong, Pentecostalism and postmodernism necessarily have an uneasy relationship at some level, since Pentecostalism requires the metanarrative of Scripture as an orienting baseline and outlook. As for Smith's article, Yong worries that Smith's preference for the pretheoretical aspects of faith would in turn galvanize those within Pentecostalism who are already suspicious of education and formal theological training and reflection.[29] One cannot help, Yong would say, but worry about how Smith's claims would be heard by those who think that the pretheoretical is all one needs in negotiating and developing a healthy theological outlook.

Admittedly, these interactions are dated, especially when one considers how these scholars have gone on to develop their careers and modify their arguments with the passing of time as expressed through the many works they have authored and edited. But notice the contours of the interaction. Noll sets up the dynamic by expressing what many already hold: Pentecostals and their kin have perpetuated a kind of anti-intellectualism as a result of "theological innovations" that involve, to some degree, revivalist emphases of divine encounter, Spirit-related happenings, and the like. Both Johns and Smith believe that Noll's charges are uncharitable, reductive, and reflecting a certain kind of mind-set that is itself predisposed to dismiss or ignore basic features of Pentecostal belief and practice. And yet Yong, in the midst of these responses, wishes to press both Johns and Smith largely on how they could be heard by Pentecostals themselves, for Yong's worry is that Pentecostals have tended to find systematic theology at odds with legitimate inquiry into the Christian faith so that an emphasis on the pretheoretical (which in a sense could be identified with spirituality) could delegitimize the theological work he and others undertake on behalf of the movement. Clearly, not simply outsiders to the movement but insiders as well are not in agreement with how to honor some of the most important features of Pentecostal life within a broader intellectual and theological framework.

28. Jean-François Lyotard is typically associated with this perspective; see his *The Postmodern Condition: A Report on Knowledge* (Minneapolis: University of Minnesota Press, 1984). Smith tackles this perspective in his *Who's Afraid of Postmodernism? Taking Derrida, Lyotard, and Foucault to Church* (Grand Rapids: Baker Academic, 2006).

29. Yong, "Whither Systematic Theology?," 87.

God and Bifurcations

The above is just but one exchange that shows the difficulties and challenges involved with discussions related to formalizing and conceptualizing Pentecostal beliefs and identity. Another interaction along these lines has an explicitly theological agenda. This one occurred between the late Clark Pinnock, a prominent evangelical theologian who had charismatic leanings, and Terry Cross, a Pentecostal theologian who is part of a second generation of Pentecostal scholars who has studied theology formally at the doctoral level. For his part, Pinnock distinguished himself in the latter years of his life as a genuine friend and advocate of Pentecostal and charismatic communities and their theologies. One of the works coming from these sympathies was his pneumatology, *Flame of Love*.[30] In 2000 Pinnock published an article encouraging Pentecostals to develop a doctrine of God, one that would reflect their experiences of God and so be both dynamic and contextual. Pinnock believes Pentecostals can "speak a strong word on behalf of the personal nature of God's relationality." They are, in Pinnock's terms, "relational theists." In a very encouraging manner, Pinnock urges: "It is time for Pentecostals to realize that they have a distinctive doctrine of God implicit in their faith and that they need to make it explicit—not just for purely academic purposes but for revival too, because Christianity is only as dynamic as its understanding of God."[31]

The backdrop of Pinnock's concerns is a theological landscape that he characterizes as being dominated by philosophical categories. Pinnock aligns himself with Pentecostals and says they can offer a "personal model of God," one that is in contrast to an "absolutist model." The latter he associates with being the result of an infiltration of categories, sensibilities, and propriety-sets from the Greek philosophical tradition. A phrase for this model would be "classical theism," and the figures Pinnock sometimes associates with it are Aristotle, Augustine, Aquinas, and those he calls "paleo-Reformed" Christians.[32]

For Pinnock, the relational model is to be preferred for a number of

30. Clark H. Pinnock, *Flame of Love: A Theology of the Holy Spirit* (Downers Grove, IL: InterVarsity, 1996).

31. Clark H. Pinnock, "Divine Relationality: A Pentecostal Contribution to the Doctrine of God," *Journal of Pentecostal Theology* 8, no. 16 (2000): 5–6.

32. This last phrase is curious. Pinnock explains it as Calvinists who "freeze the tradition at a certain date, say, at the Westminster Confession and opt out of all the positive developments of Reformed theology since then" ("Divine Relationality," 22–23n41).

reasons. First, it tends to be in line with the shape and dynamic of revelation history as found in the Bible. On many occasions, God is portrayed in Scripture as changing God's mind, altering courses of action on the basis of prayer, and so on. Pinnock believes a relational model is well-suited to account for these features of the biblical testimony. In Pinnock's view, to be relational means to be responsive and changeable in light of circumstances. God is not all-controlling in these depictions, for God allows Godself to be rejected and God's plans to be thwarted by human agents. Pinnock does acknowledge that God is beyond the world, but he is also inclined to emphasize that God is in it in genuine and self-involving ways. Pinnock believes God uses Pentecostals mightily because they take God so seriously precisely in this way. For them, the narrative of Scripture *is* the narrative of reality: if God was active and engaged in the biblical accounts in the marvelous ways depicted therein, then Pentecostals dare believe that is how God works today.

Cross responded to Pinnock in the same *Journal of Pentecostal Theology* issue that published Pinnock's contribution. For his part, Cross notes that, before Pentecostals can respond to the promptings by Pinnock, they need to overcome their "ambivalence toward reflection in the theological task and develop a theological method commensurate with [their] experience." In short, they "need to examine the role of experience and spirituality in [their] theological endeavor." From these observations, Cross proposes a spectrum with two polarities: an unreflective spirituality on one end and an exceedingly intellectualized theology on the other. For Cross, Pentecostals necessarily require the spectrum because of their linking of spirituality to theology. They see the need of experience for theological reflection, since they are committed to the point that "how one experiences God influences the way one reflects on God," but Cross also wishes for Pentecostals to avoid extremes with such an approach.[33]

As a way of grounding the exercise, Cross raises the question, "So what is Pentecostal theology?" His thoughts in this particular article include the following remarks: "Theology is a human construction of reflection on God and his relationship with his creatures. It is based on the primary event of the revelation of God as recorded in Scripture and on the secondary event of the Spirit's revelation of the truth of that primary event to our lives. Pentecostal theology, therefore, is fundamentally a second-order

33. Terry L. Cross, "The Rich Feast of Theology: Can Pentecostals Bring the Main Course or Only the Relish?," *Journal of Pentecostal Theology* 8, no. 16 (2000): 34–35.

reflection on the primary narrative of God in revelation coordinated with a reflection on the experience of God in our lives."[34] From this elaboration, it is clear that theology is largely a reactive enterprise, one that is responsive to (and so following) God's initial self-revelation.

Given the limits of language and human thought-forms, this revelation is often apprehended and categorized in terms of contrastives. In fact, Cross sees in Pinnock precisely a dualism or binary that is problematic. He agrees with Pinnock that an absolutist model is not helpful, but he believes that Pinnock's preferred relational model is perhaps inadequate as well, in that Cross equates or at least aligns it with A. N. Whitehead's broad metaphysical proposals and the theological field that is derived from them—process theology. Cross's way forward is to utilize the method of dialectic, largely along Barthian lines. Through this mechanism, Cross hopes to maintain appropriately both polarities at work in Pinnock's proposals (although Cross prefers the language of the "perfection of God" and the "relationality of God" to describe them). Toward the conclusion of his article, Cross remarks of the Christian God: "This is a God far beyond our 'either/or' language—this is a God before whom we can only stammer with the stutter of paradox."[35]

Pinnock's presentation is more subtle and nuanced than Cross would have it, but interestingly, they both share very strong affinities. In the first place, both Pinnock and Cross explicitly speak of the mystery of God. For his part, Pinnock notes that Pentecostals tend to "resist neat systematic closure on issues of interpretation and experience . . . not due to illogicality on their part, owing to the emotional nature of their faith, but . . . [due to] the mystery of Yahweh, the biblical God." On this, Pinnock remarks that Pentecostals may in turn be ready to accept more tension than he does in his own proposals; they may be more disposed to leave certain things unresolved, to which Pinnock comments: "This is fine, except that I would exhort them not to dignify bad ideas with the noble category of mystery."[36] From his end and in response to Pinnock's models, Cross remarks that "perhaps the mystery that is God is beyond this kind of 'either/or' dichotomy."[37] Cross is aware of the inadequacy of the dyad he sees in Pinnock, since he affirms that God is mysteriously beyond such category reductions.

34. Cross, "The Rich Feast of Theology," 36.
35. Cross, "The Rich Feast of Theology," 46.
36. Pinnock, "Divine Relationality," 11.
37. Cross, "The Rich Feast of Theology," 42.

Their second affinity, however, is more theologically significant and, I would argue, problematic. Pinnock and Cross actually share a penchant to work in terms of binaries. Such has already been noted in Pinnock with his "absolutist" and "relational" models for God. But such is also the case with how he conceives of theology as a whole. Pinnock begins his article with the claim that experiences of God come first, whereas theological treatments tend to follow. In his words, "It is natural that preaching would come first and then theological reflection." In phrasing similar to Smith's mentioned above, Pinnock advocates for the primacy of experience over theory.[38] As for Cross, he critiques the two models of God he detects in Pinnock's work, but as noted above, he himself continues with a dyadic presentation of the theological task. For Cross, there is the "primary narrative of God in revelation"—a first-order kind of knowledge—and subsequently there is human reflection on that revelation, an activity best understood as second-order critical inquiry;[39] it is this latter kind of theology that can best account for what theology is from Cross's point of view.[40]

It is clear from this programmatic article by Pinnock and its response by Cross that, once again, the spirituality-theology divide plagues discussions related to the manner in which Pentecostals understand and pursue theology. One can see it to some degree in the articles prompted by Noll's work, but it is even more obvious in these last articles devoted to the doctrine of God. Both Pinnock and Cross recognize the mystery of God as in some sense qualifying theological work, but what they continue to be saddled by is the conceptual commitment that spirituality and theology operate within different domains. Spirituality has to do with experiences of God and the self-revelation of God; theology, in contrast, involves conceptualization, categorization, and the like, which humans undertake in some subsequent, responsive gesture. Pinnock seems to think he has solved the dilemma from the theological side by offering a master, integrative category (relationality), whereas Cross prefers to advocate a dialectical ten-

---

38. Pinnock, "Divine Relationality," 3–4, 11.

39. Cross finds this approach to be quite popular in the literature; he cites the following examples: Stanley Grenz, *Revisioning Evangelical Theology: A Fresh Agenda for the Twenty-First Century* (Downers Grove, IL: InterVarsity, 1993), 78; Daniel Migliore, *Faith Seeking Understanding: An Introduction to Christian Theology* (Grand Rapids: Eerdmans, 1991), 9; and—further confirming the point above—Clark Pinnock, *Tracking the Maze: Finding Our Way through Modern Theology from an Evangelical Perspective* (San Francisco: Harper & Row, 1990), 182. See Cross, "The Rich Feast of Theology," 36n26.

40. Cross, "The Rich Feast of Theology," 36.

sion in which two poles (God's perfection and relationality) are juxtaposed. Both, however, fail to challenge the bifurcation itself between spirituality and theology. I believe that precisely this kind of problematization of the theological task is one of Pentecostalism's great gifts to the theological academy in the current intellectual climate. It is a gift, however, that must be refined and clarified, given the different twists and turns Pentecostal scholarship has taken over the years.

Pentecostal Systematics?

For those who have followed the development of Pentecostal scholarship over the last half century, an early stage is especially clear: the first generation of scholars within the movement—those who pursued doctorates in theological disciplines broadly conceived—were usually those seeking to be specialists in New Testament studies. One reason for this concentration was the sensed need to legitimate the Pentecostal movement, particularly the Pentecostal experience of Spirit-baptism, through exegesis, usually via the Lukan and Pauline strands of the New Testament witness. Therefore, early Pentecostal theological scholarship was largely framed by the field of biblical studies.

For this reason and others, works written by Pentecostals that could be deemed theological or doctrinal in nature were written sporadically and were often pursued as elaborations of Scripture. The term "Bible doctrines," for instance, was sometimes used to express the point.[41] The presentation in these offerings was more explicitly aligned to an order associated with systematic theology, yet the content of these studies was based on a biblically inductive methodology.[42] This tradition has been around for some time and continues to be perpetuated by Pentecostals and charismatics alike.[43] Interestingly, Yong has recently noted that, in the

41. See Myer Pearlman, *Knowing the Doctrines of the Bible* (Springfield, MO: Gospel Publishing House, 1937).

42. Pearlman remarks about *Knowing the Doctrines of the Bible* that the book involves both biblical and systematic theology, but notice how the author describes the function of each qualifier: "It is Biblical in that the truths are taken from the Scriptures and the study is guided by the questions: What do the Scriptures say (exposition), and what do the Scriptures mean (interpretation)? It is systematic in that the material is arranged according to a definite order" (12).

43. Examples would include Ernest S. Williams, *Systematic Theology*, 3 vols.

case of three single-volume works in charismatic systematics,[44] all have the appearance of "evangelical theologies plus"—meaning that "each follows a basic evangelical theological pattern and methodological approach and . . . is devoted explicitly to few topics related to pneumatology and recognized as central to renewal spirituality."[45]

With the coming of subsequent generations, the question arises: Can there be a Pentecostal systematic theology? Furthermore, should there be such a thing? If so, what should it look like? In a subsequent paper to the article referenced above, Cross addresses these questions directly. At points, he highlights the importance of Pentecostal spirituality for such activity and mentions Land's *Pentecostal Spirituality*. Cross remarks: "I see Land's work as explicating the theological basis of our spirituality, but it does not do the work of systematic theology as traditionally understood. The question remains: Do Pentecostals need to write a systematic theology or is reflection on spirituality all that is required? Do we need to go beyond Steve Land's work?"[46] Obviously, such a remark has some key judgments that need explicit clarification. For instance, it is not really clear what it means for Land's book to be described as "explicating the theological basis" of Pentecostal spirituality and how that is somehow outside the purview of systematics. More pressing for present purposes, however, would be the following: most assuredly, Land's book does not do "the work of systematic theology as traditionally understood," but precisely what work would that be? And is that work useful and worth extending, particularly when the matter is being broached within a self-consciously Pentecostal idiom and ethos?

Furthermore, it is not clear what it would mean "to go beyond" Land's

---

(Springfield, MO: Gospel Publishing House, 1953); J. Rodman Williams, *Renewal Theology: Systematic Theology from a Charismatic Perspective*, 3 vols. (Grand Rapids: Zondervan, 1996); French L. Arrington, *Christian Doctrine: A Pentecostal Perspective*, 3 vols. (Cleveland, TN: Pathway, 1992–94); and Stanley M. Horton, *Systematic Theology: A Pentecostal Perspective* (Springfield, KY: Logion, 1995).

44. In addition to Williams's *Renewal Theology*, Yong includes in this list Wayne Grudem, *Systematic Theology: An Introduction to Biblical Doctrine* (Grand Rapids: Zondervan, 1994), and Larry D. Hart, *Truth Aflame: Theology for the Church in Renewal* (Grand Rapids: Zondervan, 2005). See Amos Yong, *Renewing Christian Theology: Systematics for a Global Christianity* (Waco, TX: Baylor University Press, 2014), 10.

45. Yong, *Renewing Christian Theology*, 10.

46. Terry Cross, "Can There Be a Pentecostal Systematic Theology? An Essay on Theological Method in a Postmodern World" (paper presented at the Thirtieth Annual Meeting of the Society for Pentecostal Studies, 2001; pagination for the paper [145–66] is from the collected papers of the conference), 147.

Pentecostal Spirituality. The present book, for instance, does not presume to go beyond Land's volume but to probe deeper into its logic, which is a certain kind of development that may or may not be considered an advance. What other horizons are there, and would a "Pentecostal systematic theology" really be a level beyond what Land has done? The goal here is not to elevate Land's contribution or somehow make it a model study, for all proposals must be probed and evaluated. The matter at hand is the particular methodological judgments at work in Cross's remarks and their repercussions for framing what theology is. What one senses is precisely the tension in methodology alluded to above. In pursuing his work, Land followed a methodological approach that was at variance with the effort understood as systematic theology; when evaluated from the perspective of systematics, therefore, it is not clear whether Land "brings the theological goods," so to speak. This uneasiness seems to be on display in Cross's case; he, like Yong, wishes to maintain the prospects of systematic theology within the Pentecostal fold.

Admittedly, the phrase "Pentecostal systematic theology" is a bit strange, with two qualifiers alongside "theology." From the phrase, it is unclear what relationship "Pentecostal" and "systematic" have. Given the way that Pentecostals, as noted above, have sometimes pursued formal theological reflection, one would think that some have believed that an exegetical approach to theological thinking would help retain Pentecostal distinctives as these are understood to be drawn from the New Testament, while at the same time chastening systematics to be more explicitly biblical and less conceptually (or perhaps, philosophically) speculative. Others may assume that "systematics" is strictly a particular way of formulating and organizing beliefs and that Pentecostals can therefore subsume their beliefs within such a framework, just as Lutherans, Presbyterians, and others have done in their own traditions. These possibilities (and perhaps many others) show how the two qualifiers can exercise various amounts of power and influence over each other and in turn lead to different outcomes. But as noted above, the difficulty detectable here is not related simply to the relationship between Pentecostalism and systematic theology per se. The matter goes deeper still to the internally disputed nature of theology itself. The pivotal questions here are:

What kind of knowledge is God-knowledge?
How is such knowledge pursued and fostered?
How can one go about stating and communicating it?

The field known as systematic theology within the theological disciplines has attempted to answer these questions in a particular way, but plenty of theologians wonder about its suitability, aims, nature, and purposes. That is, theologians are often at odds with one another on how to define and understand their discipline, so much so that people can use the heading "systematic theology" to speak of very different things. No less a theological figure than Karl Barth openly questioned the phrase.

> [The term "systematic theology"] is based on a tradition which is quite recent and highly problematic. Is not the term "Systematic Theology" as paradoxical as a "wooden iron"? One day this conception will disappear just as suddenly as it has come into being. . . . I could never write a book under this title. . . . A "system" is an edifice of thought, constructed on certain fundamental conceptions which are selected in accordance with a certain philosophy by a method which corresponds to these conceptions. Theology cannot be carried on in confinement or under the pressure of such a construction.[47]

Barth's definition is quite specific, and some may find it reductive as a result. For instance, in Barth's definition one notices a kind of methodological stereotyping that could work well with the approach of foundationalism, according to which an edifice of thought is constructed on certain fundamental conceptions in line with a kind of philosophy. Others believe that systematic theology can be undertaken without such a foundationalist orientation. Their tendency would be to highlight an open-endedness to the theological task that would be developed as various theological authorities are brought together in an orderly, or "systematic," way.

This last approach would seem to be the way Yong perceives of the field; his *Spirit-Word-Community*, for example, offers a communitarian, or intersubjective, realism within a nonfoundationalist framework.[48] In many ways, the crux of this approach would be how to secure and relate this realism in a fitting way theologically. By returning to Yong's early article in response to Johns and Smith, we can see some of the challenges involved. In response to Johns, Yong states, "But traditionally, at least,

---

47. Karl Barth, "Foreword to the Torchbook Edition," in *Dogmatics in Outline* (New York: Harper & Row, 1959), 5.
48. Amos Yong, *Spirit-Word-Community* (Eugene, OR: Wipf & Stock, 2002). My thanks to Yong for personal correspondence that helped me clarify his approach.

systematic theology has been understood as the deliberate organization of ideas integrating biblical revelation on God, self, and world that aims at universal truth."[49] On this score, theological realism is secured on the basis of biblical revelation related to God, self, and world, which is subsequently organized by the systematician. Yong further stresses:

> Systematic theology is therefore best understood as a reflective enterprise that encompasses the three horizons of God, self, and world and attempts to comprehend their relationships, and that gets accurately at the realities that they claim to engage. This theological enterprise is now accountable to diverse narratives that need to be correlated in its search for norms, its quest for truth, and in its effort to articulate our experience and synthesize it within a coherent framework of belief and understanding. Systematic theology is thus the truthful integration of Pentecostal faith, spirituality, praxis, and thought—making coherent its plausibility structures, ensuring that its understanding corresponds to the way things are, and giving guidance to Pentecostal life.

The difficulty with this basic definition of systematic theology is that it puts the systematician "in the driver's seat," so to speak. It grants a place of privilege to the systematician to encompass, comprehend, get accurately at the realities in question, articulate, synthesize, integrate, and make coherent the sum of Pentecostal life—all without much by way of accounting for how or on what grounds the systematician does so. Furthermore, both in terms of the "biblical revelation on God" affirmed above, as well as the "horizon of God" alluded to in the immediate past definition, it would seem that God is simply one datum among others that needs to be accounted for in the systematic task. Within this perspective, God and God's self-revelation are features (among others) that are in need of being brought together in an orderly way by the hand of the systematician. As such, "God" represents but one feature of such a task.

I would argue that, in these early claims by Yong, two implicit features of theologizing from the Pentecostal ethos need further clarification and development. The first is that one's theologizing is only as legitimate and as truthful as one's own spiritual journey (or what some might colloquially refer to as one's prayer life). On Pentecostal terms, the life of piety is the essential and orienting grounding for one's work of theological reflection.

49. Yong, "Whither Systematic Theology?," 89.

This way of putting the matter may sound altogether too pietistic for some, but early Pentecostals were explicitly disposed to consider theological effort as necessarily dependent upon something greater than intellectual prowess and creativity. There was something vitally at stake for them in assessing and taking into account a person's Spirit-imbued power and anointing before moving on to evaluate his or her theological proposals. The theologian, in other words, had to be located within a broader context and reality, one in which spiritual matters were front and center. To use the old-time language of Azusa, a theologian in the Pentecostal tradition would need to have, and work out of, a "personal Pentecost" because such an experience opened up theological horizons (both imaginative and intellectual) and provided urgency for Pentecostal witness. [50] Implicit in this orientation is the idea that, methodologically speaking, theologizing is a kind of moral-theological activity whose character is directly tied to the character of the practitioner. [51] The "life of the mind" on Pentecostal terms is directly related to "life in the Spirit."

This life in the Spirit operates from a doxological modality, or, we could say, a context of worship. In this case, specification is needed so as to avoid misunderstandings. Worship here is not being spoken of as simply an activity at a church or revivalist service; rather, it is a way of perceiving, interacting, and behaving in the world (which would include, but not be limited to, such church or revivalist activities). Pentecostals have always located themselves within the drama of God's unfolding

50. In a section devoted to distinguishing fanaticism and defending the truthfulness of the Pentecostal movement, the *Apostolic Faith* remarks that the confirming signs were divine love, humility, and holy lives; these indicators were how one could know whether the Pentecostal movement was true. The section ends: "There is a Holy Ghost shine on the faces of the workers. Is this the work of the devil? Friends, if you profess to know the Spirit of God and do not recognize Him when He comes, there is cause for you to be anxious about your own spiritual condition" (*Apostolic Faith* 1.2 [1906]: 6). This kind of "epistemological reversal" is quite common in Pentecostal contexts; it makes the somewhat circular point that one can recognize God only if one truly knows God from a worshipful context.

51. In this and what follows, I follow arguments that I have presented in *Revisioning Pentecostal Ethics—the Epicletic Community* (Cleveland, TN: CPT Press, 2012). There I made the case that thinking of ethics on Pentecostal grounds must stem from precisely a doxological modality, which I developed in terms of "abiding" and "waiting" on the Spirit in an "epicletic" ("calling upon") manner. Corollaries can be made from that work to the theological task as a whole, since, as I see them, both tasks (the ethical and the theological) are undertaken within a broader rendering of the nature of God-knowledge.

purposes in the world.[52] This orientation has come from their view that the self-presentation of God in their lives makes them first and foremost God-related and God-directed participants in the economy of the Spirit's work. What they went on to say, preach, do, feel, and think was all self-consciously grounded in a perceived God-saturated reality. This kind of consciousness and intentionality allows this Pentecostal way of "being-in-the-world" to be called worshipful or doxological.[53] Put in another way hinted at by Hollenweger above, Pentecostals have always followed the logic inherent in the motto *lex orandi, lex credendi* ("the law of prayer [is] the law of faith"); they can also agree with an expression in Eastern Orthodoxy associated with Evagrius: "If you are a theologian, you will pray truly. And if you pray truly, you are a theologian."[54]

Necessarily, then, this commitment would make theology a kind of spiritual activity. As Eric Springstead remarks in an essay related to the interrelation of theology and spirituality: "Theology is spiritual because it involves an improvement, or is tied to an improvement, of the spirit. That theology has something to do with spirituality, therefore, means that we not only think of God, but by thinking of God truly at all we are at the same time involved with [God] in such a way that our spirits are improved by that involvement, by that thinking."[55] Springstead continues by noting that thought is related to change and that thinking of God is a kind of relating to God. I believe that Pentecostals would be comfortable with all of these claims. For Pentecostals, to be human is to be first and foremost a worshiper. Whether this perspective can be integrated into a systematics is an open question, but on this matter, Pentecostals would agree that the qualifier "Pentecostal" needs to qualify "systematic."

The second point worth pursuing in Yong's proposals as they are cited here would be that God and the experience of God are inherently irreduc-

---

52. And perhaps Pentecostals did so exceedingly; one cannot help but wonder why so many early Pentecostals thought they were front-and-center for massive changes in universal history.

53. This point appears repeatedly in Smith's *Thinking in Tongues*, but it also fits well with the broader arguments he makes in his Cultural Liturgies series, as first addressed in his *Desiring the Kingdom: Worship, Worldview, and Cultural Formation* (Grand Rapids: Baker Academic, 2009).

54. Evagrius, *On Prayer*, 61, in *The Philokalia*, ed. and trans. G. E. H. Palmer, Phillip Sherrard, and Kallistos Ware (New York: Faber & Faber, 1979), 1:62.

55. Eric O. Springstead, "Theology and Spirituality; or, Why Theology Is Not Critical Reflection on Religious Experience," in *Spirituality and Theology: Essays in Honor of Diogenes Allen*, ed. Springstead (Louisville: Westminster John Knox, 1998), 49–50.

ible at the conceptual level. Plenty of Pentecostals have been repeatedly at a loss to articulate what it is that they witness and experience in Pentecostal worship. Early adherents often simply referred to the "power of God" as a way of accounting for its all-enveloping scope. Yet, they were also inclined to acknowledge that the happenings they were witnessing were "beyond description."[56] This kind of speech shapes a particular theological sensibility over time. It can be expressed as follows: the experience or encounter with God is beyond the typical categories people use to relate and explain their otherwise mundane reality. Pentecostals often stumble and even resort to dramatic and apocalyptic imagery to convey all that is involved in what they apprehend during such encounters. Words simply do not do justice to what they traditionally believe to be involved in such "Spirit-encounters."

In addition to the points noted in relation to Yong, one should also consider Cross's contribution, especially since he raises so prominently the question of the viability of "Pentecostal systematics." Cross pursues the legitimacy of an ongoing demarcation between spirituality and theology, but his program does not take account of the complexity of the relationship as Pentecostals typically understand it. Cross's demarcation is evident on a number of fronts. When speaking of the disarray postmodernism has created for systematics, Cross notes in passing, "To imply *systematic* theology is in peril as a discipline does not mean theology itself is in peril, rather that a systemless theology that no longer explicates and organizes a revealed set of truths but instead offers a series of testimonials of one's spirituality is on the rise."[57] With regard to Pentecostals, he remarks, "Theology for Pentecostals might take on the appearance of a theology of spirituality rather than an overarching system of doctrine." At this point we have footnoted remarks that he makes about Land's project—in particular, that Land offers a "theological basis of [Pentecostal] spirituality but [his book] does not do the work of systematic theology as traditionally understood."[58] From all that we have surveyed about Cross's views, it seems that spirituality is something that can be theologized about but ultimately something distinct from theology, even if at the end of the day it is the ground of theology. Here I would argue that Cross has fundamen-

56. *Apostolic Faith* 1.1 (1906): 1.
57. Cross, "Can There Be a Pentecostal Systematic Theology?," 147n11 (emphasis original).
58. Cross, "Can There Be a Pentecostal Systematic Theology?," 147, 147n13.

tally misunderstood Land's proposals: Land was not simply trying to theologize about Pentecostal spirituality; more significantly, he was aiming to explore how spirituality determines the manner and shape of Pentecostal theologizing. In other words, Land's contribution was methodologically productive in a way that Cross does not sufficiently recognize, perhaps since from the beginning Cross associates spirituality fundamentally with experiences that may be theologically fruitful at some point in time but only as they are taken up within a particular, methodologically defined theological structure.

Cross is aware that Pentecostal theology must be distinctive from other kinds. In fact, he makes several points that are in line with the project being pursued here. For instance, he distances Pentecostal theology from evangelical theology, citing no less a figure than Carl F. H. Henry in doing so.[59] Cross is also keen to emphasize the pneumatological character of Pentecostal theology. But most surprisingly, he comes closest to the agenda of the present work when he draws from Springstead to say that theology must be something that shapes the thinker. Cross remarks that "theology is spiritual" and that the basis for this conviction is that, "for there to be knowledge of God, one must interact with God. Thus, theology (or something akin to the knowledge of God) has spirituality at its root." Further elaborating on Springstead's work, Cross notes that, in weaving together *speculativo* (intellection) and *speculatio* (contemplation), Springstead "wants to create a place where God is the object of our intellectual apprehension and yet still affects humans who are encountered by him. God is 'spiritually fecund' and therefore draws us toward perfection by his very nature." Finally, Cross points to Springstead's use of Simone Weil, an important figure with regard to discussions of mystical theology. Cross states, "Humans wait on God or pay close attention by focusing on [God]. This 'non-active action' transforms them. The intellect and spirit are not split in this response, but the whole being is changed, drawn upward towards God." Cross concludes: "Therefore, theology's task is not merely reflecting on one's religious experience, but waiting on God, being transformed by [God], and made fit for participation in the divine life." Cross then cites both Ellen Charry and Land as supporting Springstead's proposals, and Cross himself admits that there is much in all of this with which he could agree. He even goes so far as to claim what could have been leveled

---

59. Henry will be a focus of chap. 3; here we note simply that Cross's critiques are similar to the ones considered there.

as a critique of his earlier work and reflections: "Pentecostal theology must sink its roots deep in the experience of the God of Pentecost. . . . Yet in turn, the development of theological reflection should also enhance one's spiritual experience. The sap flows both ways in this Pentecostal tree."[60] All these claims by Cross are very promising.

And yet, Cross cannot resist. The question that forms the title of his essay presumably needs answering, and the pressure to answer it in a certain way is considerable. Right after the line quoted immediately above, Cross continues: "The question remaining, then, is whether such Pentecostal theology can be *systematic*."[61] Why does this question remain? A few lines later, Cross comments, "Almost every theology has an integrating principle or motif around which it operates." He does not want a scholasticizing approach, such as one finds in some evangelical works on systematic theology, but he does wish for Pentecostal theology to avoid being "a collection of miscellaneous testimonies or scattered narratives highlighted from Scripture." What Pentecostals need is an "organizing skeleton to build upon so that there is some substance of content and consistency of approach in their theological endeavor." Cross goes further in suggesting at this point that "integrating principles are necessary" for securing coherence and meaning. Without these principles, knowledge cannot hold together and be communicated. As a result, "Pentecostal systematic theology needs to offer an integrating principle for the sake of clarity of presentation and coherency of content, both to the Church and the world."[62]

What could such an integrating principle be? Cross surveys the fourfold/fivefold paradigm and its use for theology as proposed by John Christopher Thomas,[63] but he goes on to mention some reservations with such an approach. Cross's alternative is to present Trinitarian theology as an integrating principle. He speaks of the Trinity as a rubric by which one can account for the encounter Pentecostals confess to have with the God of their worship, as well as one around which Pentecostals can craft their

60. Cross, "Can There Be a Pentecostal Systematic Theology?," 160, 162. Interestingly, this elaboration of Springstead's work problematizes to some degree Cross's own logic of subsequence within the spirituality-theology dynamic.

61. Cross, "Can There Be a Pentecostal Systematic Theology?," 162 (emphasis original).

62. Cross, "Can There Be a Pentecostal Systematic Theology?," 162.

63. John Christopher Thomas, "Pentecostal Theology in the Twenty-First Century," *Pneuma* 20 (1998): 3–19.

theological reflection. In a telling line, Cross concludes a point by stating, "The richness of trinitarian life becomes the integrating, systematic principle for a Pentecostal theology."[64] The promise hinted at earlier in Cross's paper has now been abandoned. Against his own intuitions, I would argue, Cross has gone on to conceptualize that which from one angle he knows cannot be.

As with Yong, so with Cross here: I wish to make two points regarding the latter's proposals in which he has challenged Pentecostal theological sensibilities. First, Cross's commitment that all knowledge—and by implication, then, all theological knowledge—requires an integrating principle to make sense sounds very close to Smith's reservations regarding Noll's project, namely, that one needs a theory in order to engage in meaning-making. In this, Cross perhaps sounds more like the evangelicals he wishes to keep at some distance than he might care to admit. I would argue that, when Pentecostals share their testimonies, they do so not out of random, willy-nilly, happenstance conditions. One senses a logic to their testimonies, but such a logic is not based on an integrating principle per se. The logic of Pentecostal testimonies rings true only when one catches a glimpse of *who* the God is whom Pentecostals proclaim—and this glimpse involves a number of registers (including a cognitive one, but certainly not exclusively so). Pentecostal testimony does not receive its coherence from being structured around a rubric or integrative principle, nor does it make sense only when it is pushed into some broader mechanism of meaning.[65] Ultimately, when Pentecostals testify, they are bearing witness to someone beyond their (and their hearers') cognitive grasp or comprehension. Their testimonies are an implicit invitation to enter into that reality, to feast on "the good things of God," to experience a baptism of love that almost kills with its sweetness.[66]

64. Cross, "Can There Be a Pentecostal Systematic Theology?," 165. One of the problems with "integrating principles" is that they always have shortcomings in application and relatability; the same rings true here: Oneness Pentecostals would have something to say as to the adequacy of this organizational motif for Pentecostal theology.

65. Granted, early Pentecostals simply assumed Scripture's metanarrative and did so within particular revivalist accents. Within this approach, various things were assumed to be the case about God, God's purposes, and God's work overall; in other words, a logic was at play. But such a move is different from the claim that the Trinitarian life is "an integrating systematic principle" or a generalized "rubric" by which to order an account of beliefs. With such kind of language and the expectations it introduces, I would say one has entered into a distinct, intellectualist (per Smith's usage above) domain.

66. *Apostolic Faith* 1.1 (1906): 1.

On this score, a second point is worth noting about Cross's propos- als, one that is quite similar to the one raised with regard to Yong's. On Pentecostal grounds, the triune life—and so the God of Christian confession—cannot be reduced to a theological *concept*. To use Cross's phrasing, "the richness of trinitarian life" is that it is in fact *a life*, and a life cannot be put to use as a rubric, integrating principle, or organi- zational skeleton that in turn serves the purpose of aiding in the con- struction of a system of thought.[67] When exposed to such a reduction, a life is objectified in such a way that it can be utilized and appropriated for any number of unhelpful ends. Rather than this approach, another possibility presents itself: a life must be encountered only from another life within the conditions of a specific time and space. These kinds of commitments hold for thinking of human intersubjectivity, but they can also be analogously maintained in the consideration of God-human interactions.

The Spirituality-Theology Interface

Yong's and Cross's persistent pursuit of the viability of Pentecostal system- atic theology is in many ways unfortunate, in that such concerns operate in response to pressures that wield significant influence in determining what theology needs to be in order to be a respectable academic discipline. In one sense, Yong and Cross cannot be faulted for raising such questions and expressing such concerns in these early works. Pentecostal theology is relatively new and unknown to the theological scene, and interactions and dialogue are very much part of growth and understanding for both insiders and outsiders alike. Cross raises important queries that many people have asked and will continue to ask, and perhaps no one has sin- glehandedly done more in recent memory to elevate the prominence of

67. What may be more fitting to say (and perhaps this is Cross's intent) is that the *doctrine* of the Trinity (and not the Trinity per se) can form the basis of a Pentecostal systematic theology. But then again, the notion of a doctrine as strictly theoretical or conceptual is itself what is being challenged here. Obviously, a conceptual dimension is involved when matters are communicated, related, and thought out, but the doctrine of the Trinity is not strictly a conceptual notion. As the next chapter will suggest broadly, doctrines such as that of the Trinity are mystical in that they move beyond theoretical cognition to participatory levels of engagement, becoming an expression of and an invitation to encounter the living God.

Pentecostal theology in the academy than has Yong. The concern being considered here is whether Pentecostal theology runs the risk of conceding too much by way of theological methodology when it tries to answer the question of Pentecostal systematics. Can theology as it is typically done do justice to some of the most important features of what Pentecostalism is? The question pushes the focus back on Pentecostals to think carefully about what makes their tradition distinctive. In other words, it calls for the task of tradition-negotiation.

One of the difficulties with such a process of tradition-negotiation (which both Yong and Cross feel and acknowledge in their respective ways) is that Pentecostal reflection has at least two significant streams in the early literature: one was published testimonies and narratives of people's experiences of God, and the other involved more expansive and elaborative works that were intentionally written as explanatory and suggestive treatises. The second category is what largely constitutes the survey that Douglas Jacobsen presented in his *Thinking in the Spirit*. Here Jacobsen highlights twelve early Pentecostal leaders who lived in the period 1900–1925 and who published significant works of theological reflection. Jacobsen used these works to summarize how these leaders were reflecting on the movement during its early years. For example, when considering Charles Parham, Jacobsen largely does so in the terms established in Parham's *Kol Kare Bomidbar*; when Jacobsen reviews Richard Spurling, he highlights *The Lost Link*, and so on. Jacobsen's remarks on these works by these twelve leaders are quite fascinating for their methodological suggestiveness:

> The point is that while pentecostal theology does indeed have a different center of gravity than many other kinds of theology, pentecostal theology does not exist in a class by itself. The stylistic difference between pentecostal theology and other forms of theology is one of degree, not of radical disjuncture. From the beginning of the movement, pentecostal thinkers have been producing theological treatises alongside their songs, sermons, prayers, and testimonies. These authors never implied that they had to give up part of their pentecostal faith to write in a systematic and logical manner, and there is no evidence that their relatively systematic style of writing forced them to set aside certain pentecostal topics simply because they didn't logically fit with everything else. They were writing as pentecostals to pentecostals for pentecostal theological purposes while trying to be just as thorough and systematic

as their non-pentecostal theological peers. It is these works that provide the focus of this study.[68]

Clearly, Jacobsen has privileged a certain kind of textual evidence in developing his understanding of Pentecostal theology. He proceeds: "The main goal of these systematic presentations of pentecostal faith was not personal transformation but truth-telling. The primary purpose was explanation, not testimony. The motivating impulse was not necessarily to lead the reader into one or another spiritual experience . . . but to explore the theological significance of those experiences." He concludes by summarizing, "While many of these pentecostal theologians could exhort and testify with the best of them, they were intent on keeping their preaching separate from their lecturing in their explicitly theological publications."[69]

In presenting his intellectual history and survey, Jacobsen needs to circumscribe his task in some way. He does so by highlighting the significance of the second strand mentioned above, even as he acknowledges that what makes Pentecostalism unique is the first strand. Jacobsen implicitly suggests as much by beginning his text with the testimony of William Durham and by explicitly noting that Pentecostalism has a "different center of gravity" than other forms of theology, given its spirituality.[70] Jacobsen is just one of many who think that Pentecostal theology, for it to be theology, must have some kind of ordered, or systematic, structure. But narratives and testimonies are assumed to be something other than proper theology, most likely the less academically respectable category "spirituality."

The reservations noted above in relation to Yong's and Cross's proposals could apply in some sense to that of Jacobsen as well. These concerns stem from the perspective first extensively argued in the contemporary

68. Douglas Jacobsen, *Thinking in the Spirit* (Bloomington: Indiana University Press, 2003), 7.

69. Jacobsen, *Thinking in the Spirit*, 7–8.

70. In this context (*Thinking in the Spirit*, 6), Jacobsen alludes to an extended comment by Harvey Cox: "As a theologian I had grown accustomed to studying religious movements by reading what their theologians wrote and trying to grasp their central ideas and most salient doctrines. But I soon found out that with pentecostalism this approach does not help much. As one pentecostal scholar puts it, in his faith 'the experience of God has absolute primacy over dogma and doctrine.' Therefore the only theology that can give an account of this experience, he says, is 'a narrative theology whose central expression is the testimony.' I think that he is right" (*Fire from Heaven* [Reading, MA: Addison-Wesley], 71). Cox does not identify the theologian he is quoting, but the insights are in line with much of what I am here proposing.

literature by Land, namely, that narrative and testimony *are* legitimate and productive theological categories in and of themselves. This position pushes Pentecostal theology to a methodological crossroads, with the various proposals coming from such a crossroads having their own supporters and rationales. According to Jacobsen, the second stream really is not all that different methodologically from other alternatives within the Christian tradition. For some, this outcome is perfectly acceptable and perhaps even appealing. My view, however, is different. I wish to highlight the *theological* significance of the first stream because I believe that it captures much of what makes Pentecostalism distinctive from other Christian traditions; it also constitutes what Pentecostalism's contribution can be to those wider publics.

If one grants the theological integrity of the first stream, several implications follow. First, this acknowledgment recognizes that theology need not be wholly captive to the tendencies and prejudices governing how academic disciplines are framed. Given that narratives and testimonies arise from life experiences and events, they can in turn expose the abstraction and decontextualization that often surround disciplinary understandings as these promote for themselves objectivity and freedom from bias. In marked distinction to the latter, theology that is attentive to the life of faith must be pursued in a unique way if its object of study cannot be abstracted or selectively held at a distance. An emphasis on the first stream would mean that Pentecostals implicitly understand that theology cannot simply be another discipline among others in a university or seminary setting.

Second, narratives and testimonies place God-knowledge front and center as that which occupies the theological task. This knowledge somehow needs to be available beyond the confines of those who speak of it, since it aims to be theological in character and not simply anthropological. Put quaintly, Pentecostals typically mean to talk about God, not simply about themselves, when they speak of their experiences. Grant Wacker makes this observation quite directly: "Stepping back in time, quietly slipping into early pentecostals' kitchens and parlors, I heard, first of all, a great deal of talk about Holy Ghost baptism . . . about the Bible, its power, its beauty, and the way it served as the final authority . . . about signs and wonders." But, he adds, "The more I listened to those discussions . . . the more I realized that most of them were really about something else. And that something else, of course, was God."[71] From such an observation,

71. Grant Wacker, *Heaven Below* (Cambridge, MA: Harvard University Press,

one can compellingly state regarding the two significant streams of Pentecostal theology noted above: the first strand can be theo-logical in ways that the second cannot.

Third, if theology is to be theo-logical (i.e., properly about God), then it must be understood as directly related to spirituality. To separate the two is always a *theological* mistake. If the object of theology is the God of Christian confession, then how and in what manner this object is engaged and known is significant. If narratives and testimonies within the Pentecostal fold are privileged in theological reflection, then we have a genuine interaction between theology and spirituality. This relation, which I will call for brevity's sake "the spirituality-theology interface," is one of the great contributions of Land's *Pentecostal Spirituality*. For those who observe the many features of the movement, the dynamic is very obvious. As Jacobsen himself admits, "Within early pentecostalism, theology and experience went hand in hand."[72]

In fact, the methodological privileging of the spirituality-theology interface in Pentecostalism—with its reliance on narratives and testimonies for its theological substantiation—simply brings many features of Pentecostal theological reflection to light that may otherwise be hidden. Some of these points have already been highlighted above, including theology's integrity being tied to a theologian's spirituality, the irreducibility of God and the experience of God, the registering of meaning beyond the positing of a baseline theoretical construct, and the affirmation that God is best understood not simply as a concept. The spirituality-theology interface also addresses the direct concern of Pentecostals to keep theological reflection in check, lest it compromise the experience of genuine faith. Repeatedly, early Pentecostals expressed caution regarding theological statements (including doctrines, creeds, and the like) and formal theological education (at least, as pursued outside their own nascent educational efforts) because they had seen repeatedly that these could obstruct or compromise the animating center of the life of faith. Of course, Pentecostals did fight and divide (excessively!) over doctrinal concerns, but overall, this regulative function of doctrine operated alongside a suspicion of doctrine. The logic of such a tension requires a paradigm that highlights the spirituality-theology interface.

2001), 11. For purposes of this study, it is important to highlight what Wacker goes on to say immediately after the line above: "Occasionally the longing to touch God bordered on mysticism, a craving to be absorbed into the One or even to obliterate one's own identity into the identity of the All."

72. Jacobsen, *Thinking in the Spirit*, 3.

Expanding the Field of Systematics

On account of these many points that stem from this particular reading—one that privileges this first strand of Pentecostal self-expression in the early literature—Pentecostalism starts to appear more like a Christian mystical tradition and less like a movement that can be conveniently circumscribed by any systematic theology. To emphasize one direction seems to inevitably depart from the other. One must recognize, however, that the language of systematics can mean different things to different constituencies; these possibilities are worth probing further.[73]

"Systematizing" can indeed mean building an architectonic system of thought through deduction, based on certain principles or axioms, as Barth suggests in the quote above on page 19. This model represents a foundationalist understanding that is reminiscent of modernist thought-forms, but its lineage can be traced back to Aristotle. Some refer to this model as Euclidean or geometric because of the way it works from a priori givens to subsequent claims. This kind of geometric reasoning can occur either within a deposit of material (making it an intrinsic kind of foundationalism) or outside of such a deposit, thereby requiring some other foundation. The kind of movement stemming from a priori foundations to subsequent axioms can also vary. For "strong" accounts of these efforts, the deduction is quite rigorous in terms of a displayed continuity and logic carried through in lockstep fashion. For others, the interconnectivity of various claims is ordered more on a network model; they are connected and interrelated in some sense, but the logic from axioms to subsequent principles is "weak."

Perhaps these possibilities are best illustrated through concrete examples from the history of theological reflection. Among early theologians, for example, Irenaeus is a different kind of systematician than Origen.[74]

73. For the following elaborations, I am indebted to Colin Gunton; see his "A Rose by Any Other Name? From 'Christian Doctrine' to 'Systematic Theology,'" *International Journal of Systematic Theology* 1, no. 1 (1999): 4–23. Gunton is partly reliant on a suggestive work that is not limited to systematic theology but certainly applicable to it: Nicholas Rescher, *Cognitive Systematization: A Systems-Theoretic Approach to a Coherentist Theory of Knowledge* (Totowa, NJ: Rowman & Littlefield, 1979).

74. This pairing is Gunton's in "A Rose by Any Other Name?" I realize that many scholars (including Gunton himself) often consider Origen's *On First Principles* the first self-conscious exemplification of the genre of systematic theology; however, I am encouraged by Gunton's comparison at this point, since Irenaeus's work can also be

Irenaeus's *On the Apostolic Preaching* and Origen's *On First Principles* are two very distinct texts in their theoretical and epistemological commitments. Both are indeed systematic accounts of the Christian faith, but they are so in different ways.

In recognition of the zeal for godliness of his friend Marcianus, to whom Irenaeus is writing, Irenaeus remarks in the preface to his work,

> We have not hesitated to speak a little with you . . . by writing, and to demonstrate, by means of a summary, the preaching of the truth, so as to strengthen your faith. We are sending you, as it were, a summary memorandum, so that you may find much in a little, and by means of this small [work] understand all the members of the body of truth, and through a summary receive the exposition of the things of God so that, in this way, it will bear your own salvation like fruit, and that you may confound all those who hold false opinions and to everyone who desires to know, you may deliver our sound and irreproachable word in all boldness.[75]

For Irenaeus, truth is associated with faith, godliness, sanctification, and the like. He adds at the end of the section, "We must keep the rule of faith unswervingly, and perform the commandments of God, believing in God and fearing Him, for He is Lord, and loving Him, for He is Father."[76] Faith, obedience, and love—these are what allow believers to have "a true comprehension of what is," to have a working sense of the "systematic" elaborations that follow in Irenaeus's work.

Origen's work is of another order; it has a different operational and methodological orientation. Origen affirms that Jesus Christ is the truth

---

considered "systematic" in a certain way. It is helpful here for Gunton to have included Irenaeus so as to nuance and vary what the modifier "systematic" can mean in theological reflection. Furthermore, I should add that Sarah Coakley has recently encouraged readers of Origen to go beyond *On First Principles* to "fill out the picture of his doctrinal vision in infinitely richer ways" (Sarah Coakley, *God, Sexuality, and the Self: An Essay "On the Trinity"* [Cambridge: Cambridge University Press, 2013], 37). As helpful as this encouragement is in Origen's case (and the recommendation applies to others as well), the point still stands that certain works from antiquity are selected and privileged as embodying the label "systematic theology." Thankfully, with the help of Coakley and others, this privileging can be shown for what it is, namely, a modern, academic bias.

75. St. Irenaeus of Lyons, *On the Apostolic Preaching*, trans. John Behr (Crestwood, NY: St. Vladimir's Seminary Press, 1997), 39.

76. Irenaeus, *On the Apostolic Preaching*, 41.

and that people have come to know and speak of this truth because of the work of the Holy Spirit. Various teachings can arise on these points, however, and Origen finds it necessary "to fix a definite limit and to lay down an unmistakable rule" regarding each of the topics of faith.[77] After summarizing some of the points of the apostles' teaching, he concludes the preface to *On First Principles* as follows:

> Every one, therefore, must make use of elements and foundations of this sort, according to the precept, "Enlighten yourselves with the light of knowledge," if he would desire to form a connected series and body of truths agreeably to the reason of all these things, that by clear and necessary statements he may ascertain the truth regarding each individual topic, and form, as we have said, one body of doctrine, by means of illustrations and arguments—either those which he has discovered in holy Scripture, or which he has deduced by closely tracing out the consequences and following a correct method.[78]

Origen is committed to establishing a summary of the faith, as is Irenaeus, but Origen believes that doing so rests largely on an intellectual work predicated upon examples from Scripture or matters deduced from tracing out consequences and following the inherent logic of a particular method.

Commitment to Christ on the part of these authors is not at issue in terms of the merits of these proposals; rather, the matter concerns how the Christian gospel is conceptually secured, ordered, and framed. Unmistakably, different methodologies are at work in these two works, but it is worth noting here that different ends and purposes are also involved. For Irenaeus, "summarizing" and "systematizing" are activities that, on the basis of the terms above, represent a kind of effort that is intrinsically network-oriented rather than deductively delineated. It is also clear, however, that *On the Apostolic Preaching* aims to strengthen the reader's faith, to help the reader bear effective witness—in short, to aid the reader in his or her godliness of mind, soul, and body. Whereas the work may be deemed "systematic" in a certain sense, its aim ultimately is beyond itself: to lead to the transformation of the reader, who is above all to be located within a God-permeated reality. As Colin Gunton notes, Irenaeus is ultimately concerned with "the economy of divine action towards and in the

77. Origen, *On First Principles*, Preface as found in *ANF* 4:239.
78. Origen, *On First Principles*, Preface, *ANF* 4:241.

world."[79] In these senses, Irenaeus is privileging a spirituality-theology interface.

Origen, in contrast, also pursues an intrinsic, foundationalist kind of project, although the form of interconnectivity within it is "strong," in that the deductive format is quite pronounced. What is Origen's goal with *On First Principles*? It seems to be to offer an account of the Christian faith that represents a single body of teaching, unified by a methodological and deductive rigor. In other words, the purpose of this work is largely considered in terms of its intellectual appeal; it is oriented toward itself—to its own integrity via demonstration and argumentation for the sake of a unified presentation.

The methodologies of these works are different, and so are their aims. They both operate out of the givenness—and so out of the restraints and possibilities—associated with the gospel narrative. But one is more rigorous in deductive logic than the other; Origen's is more inclined to look to itself, whereas Irenaeus's is outward directed in terms of God's engagement and work, which would include, among other things, the reader in his or her own particular circumstances. The systematic weakness evident in Irenaeus's proposals appears to be strategic. Origen strives after consistency within a given methodology, and his starting point includes a rationalistic rigor. Irenaeus, in contrast, is striving after faithfulness within an economy of holiness—the theater of God's participation and engagement with the world that leads to its healing and divinization.

As I understand them, Irenaeus's vision and those like it will typically be appealing to Pentecostals. This vision calls for the systematic theologian and his or her writing, speaking, and conceptualizing (i.e., systematizing) to be located within the economy of God's activity and purposes. On this score, sanctification is a more fundamental category than scholarly completeness—conviction and passion are more determinative here than coherence and rationality. What sets the tone for Pentecostal theologizing is the reality and confession that God is at work in the world, including the academic realm. With such a baseline and orienting claim, Pentecostals cannot help but think that falling prostrate on one's knees in prayer is more basic to a faithful form of engagement than typing one's thoughts on a keyboard. The prayer-logic, however, can be sustained to a deeper level still: typing on a keyboard can in some sense—when it is construed as an activity within the framework of God's self-presentation and work—be a

79. Gunton, "A Rose by Any Other Name?," 9.

prayerful act of faithfulness. The importance highlighted here is not so much on a specific activity (e.g., typing) as it is on the context of the activity within the economy and purposes of God's self-disclosure.

Again, intellectual effort is not necessarily antifaith; many have benefited from Origen's *On First Principles* over the centuries, and others have successfully followed in its wake. But there are diverse ways of engaging the rule of faith. Intellection, conceptualization, description, explanation, analysis—these kinds of activities are important, but on Pentecostal terms they are theologically significant only when they are sustained *coram Deo*, that is, with a full awareness that they are pursued in hopes of apprehending God and living within God's purposes. Reason and revelation need not operate in different domains, but as Murray Rae notes, "Revelation is not at reason's disposal."[80] For Pentecostals, systematization must be in tune with the economy of God's self-presentation, and such a framework inherently implies that the spirituality-theology interface is live and operative.

Conclusion

This chapter attempts to clear the methodological air within Pentecostal theological reflection. Without question, different proposals are on offer within Pentecostalism as to how to conceptualize its basic and orienting commitments. From the arguments considered to this point, this work situates itself within the trajectory of efforts that find spirituality to be intimately connected to theology. Sadly, that orientation is sometimes marginalized on the contemporary scene as promoting subjective bias or novelty, but a wider awareness of the history of Christian thought casts a different picture. Pentecostalism is in sundry ways vitally relevant to the challenges of today because it shows instincts that can be located within the many expressions of Christian mysticism across the ages.

80. Gunton, "A Rose by Any Other Name?," 16, citing Murray Rae, *Kierkegaard's Vision of the Incarnation* (Oxford: Clarendon, 1997), 112.

CHAPTER 2

A Mystical Tradition?

M any if not most Pentecostals would hesitate to identify themselves as modern-day mystics. The label "mysticism" could be understood as too esoteric, self-absorbed, archaic, or—worst of all—pagan. But in chapter 1, the argument was made that Pentecostals would resist the many bifurcations within the theological disciplines today. In particular, Pentecostals would reject the division between spirituality and theology, seeking instead a genuine interface between the two, with each conditioning the other in a mutually authenticating manner. This attitude stems largely from how Pentecostals think of God-knowledge. For Pentecostals, God-knowledge is not so much cultivated through actions of the intellect as it is through holistic engagement. Insofar as these features of the Pentecostal ethos continue, I would argue that the use of the language of mysticism could very well contribute toward a richer understanding of God-knowledge for Pentecostals.

Of course, it is critical how we ultimately define "mysticism" as it relates to Pentecostalism's unique theological character. Much of this task is the focus of the present chapter, which considers how mystical language can be employed theologically in a way that Pentecostals would find useful.

To begin with, the claim that Pentecostalism represents a mystical tradition within the church catholic assumes that mystical traditions within Christianity have historically existed and presumably can exist today. Such a claim is not difficult to sustain, at least historically. Many people with some working sense of Christian history recognize the names of, say, Pseudo-Dionysius or Hildegard of Bingen. Despite the relative prominence of such figures, however, mystical figures and movements have largely been on the edges of the theological mainstream as it has typically been understood, especially since the modern era. And so we need to ask, Just how significant is mysticism for Christian identity? Can Christianity be understood to be at its core a mystical faith, or are these figures and movements just tangential and highly idiosyncratic "takes" on a religion that is on the whole something else?

Given the way that Christianity has been repeatedly framed as very much a "public faith"—as we see, for instance, in the writings of the early apologists and of those throughout the various expressions of Constantinian privilege that Christianity has enjoyed in the West—it might seem that a mystical approach to Christianity is not only a minority effort but one that is largely irrelevant and insignificant. I would reply that, for the first generations of Christians, there was no getting around mystical motifs. Much of the language, happenings, and practices of the first Christians and the early church can be understood as inherently and thoroughly mystical. Consider the farewell discourses of the Gospel of John, the Day of Pentecost happenings as recorded in the Book of Acts, the early practice of sacraments such as Eucharist and baptism, and even the formulation of such doctrines as the incarnation and the Trinity—these all can be said to have mystical dimensions and qualities.[1] No wonder, then, that mystical impulses repeatedly appear in Christianity, whether cultivated in local churches, embodied by venerable figures, or manifest within schools, abbeys, and revivals of various sorts.

To turn to the immediate agenda at hand, I wish to argue that Pentecostalism represents a particular kind of resurgence of these mystical dimensions of Christianity within a largely Western context, and increasingly a global one as well. Their rise in this setting is important, since the West has often been unable to account for things that are inconsistent with the tenets of its preferred epistemology. The rise and prominence of a dynamic Pentecostalism over the last decades has been something of an unexpected occurrence. Many of its qualities, however, have been consistent with long-standing features of mystical Christianity. I am not the first to make this claim. I do hope, however, to extend this thought in a more directed, critical, and sustained fashion. I also aim to clarify what the language of mysticism can mean in a self-conscious Christian con-

1. Andrew Louth considers these as "mystical doctrines formulated dogmatically" (*The Origins of the Christian Mystical Tradition: From Plato to Denys* [Oxford: Clarendon, 1981], xi). I agree with this evaluation, given that these doctrines have as their subject matter the God of Christian confession, who is known only as this One has disclosed Godself.

text, given that it is variously understood; these variations can be either helpful or deleterious for its recovery as a viable category within Christian theology. Much of this work can take place only if we note carefully how theology has undergone significant changes and mutations in the West, for these have often had implications for the understanding of mysticism on the whole.

A Category Deemed Applicable by Insiders and Outsiders

Occasionally, writers on Pentecostalism have referred to the movement as a mystical tradition. In James K. A. Smith's groundbreaking *Thinking in Tongues*, he speaks of Pentecostalism's expressed need of the affective core of a person being reached in discipleship, to which he appends the following footnote: "It is this, I think, that makes pentecostalism a 'mystical' tradition as expressed, say, in the disciplines of Saint John of the Cross, *Dark Night of the Soul*."[2] Another scholar who has made this connection is Margaret Poloma, who used "mystics" in the title of one of her books on Pentecostalism.[3] Also, Dale Coulter, a Pentecostal scholar specializing in medieval studies, has drawn connections between Pentecostals and mystical thinkers in terms of medieval exegesis and hermeneutical practices, and Simon Chan has also significantly developed this point.[4] Perhaps the scholar who has made the point most strongly has been Daniel Albrecht.[5] Such a list could be extended further.

A figure who makes a sustained case for Pentecostals as mystics is an outsider of sorts: Harvey Cox, Hollis Research Professor of Divinity at Harvard Divinity School. Cox made a significant contribution to Pentecostal

2. James K. A. Smith, *Thinking in Tongues* (Grand Rapids: Eerdmans, 2010), 77.

3. Margaret M. Poloma, *Main Street Mystics: The Toronto Blessing and Reviving Pentecostalism* (Lanham, MD: Altamira Press, 2003).

4. Dale Coulter, "What Meaneth This? Pentecostals and Theological Inquiry," *Journal of Pentecostal Theology* 10, no. 1 (2001): 38–64; Simon Chan, *Pentecostal Theology and the Christian Spiritual Tradition*, Journal of Pentecostal Theology Supplement 21 (Sheffield: Sheffield Academic Press, 2000).

5. Daniel Albrecht, *Rites in the Spirit: A Ritual Approach to Pentecostal/Charismatic Spirituality*, Journal of Pentecostal Theology Supplement 17 (Sheffield: Sheffield Academic Press, 1999), 238–40. Albrecht's study is in ritual studies, but at one point he makes the same theological claim made in this work, namely, that "though Pentecostals seem largely unaware, they participate in a rich heritage of Christian mysticism" (238–39).

studies through his work *Fire from Heaven*. His is a unique perspective and contribution. In this chapter I focus particularly on Cox's work, which will be helpful in describing mysticism in a way that clarifies Pentecostalism's theological identity.

Cox's volume is significant both in what it says and in the circumstances of its writing. This established theologian presents a critical yet sympathetic reading of a worldwide Christian phenomenon. Not surprisingly, given their persistent marginalization, Pentecostals found Cox's approach and overall tone to be a refreshing change. In it they were being recognized by the establishment in a way that affirmed that their voices mattered—that they had something to say and should be considered seriously on the religious and cultural scene. *Fire from Heaven* took the form it did not only because of Pentecostalism's worldwide growth and relevance but also because of Cox's amicability, curiosity, and humility. For instance, Cox recognizes in this work that he might have paid too much attention to sociological prognosticators when he wrote *The Secular City*, given the upsurge of religiosity (particularly of the Christian charismatic variety) across the globe since its publication in the 1960s. As for its broader impact, *Fire from Heaven* has helped Pentecostalism gain a greater foothold within the theological academy. It is now quite common to see conferences, working groups, and similar academic efforts focusing on and taking seriously the concerns of Pentecostals and charismatics. Cox and his work undoubtedly have helped contribute to this upsurge.

As for the book's content, Cox begins by drawing from his boyhood days. He notes that, because of an early experience at a church he attended with a young friend, he came to realize that "eros and agape, the erotic and the spiritual energies of life, may not be as distinct as some theologians would have us believe." The church in question, most likely a Holiness church and yet one that had significant corollaries to what Cox would come to associate with Pentecostalism, was filled with passionate people who used their bodies and emotions explicitly in their worship. Such happenings never occurred in the Baptist and Quaker congregations Cox knew as a young man. Cox mentions how the groups that attend to the "religious affections" were especially appealing to him, including Pentecostalism, which represents "the most experiential branch of Christianity."[6]

Despite these sympathies, Cox admits that, once he began to delve

---

6. Harvey Cox, *Fire from Heaven* (Reading, MA: Addison-Wesley, 1995), 10, 14.

into the primary documentary evidence of the Pentecostal tradition, he found himself at a crossroads. At first, he confesses that he was disturbed by the sensationalism of some of the accounts he was reading, and as a result he was not sure how to proceed. Eventually, he decided to "let himself go" as he read the primary literature. This decision led to a significant change:

> I quickly found that my new attitude allowed me to follow the spectacular spread of Pentecostalism better than either credulity or skepticism could. As I pored over these archaic accounts, it became clear to me that for those early converts, the baptism of the Spirit did not just change their religious affiliation or their way of worship. It changed everything. They literally saw the whole world in a new light. Spirit baptism was not just an initiation rite, it was a mystical encounter. That is why they sometimes sounded like Saint Teresa of Avila or Saint John of the Cross, although they had probably never heard of either one.[7]

Later, Cox comments on the "magical realism imbuing many pentecostal testimonies." This "enchanted" feature of Pentecostal experience "is so total it shatters the cognitive packaging."[8]

As an outsider looking in, Cox grapples with a number of possibilities as to why Pentecostal religiosity has become so popular over the last few decades. We see his theory in the following summary: "It has succeeded because it has spoken to the spiritual emptiness of our time by reaching beyond the levels of creed and ceremony into the core of human religiousness, into what might be called 'primal spirituality,' that largely unprocessed nucleus of the psyche in which the unending struggle for a sense of purpose and significance goes on." Cox proceeds to extend this language of primality by stating that Pentecostalism has helped people recover an "elemental spirituality" that consists of "primal speech" (glossolalia, ecstatic utterance, language of the heart), "primal piety" (mystical experience, trances, dreams, and other "archetypal religious expressions"), and "primal hope" (an expectation for a better future). This focus on primality means that Pentecostalism is not an aberration but "part of the larger and

---

7. Cox, *Fire from Heaven*, 70–71. Cox also makes significant reference to Catherine of Sienna later in the book (204ff.), as he goes on to document his growing appreciation for the contemporary turn to primal spirituality.

8. Cox, *Fire from Heaven*, 71. Smith, in *Thinking in Tongues*, speaks of this point in terms of an "enchanted" view of reality.

longer history of human religiousness," which works from the universal, deep sense that we are *homo religiosus*.[9]

Other remarks that Cox made are interesting. When addressing primal speech, Cox talks about how tongues-speaking relates to the "ecstasy deficit" that we in contemporary secular Western societies cultivate because we have both shielded ourselves from our deeper registers and resisted lowering our perceptual barriers so that "deep [can speak] to deep."[10] Through this kind of speech, Pentecostalism shows its power to "tap into a deep substratum of human religiosity and [signifies] another radical departure from evangelical or fundamentalist protestantism in which neither tongue speaking or links to other religions are condoned." However, Pentecostals, by using the biblical framework, allow for a familiarity to drape this broader, numinous element, one that is based on an overriding claim: "The Spirit of God needs no mediators but is available to anyone in an intense, immediate, indeed interior way."[11]

This intensity for Cox is best understood in mystical terms. Cox broadens the parameters of consideration by stating, "I believe that the inner significance of speaking in tongues or praying in the spirit can be found in something virtually every spiritual tradition in human history teaches in one way or another: that the reality religious symbols strive to express ultimately defies even the most exalted human language. Virtually all the mystics of every faith have indicated that this vision they have glimpsed, though they try desperately to describe it, finally eludes them."[12] Cox applies this broad comment to Pentecostalism in particular: "It seems ironic that pentecostalism, the religion of the poor and the unlettered, should in this respect be closer to the most sublime forms of mysticism than are the more respectable denominations that sometimes look down on it." Slightly later he adds, "It is precisely this ragtag religion from across the tracks that is now bearing the mystical torch with most vigor."[13]

9. Cox, *Fire from Heaven*, 81, 82–83.

10. Cox duly notes later that these barriers were erected within Western civilization between "the cognitive and emotional sides of life, between rationality and symbol, between the conscious and unconscious strata of the mind" (*Fire from Heaven*, 100–101).

11. Cox, *Fire from Heaven*, 91, 87.

12. Cox, *Fire from Heaven*, 92. In chap. 4 we consider the connection between tongues-speech and mysticism.

13. Cox, *Fire from Heaven*, 92, 93.

Pressing Deeper into the Term "Mystical"

What should we make of Cox's analyses and considerations? Again, one cannot help but note the tone Cox employs throughout his book. He immersed himself sufficiently within the traditions of Pentecostalism to understand significantly its passions, virtues, fears, and concerns. Overall, he tries to be charitable and gracious, noting both the successes and the shortcomings of the movement as he has experienced it. For all these reasons, he is a valuable dialogue partner for Pentecostals. Nevertheless, because of how Cox uses the label "mystical," I believe that Pentecostals would hesitate to use it in describing themselves. Pentecostals could accept much of the descriptions that Cox gives, but there are some features of his narrative—the more theoretical and explanatory comments—that would most likely sound strange and off-putting to many if not most of them.

In broad terms, to use "mystery" in speaking of Pentecostalism is useful for Cox in that it helps indicate continuity between Pentecostalism and other Christian traditions that highlight Christian spirituality, ones that are often muted in Christianity's modern Western forms. Early Pentecostals often thought of themselves as participating in a restorationist movement, that is, one that would reestablish basic features of New Testament Christianity. With the passing of years, however, Pentecostal scholars have been more inclined to note continuity with other Christian traditions across the centuries.[14] Cox sympathetically joins these efforts by drawing the connection between Pentecostalism and past voices in Christian mysticism.

But we need to ask, What precisely is meant by mysticism? To answer

14. A pioneer in this regard is Stanley Burgess. However, the point of this being a recent development should not be pressed too strongly. For instance, the *Apostolic Faith* was willing to recognize the flowering of charismatic signs in other Christian movements; for example: "At the beginning of the Eighteenth century, among the French Protestants, there were wonderful manifestations of the Spirit power accompanied by the Gift of Tongues. The early Quakers received the same powerful religious stimulus and had the Gift of Tongues. The Irvingite church, about 1830, had the baptism with the Holy Ghost, and spoke in other tongues. In the Swedish revival in 1841–43 there were the same manifestations of the Spirit and also the Gift of Tongues. In the Irish revival of 1859 there is the record of the power of the Spirit in winning souls and the speaking in tongues by Spirit filled men and women" (1.1 [1906]: 3). Clearly, an impulse, however strong, was noticeable among some early Pentecostals to ground their experience and beliefs within the continuous story of the Christian church and not simply within first-century happenings.

this difficult question will help us understand Cox's portrayals, and it will serve broader purposes as well. We can start by considering the definition given by Andrew Louth, a respected Orthodox scholar who characterizes mysticism as "a search for and experience of immediacy with God. The mystic is not content to know *about* God, he longs for union with God." He adds, "Yet the search for God, or the ultimate, for His own sake, and an unwillingness to be satisfied with anything less than Him; the search for immediacy with this object of the soul's longing: this would seem to be the heart of mysticism."[15] Louth's definition is curious, since it says little about the object being sought through mystical efforts ("God" and later "the ultimate") but much about how one comes to engage with and pursue this object. It is almost as if the term "God" is a placeholder in these definitions—an amorphous end or goal that can be easily exchanged with another phrase (such as "the ultimate").

If we remove "God" and "the ultimate" from such statements and leave the referent open, then this definition of mysticism would be acceptable to a variety of religious traditions. Such terms as "search," "experience," "immediacy," and "union" would be common in describing mysticism. For instance, the great Hindu thinker Adi Shankara could be termed a mystic, for he expounds on nonduality (*advaita*) as pressing through appearances (*māyā*) inwardly to the soul (*ātman*) and on to "Brahman" (the eternal being, or ultimate reality)—a journey of searching and a desire for meaning and union. And yet, if we were to replace the Sanskrit terms with others more familiar to Westerners, we could fit the teachings of Plotinus here, or perhaps the reflections of someone like Meister Eckhart. In fact, Rudolf Otto makes a number of connections between Shankara and Eckhart in a comparative study. He points to several similarities, one of them the following: "An almost identical metaphysic could be built up from them in this way. More astonishing still, both mystics express themselves in a metaphysic which seems to be essentially 'ontological,' essentially a speculation as to the nature of Being, using methods which are startlingly alike, and a still more similar terminology."[16] Religious

15. Louth, *The Origins of the Christian Mystical Tradition*, xv.
16. Rudolf Otto, *Mysticism East and West: A Comparative Analysis of the Nature of Mysticism* (Wheaton, IL: Theosophical Publishing House, 1987), 8. Otto is quite bullish on the possibilities; he notes on the same page: "It would be possible to treat Eckhart just as we have here dealt with Sankara. . . . Sentences could be taken unchanged from his works, or others could be formed in line with his thought, exactly corresponding to those of Sankara."

studies scholars could debate the merits of this assessment and comparison; however, Otto and others with a similar methodological orientation find this kind of work to be ultimately helpful. For his part, Otto is convinced the similarities exist because of his belief that humans share a common *intuitus mysticus* ("mystical intuition") that ranges across widely different contexts.

This proposal and others show that mysticism has become a frequently used category within religious studies to encompass a wide range of phenomena, including Muslim mystics (Sufis) and Jewish mystics (Kabbalists). The great range of texts, figures, themes, and practices in the world's religions that can all be labeled "mystical" tends to make the differences among the various traditions less pronounced.

As useful as the category "mysticism" may be phenomenologically, it nevertheless is limited by the one observing the phenomena. After all, each one of us has a context—a lens or a worldview—in which we operate, and so how something is read, narrated, and categorized as mystical will necessarily reflect this orientation. Ironically, the tendency for observers to think that "mystery" is a great umbrella category that embraces a broad range of experiences reflects a particular mind-set, culture, and worldview.[17]

Cox manifests this religious studies tendency when he moves from ethnographically documenting Pentecostal speech and lives to describing their warrants and logic—in other words, when he seeks to explain and make sense of Pentecostalism as a worldwide religious movement within a conceptual, linguistic, and explanatory framework that is different from what Pentecostals themselves hold. Consider the following remarks by Cox: "Almost all religious traditions have now, or have had at one time or another, the basic phenomenon of what might best be called 'ecstatic utterance.' They have explained it in a wide variety of ways and created innumerable theologies about it. . . . What links these religious traditions to each other, and what connects one century to another or even within a single tradition, cannot lie in the theological explanations . . . but is to be found in the searing realization that the reality of God utterly transcends

---

17. One might say, for instance, that it pivots on a Kantian-like distinction between the phenomenal and noumenal realms. For a perspective that takes this tack in reference to the work of John Hick and Wilfred Cantwell Smith (among others), see Kenneth Surin, "'A Politics of Speech': Religious Pluralism in the Age of the McDonald's Hamburger," in *Christian Uniqueness Reconsidered: The Myth of a Pluralistic Theology of Religions*, ed. Gavin D'Costa (Maryknoll, NY: Orbis Books, 1990), 192–212.

our puny capacity to describe it."[18] Cox essentially locates Pentecostalism, ecstatic utterance/experience, and the reality of God all within the larger framework of religious phenomenology. Within this perspective, the theological explanations of Pentecostal practitioners are simply expressions of supposedly more fundamental realities.

In Cox's view, we humans can, at the end of the day, be classified as *homo religiosus*. That is, humans are religious beings at their core, and we express this feature of ourselves differently across time and place. The roots of mysticism lie in this fundamental conviction about what it means to be human. Given this approach, Cox can readily draw connections among many religious traditions and speak of the primal spirituality that he sees at work among Pentecostals and others. His perspective is largely theologically agnostic. Cox occasionally uses explicitly Christian terms to frame this religious impulse (e.g., in one place he mentions the logic of *imago Dei*), and he intermittently uses God language to label what can otherwise be a broad reference to the numinous or the holy (to use the wording made popular by Otto, Mircea Eliade, and others). But such usage is largely generic. Without theological specificity, these proposals shed no light on their subject matter. In fact, one could make the case, as Nimi Wariboko has, that Cox's main focus in *Fire from Heaven* is not Pentecostalism per se but this amorphous category of primal spirituality that Cox believes Pentecostalism exemplifies.[19]

These complexities surrounding the use of "mystical" may appear insurmountable. Where does this leave us? Broadly, I believe that Pentecostals cannot use the language of mysticism as religious scholars typically do. These two groups simply operate from different "confessional" standpoints. Pentecostals may try to appropriate religious studies discourses for their particular ends (e.g., as they attempt to form particular proposals within a theology of religions), but they would have to do so in a markedly unique way. Why? Because given their ethos—the very core

18. Cox, *Fire from Heaven*, 95–96.

19. "Even if the book is coded as a Pentecostal study, it is about Cox's worldwide pilgrimage into the inside, the mystery of the human being, and the nature of primal spirituality in the twentieth century. Cox, the *homo quaerens*, was probing the depth dimension of the human spirit as it is laid bare by the Pentecostals. He was not really interested in their doctrines, beliefs, or theologies. The thrill was in investigating their particular expression of the encounter with 'ultimate concern,' a particular display of *mysterium tremendum et fascinans*" (Nimi Wariboko, "*Fire from Heaven*: Pentecostals in the Secular City," *Pneuma* 33, no. 3 [2011]: 403).

of their identity—Pentecostals cannot be theologically agnostic. Quite the contrary. Whereas various definitions of mysticism use anthropological descriptions (that we as humans are *homo religiosus* or have a *mysticus intuitus* or have a sense of the holy or the numinous), Pentecostals insist on describing themselves in terms of *theological* concern. Ultimately, Pentecostals focus their attention, testimonies, and passions on *who God is* and *what God is doing*, and they specify "God" as none other than the One proclaimed by and at work in Jesus through the power of the Holy Spirit. This distinction is not incidental or ancillary to the task at hand; quite the contrary, it points to a methodological crossroads.

If the term "mysticism" is to be of any use for Pentecostals, it will have to be conceived, appropriated, and applied largely in emic (i.e., insider) ways. "Mysticism" would have to be a term Pentecostals use of themselves to affirm their identity as distinct from, and yet part of, the larger Christian world. It would have a use different from that of religious studies scholars. Such distinctions are difficult, if not impossible, to maintain for those who both use and hear the term. Many contemporary discourses tend to overlook such distinctions, even while claiming to be accommodating uniqueness, diversity, and openness. But such is the challenge with any range of terms, including "scripture," "tradition," "experience," "spirit," "the sacred," "charisma," and "sect." For widely employed language to be useful for specific ends, it must be deliberately and determinedly limited. The running assumption in what follows is that this process can and should happen in the case of "mysticism" as Pentecostals articulate their identity in productive ways.

Parameters for Mysticism as a Theological Category

So far, we have considered mysticism as a category used by religious studies scholars to draw comparisons across religious traditions largely on phenomenological grounds. But we should also note that, within Christian discourse, the term is also highly contested and variously used. For instance, I sometimes point out to my students that Protestant primers of theology commonly have a first chapter on revelation or the Bible, whereas their Orthodox counterparts often start with a treatment of mystery. The differences here no doubt relate to the various ways that theologians view God-knowledge. Whereas some Christians may be suspicious of the term "mystery," a renowned theologian like Vladimir Lossky can make the following claim: "In a certain sense all theology is mystical, inasmuch as it shows forth the divine mystery."[20] For such an assertion to make sense, we need to recognize a certain epistemological sensibility present here involving how we form and develop God-knowledge.

This particular sensibility can be explored with the aid of a recent proposal. Steven Boyer and Christopher Hall have delineated possibilities for what the term "mystery" can mean in English and its implications for theological knowledge. They have duly noted that this term is quite flexible and can go beyond the larger, dictionary understanding of something that resists or defies explanation. Boyer and Hall begin by introducing two broad distinctions. One is the understanding of mystery as a puzzle to be solved. They refer to this sense when speaking of detective fiction, but also of certain philosophical work that aims at proving the existence of God. They use the category *investigative mystery* to elaborate this sense, and they emphasize that its primary characteristic is what is unknown. Mysteries of this kind need to be unraveled or explained away.

Boyer and Hall believe that this understanding of the word "mystery" is not very helpful for theology, in that one's primary disposition toward God and God's purposes should not be explanation or sought-after resolution. Rather, a theological account of mystery must be of another order. They argue that God is a mystery who reveals Godself through what God does within various contexts; that is, God is a *revelational mystery*. On this score, the mystery in question is to be considered primarily in terms of what is known: Christians behold a self-disclosing God, and within such moments of disclosure God is apprehended as One who defies categorization and definition. Notice the distinction: people approach an investigative mystery out of ignorance with the goal of finding more so as to explain it away, whereas a revelational mystery involves some basis of knowledge that over time reveals ever deeper and richer dimensions that cannot be adequately categorized or defined. Boyer and Hall summarize the point as follows: "A revelational mystery is one that remains a mystery even after it has been revealed. It is precisely in its revelation that its distinctive character as mystery is displayed."[21] They cite a number of themes that illustrate such an understanding, all from biblical passages,

---

20. Vladimir Lossky, *The Mystical Theology of the Eastern Church* (Crestwood, NY: St. Vladimir's Seminary Press, 2002), 7.

21. Steven D. Boyer and Christopher A. Hall, *The Mystery of God: Theology for Knowing the Unknowable* (Grand Rapids: Baker Academic, 2012), 6.

including the resurrection of Jesus, the union of husband and wife, and the person of Christ.

The distinction between the two kinds of mystery delineated by Boyer and Hall is important for a number of methodological reasons. First, one could approach an investigative mystery in similar ways, regardless of the object in question. In other words, one could use various rationalities and methodologies (e.g., empirical investigation, trial and error, varying forms of analysis) so as to explain away these kinds of mysteries—whether cold cases, the cause of climate change, the origins of diseases, and so on. But a revelational mystery requires an object-specific rationality and methodology, given that it is available (or revealed) within frameworks and terms determined by its object. Put another way, a revelational mystery is assumed to be knowable in some specific way from the beginning of its consideration; the way it is to be known would depend on its own manner of self-presentation.

A second point worth making is that, with an investigative mystery, one imagines that the category "mystery" is an unsettled and to some degree intolerable category for the long haul. Given that the energies associated with investigative mysteries are directed to unraveling and thus eliminating their mysterious quality, the category of mystery in this case functions as an impediment—something to be overcome or awaiting resolution. People typically are uneasy sitting in investigative mysteries because ignorance is depicted here as something negative—as an exposure of human frailty and weakness.

Quite the opposite, however, is true for revelational mysteries. Here the mysterious sense is not something to be overcome but, rather, something to be apprehended and taken into account *as such*. This prospect is not to be lamented but rather championed and celebrated in that a revelational mystery, by continuing to retain its mysterious quality, has an available storehouse of riches to be perpetually discovered and mined. The specific kind of ignorance at work in this case is not so much an exposure of human frailty as it is an invitation to anticipate surprise, awe, wonder, and amazement. A revelational mystery has the potential for being beautiful, true, and good in that it can enrapture and enchant those engaging it.

Boyer and Hall go further in discussing mystery by distinguishing three subdivisions of revelational mystery. First, such a mystery can be subcategorized as an *extensive mystery*. In this sense, something is quantitatively inexhaustible. An extensive mystery is simply too much to account for in terms of standard metrical registers. Boyer and Hall speak of a second kind of revelational mystery in terms of "nonrational opaqueness." Rather than quantitatively excessive, this sense has to do with a unique qualitative character, one that they try to capture via the language of *facultative mystery*. With certain mysteries, a different perceptual register or capacity is needed, given that some things simply defy consideration in typical ways. And finally, Boyer and Hall have a third subcategory: the *dimensional mystery*. This last category tends to be their preferred category for thinking of God. In this sense, something is mysterious on account of "an unclassifiable superabundance that transcends but does not invalidate rational exploration."[22] They use as an illustrative example the notion of a two-dimensional figure looking at a circle that happens to be the end of a cylinder; given the gaze of the two-dimensional figure, all that can be seen is a circle, but for us who are not limited to such a gaze, we can see both the circle and something more expansive.

Boyer and Hall's work in specifying additional dimensions within a revelational mystery is quite helpful, although some of their discussion is unclear. On the one hand, one can see how an extensive mystery is dependent upon a sense of scale, and this dependence itself represents a kind of limitation if it is simply left to stand cataphatically (i.e., as a positive statement about the mystery). On the other hand, their slight dismissal of a facultative mystery as unsuitable for theological work is somewhat unclear, and one cannot help but link this conclusion with how they go on to speak about a dimensional mystery as being of such a nature that it "transcends but does not invalidate rational exploration." They go on to say: "Rational exploration is certainly possible, and yet it is pursued in light of a deeper or denser or more complex substantiality than reason is familiar with."[23] What could have been posed as a complementary relationship between a facultative and dimensional mystery is depicted as a privileging of the last, which also retains some uneasy relationship with reason. But why is this championing of reason (whatever it means in this case) relevant here? Furthermore, how can one know that reason has been transcended, apart from some sensory or facultative capacity? With reason being mentioned even in terms of a dimensional mystery, it seems that a revelational mystery could somehow become an investigative mystery. In fairness, perhaps Boyer and Hall are trying to maintain discursivity and the potential for evaluation and assessment with their appeal to rea-

22. Boyer and Hall, *The Mystery of God*, 8, 11.
23. Boyer and Hall, *The Mystery of God*, 11.

son when speaking of a dimensional mystery. Perhaps they are trying to avoid a latent Gnosticism or an operative privatization that would open the door to the language of experience unhelpfully becoming part of these discussions. But an appeal to reason may not be the best way to avoid these problematic alternatives.

More promising, it would seem, is the way Boyer and Hall conclude a summary of their views:

> When we speak of "mystery" from now on, we are speaking of a revelational mystery that is dimensional in character—that is, of mystery that is impenetrable even after it is revealed, not by virtue of its quantitative magnitude, nor by virtue of its existential uniqueness, but by virtue of an unimaginable depth or density that transcends our rational capacities and all of our other capacities as well. And to speak of the "mystery *of God*" is to insist that, for finite creatures like ourselves, God the Creator, the living God of Christian faith, is just this kind of mystery.[24]

This last way of expressing the point hints at an important feature of the senses of mystery for theological purposes. Boyer and Hall quite appropriately find themselves brushing up against the Creator-creation interface when speaking of the fittingness of mystery for speaking of God. Essentially and ultimately, when Christians dare speak of their God, they do so within the conditions of their creaturehood; they attempt such work as creatures who are struggling to account for their source, their Creator. Such conditions make the category of mystery quite fitting for describing God, given that creating is a unique kind of activity and that creaturehood is a category largely registered in terms of limitations or boundaries.[25]

Consider the last point first. Anthropologically, Christians necessarily encounter their own limits, biases, and contextualizing conditions when they speak of God. To recall the illustration used by Boyer and Hall, the limit does not lie with the end of the cylinder that appears to be only a circle to a two-dimensional figure; the limit would be two-dimensionality itself, in which the two-dimensional figure subsists. Analogously, it is not so much that God is like the cylinder but that we are like the two-dimensional

---

24. Boyer and Hall, *The Mystery of God*, 13 (emphasis original).

25. See Norman Wirzba, "The Art of Creaturely Life: A Question of Human Propriety," *Pro Ecclesia* 22, no. 1 (2013): 7–28.

figures; we can account for only so much, given that we are creatures who nevertheless attempt to speak and think of what is ultimately beyond us.

As to the first point, God is an infinitely rich, superabundant mystery. Such is what is involved when confessing God as Creator. Too often the radicality of this confession is lost in the midst of other pressures and tangents associated with the language of creation. But the claim that God is Creator assumes that creating ex nihilo is a unique act undertaken uniquely by a unique Agent.[26] These claims underscore the point of God's transcendence. We must make the claim of God's transcendence noncontrastively or noncomparatively, for only in this way can God be spoken of as fittingly engaged and involved with all that is.[27] Such a portrayal makes the question of availability all the more pressing.

Mysticism and Encounter

If mysticism is an appropriate category for describing theological efforts that concern God primarily—sometimes called theology proper—then one also must account for how one comes to engage God. As noted above, God is a mystery on account of God's revealedness. As God is made known, one comes to see ever deeper features of the divine life. But this process raises a question: *How* is God known? The issue is timely because, with the dawning of modernity, epistemological concerns have occupied philosophers and theologians alike. The need for securing knowledge on the basis of generalizable foundations is part of the heritage that colors contemporary efforts in theology. Different stages of this discussion can be seen across the myriad of scholarly debates today, and the discourse can be quite technical and sophisticated, often with very little to show by way of results.

But if one works within the dynamic of the Creator-creation interface, accepting that revelation is in fact the condition for knowing this ever-deep, superabundant life, then divine self-presentation is re-

26. The matter is underscored by Herbert McCabe's insistence on the difference between "making" (to actualize a potentiality) and "creating" (to produce both a potentiality and actuality); see *God and Evil in the Theology of St. Thomas Aquinas* (New York: Continuum, 2010), 104. For a recent treatment of this doctrine, see Ian A. McFarland, *From Nothing: A Theology of Creation* (Louisville: Westminster John Knox, 2014).

27. For more on this point, see Kathryn Tanner, *God and Creation in Christian Theology* (Minneapolis: Fortress, 1988), 45–48.

quired. To put it starkly: God has to make Godself known in order to be known, and the way God wishes to be known makes all the difference as to whether God is known at all. The initiative must come from God's side, since human striving cannot bridge the gap between Creator and creation. All these points lead to the conclusion that knowing God is not a human achievement but a kind of participation in grace. The solving of an investigative mystery brings with it the accolades of human achievement, but with knowledge of a revelational mystery, a sense of devotion, attentiveness, and dependence to that which is *given* is crucial to acknowledge.

This kind of attentiveness in God-knowledge is illustrated by Louth through two different analogies. One is interpersonal, or relational, dynamics. Within this way of understanding (perhaps better, beholding), one cannot simply know about God from the testimonies or ideas of others. Just as it would be insufficient to know a person simply by what others say about him or her, so in this case (again analogously) one has to know God and not simply *about* God if one's account of God-knowledge is to be fitting.[28] A kind of firsthand account is called for, which bespeaks of a particular kind of engagement. A second broad analogy Louth offers is aesthetic experience. When one sees a work of art, one is presented with a unique experience of beholding something else. The dynamic here involves alterity (the work of art is different from the one viewing it), as well as event-laden understandings (the work of art and its beholder come together in time, i.e., at a particular moment). The analogy presents itself similarly to God once more: there is no substitute for experiencing God for oneself, a kind of event that Hans-Georg Gadamer would call a fusion of horizons (*Horizontverschmelzung*).[29] The influence, engagement, and interchange made possible through such an event are unavailable in other ways. As one person will say to another about a particular work of art, "You just have to see it for yourself!"

For both analogies, we can speak of *encounter*, a motif that Louth does not consider extensively but that often appears in the literature surrounding these themes. One must encounter and be encountered by the mystery of the triune God so as to be captivated, moved, and struck by the Trinity's beauty and glory. The event must be a genuine encounter, one in which

28. Andrew Louth, *Theology and Spirituality* (Oxford: SLG Press, 1978), 2.
29. Hans-Georg Gadamer, *Truth and Method*, 2nd rev. ed. (London: Continuum, 1989).

Buber's "I-Thou" dynamic is at work.[30] When people relate to others or to works of art, a realism is necessarily at play—someone or something exists outside of one's gaze. Applied to our main concern, God cannot simply be a projection of one's desires or a form of wish fulfillment. God must be a truly self-subsistent Other. And yet a touchpoint or connection of sorts must be at work as well. In some fashion, a genuine engagement must take place. Of course, on both scores—alterity and connectedness—these features of encounter are complicated, given that God is being considered. God cannot simply be a Thou like other persons or subjects, nor can we simply speak of meeting or finding God, since God is the ground of our being. Again, the analogous nature of this exercise (and of all theological language for that matter) must be recognized.

At the same time, however, without something like the theme of encounter, one is left to ask: How can one talk of knowing and experiencing God? How else can one go on to claim with a degree of holy boldness that God is at work, that God is speaking, or that God's will is one way or the other—if somehow God is not manifest and not claimed as such? This issue is perhaps one of the most difficult in the reorienting of theology toward its proper subject matter. As Louth notes in the first part of his fine pamphlet, academically speaking, it is assumed to be much easier to analyze other people's views of God or the idea of God itself, or to pursue other strategies that at some level avoid the question: Who is this God?[31] But this hesitation indicates precisely the problem before us. Academic theology is saddled with an inability to claim confidently its subject matter. Such difficulties can foster any number of holy tempers and virtues, including humility, the fear of the Lord, and gratitude. Typically in academic circles, however, this recognition leads to deferral or evasion. This state of affairs has not always been the case, but it persists in the current climate, which suggests that the plausibility structures of our contemporary imagination cannot contemplate the theology-spirituality interface.

As challenging as the point may be, Christian theologians, if they are to consider God as a revelational mystery as opposed to an investigative one, require some account of God coming to us or made manifest to us so that God can be said to be known in a genuine and truthful way. A possibility for securing this point is via a theme closely related to mysticism, namely, spirituality.

30. Martin Buber, *I and Thou* (New York: Touchstone, 1970).
31. Louth, *Theology and Spirituality*, 1–3.

Mysticism and Spirituality

If "encounter" can be helpful in speaking of the manner and shape of apprehending the mystery that is the triune God and this One's works, further questions present themselves in terms of how to think of this encounter, including when, how, and for what end it happens. In light of these questions, it is perhaps best to distinguish mysticism and spirituality within Christian discourse. If mystery has to do with encountering the superabundant, self-disclosing God of Christian confession, then spirituality can denote the wider gamut of practices and activities that have such an encounter as their ground, purpose, and goal.

As Louth notes, the experience of God cannot be evoked, but it can be prepared for in terms of the efforts that cultivate openness and waiting in stillness for God.[32] In these comments, Louth is approximating what was said earlier in terms of an epicletic disposition, one that marks the life of those seeking to be "in the Spirit." The language of epiclesis in particular helps to make the point, given that it is a term stemming from the church's liturgical life, thereby affirming the doxological modality needed for Pentecostal theology. The ecclesial dimension is crucial because it involves a dynamic wider than an individual and his or her subjective experience. In fact, it denotes a context (which would involve a particular Thou) in which to situate an "I" so that the "I" can be identified, understood, shaped, and potentially transformed as a result. This wider gamut is what best describes the notion of spirituality. According to Mark McIntosh, spirituality "is not something the believer has but is a new pattern of personal growth taking place in the community of those who have been sought out, converted and cherished by the risen Christ." He also states that spirituality "is inherently mutual, communal, practical and oriented towards the God who makes self known precisely in this new pattern of life called church."[33] With such emphases on community and practice, McIntosh asserts that spirituality represents a kind of culture that promotes the honing of particular capacities and skills in which discernment and the formulation of the meaning of mystical encounter can occur over time. The point is significant, since the notion of mystical encounter—perhaps even more so in our current-day climate than in earlier eras—is an unwieldy topic prone to all kinds of excesses and misunderstandings.

---

32. Louth, *Theology and Spirituality*, 3.
33. Mark A. McIntosh, *Mystical Theology* (Malden, MA: Blackwell, 1998), 6, 7.

Rowan Williams captures the dynamic between mysticism and spirituality quite well: "Every Christian thinker, if he or she at all merits the designation, begins from the experience of being reconciled, being accepted, being held (however precariously) in the grace of God. And this is mediated in the objective form of a shared life and language, a public and historical community of men and women, gathering to read certain texts and perform certain acts."[34] The dynamic, as Williams presents it, does have internal-external or subjective-objective features, but they overlap significantly in terms of the life both share. Through encounter and embodiment, an individual is called to participate in a way of life in community so as to propel an ethos of sorts in which the fullness of human lives can be situated within the fullness of God's triune life.

Spirituality and Theology

Rather than use the language of epiclesis, Louth prefers to view spirituality in terms of prayer generally, which is typical of an Orthodox approach. Historically, this move is traceable to the statement by Evagrius noted earlier: "If you are a theologian, you will pray truly. And if you pray truly, you are a theologian." On Louth's reading, this expression made sense from the early church fathers to Anselm of Canterbury and the Victorines, without the drawbacks that it often meets on the contemporary scene. It was able to do so in part because epistemic commitments had not faced the kind of challenges associated with modernity regarding the plausibility of God being an object of knowledge. The crises that complicate this work, as they have particularly been formulated and felt in the West, stem largely from the Middle Ages. Theology as a discipline has yet to recover from such shattering developments and their epistemologically fragmenting consequences. They very much mark today's theological landscape.

But before examining those difficulties, it should be clear why in a sense this division is deeply problematic. If spirituality has to do with the lives led by Christ-followers and theology has to do with the speech and concepts used by Christians to account for their lives as such, then

---

34. Rowan Williams, *The Wound of Knowledge: Christian Spirituality from the New Testament to Saint John of the Cross*, rev. ed. (London: Darton, Longman & Todd, 1990), 12.

it makes perfect sense how, at least formally, the two can and should be complementary and mutually constituting. Experience and imagination, consciousness and language—these are simply coinhering features of a sustained identity over time. They are connected aspects of Christian lives because at the center of theology and spirituality is the God of Christian witness and confession, who in turn is contemplated and beheld by the totality of a creature's being. In terms of this subsection, one's embodied life—including one's practices, activities, and loves (spirituality), as well as one's ideas, concepts, and categories (theology)—is representative of the totality required in the beholding of this revealed mystery.

As difficult as it may be for some modern-day Westerners to imagine the bond between theology and spirituality in such a way, one sees examples for such possibilities from the witness of the church across its many ages. For instance, two key words that designate this enlivening link are "contemplation" and "wisdom." The former has a long, revered history in Christian reflection. Its purview includes what is often disjoined, namely, what McIntosh calls "the affective or loving impulse," as well as the "intellectual or knowing impulse."[35] Both McIntosh and Louth are fond of quoting and elaborating Richard of St. Victor's definition, which they believe captures this dynamic: "Contemplation is a free and clear vision of the mind fixed upon the manifestation of wisdom in suspended wonder." Several features of this definition are worth elaborating, including the following:

1. the freedom and clarity of vision bespeak of an intensity and focus that is outwardly directed;
2. the gaze and modality associated with "suspended wonder" recall the infinite and superabundant riches of the divine mystery; and
3. references to the mind and to wisdom suggest an expansive and richly textured shape for understanding.

One of these last terms, "wisdom," is helpful in its own right as another possibility for keeping spirituality and theology together in some mutually conditioning and enlivening way. Wisdom is both personified in Scripture as very much a God-related term, but it is also characterized in affective terms ("the fear of the Lord is the beginning of wisdom"), as well

35. McIntosh, *Mystical Theology*, 11.

as associated with deliberative dimensions that involve experience, praxis, and time. One proposal defines wisdom as the integration of "knowledge, understanding, critical questioning and good judgment with a view to the flourishing of human life and the whole of creation," with theological wisdom attempting "all that before God, alert to God, and in line with the purposes of God."[36] With contemplation and wisdom, one encounters themes that are neither anti-intellectual nor intellectualist; rather, they point to an expansion and contextualization of the cognitive register within the totality of the human self before God.

Sadly, such words as "contemplation" and "wisdom" are difficult to recover on the contemporary scene. The consequences of not being able to count on words that envision the unity of theological knowledge include not only its dissolution into splintering parts but also (and most severely) its impoverishment and deformity. In a manner of expression that McIntosh recognizes as blunt, he remarks: "Theology without spirituality becomes ever more methodologically refined but unable to know or speak of the very mysteries at the heart of Christianity, and spirituality without theology becomes rootless, easily hijacked by individualistic consumerism."[37] The interrelation between spirituality and theology allows for both a critical and a legitimizing process that keeps each honestly directed to its proper subject matter—the God revealed in Jesus Christ by the power of the Holy Spirit. The divorce between theology and spirituality has been none the better for either.

The Division of Theological Knowledge

In the second volume of his much-respected work *A History of Philosophy*, Frederick Copleston offers a sobering reminder to both philosopher and theologian alike when he states that "Christianity came into the world as a revealed religion." Christianity emerged and operated more as a way of life than as a theoretical school. Christ sent out his disciples "to preach, not to occupy professors' chairs."[38] And yet quite early in its existence Christianity felt the pressure, both externally and internally, to pursue

36. David F. Ford and Graham Stanton, "Introduction," in *Reading Texts, Seeking Wisdom*, ed. Ford and Stanton (Grand Rapids: Eerdmans, 2003), 2–3.

37. McIntosh, *Mystical Theology*, 10.

38. Frederick Copleston, *A History of Philosophy*, vol. 2: *Medieval Philosophy* (New York: Image Doubleday, 1993), 13.

more sophisticated intellectual accounts of what was assumed to be available through revelation. The external pressure involved the clarification of misunderstandings and suspicions held by the wider culture of the Roman Empire. Internally, Christians found it important to press deeper into cognitive domains concerning their faith and to use them in describing all of one's life and world. Both kinds of pressures were at work (and to some degree difficult to distinguish) already during the apologetic era. It cannot be stressed enough that, astonishingly, as early as the second century, Christians were engaged in reflective efforts to understand the Christian faith as the one, true philosophy. For instance, Copleston mentions Marcianus Aristides, whose *Apology* (ca. 140) takes into account the order and design of the universe and on that basis infers that none other than the Christian God is behind it all. Furthermore, both Justin Martyr (ca. 100–164) and Clement of Alexandria (ca. 150–ca. 215) thought philosophy was a gift of God that served to facilitate the reception of the gospel; interestingly (and infamously), they both believed that Plato borrowed from Moses and the Prophets for his own thought.

The issue, then, did not revolve around whether Christians were going to engage the wider culture, thereby choosing either to separate from it or capitulate to it. Rather, for Christianity to have emerged in the context that it did meant that philosophical terms, sensibilities, and inclinations of the time period were appropriated by those Christians who wished to pursue public accounts of their identities as Christians. Such inclinations are quite obvious in a figure like Minucius Felix, who argued that "God's existence can be known with certainty from the order of nature and the design involved in the organism, particularly in the human body, and . . . the unity of God can be inferred from the unity of the cosmic order."[39] Felix believed that this inference could be made by both Christians and the Greek philosophical tradition. But such inclinations were also on display in a figure like Tertullian (ca. 160–ca. 225), who—despite being famous for asking rhetorically what Jerusalem has to do with Athens—was explicitly indebted to the Stoics, Zeno, and Cleanthes. Again, by way of underscoring how early these tendencies were, both Felix and Tertullian were writing in the second and third centuries.

From these early times up to the medieval ages, Christian intellectuals did not maintain rigid demarcations between theology and philosophy. They avoided doing so because of the thought-world they inhabited

---

39. Copleston, *A History of Philosophy*, 23.

and the manner in which they engaged it. These figures believed that God was the source of all truth, which includes both faith and reason, and they therefore often pursued their vocation in ways that seem to be more philosophical than theological, at least when measured by contemporary standards. Such has been the history of Christian thought. From the origins of the Christian intellectual tradition, a diversity of strands and trajectories have arisen, and these over time have shifted, changed, and morphed, given the rise of different challenges and the promulgation of various paradigm shifts.

A comprehensive narrative of these many strands goes beyond the limits of the present book, but we should consider how the role of saintliness was typically not incidental to this intellectual work. In other words, not only were theology and philosophy not consistently demarcated during this time period, but often neither were theology and saintliness. As Hans Urs von Balthasar noted in an important chapter for this discussion, up to the period of Scholasticism, the great saints of the church were also theologians. These individuals "were 'pillars of the Church,' by vocation channels of her life: their own lives reproduced the fullness of the Church's teaching, and their teaching the fullness of the Church's life." This collective witness made an indelible contribution. Onlookers could be built up in their faith as a result of looking to these church leaders; people could see in these saints' lives how God-knowledge is both intellectually demanding and soul-purifying. In short, these pillars helped communicate a certain account of gospel truth. Balthasar comments that these leaders helped render a "complete concept of truth . . . [consisting] precisely in this living exposition of theory in practice and of knowledge carried into action." He later adds, "From the standpoint of revelation, there is simply no real truth which does not have to be incarnated in an act or in some action, so that the incarnation of Christ is the criterion of all real truth and 'walking in the truth' is the way the believer possesses the truth."[40] Put another way, the revelational beginnings of the Christian faith, as well as the faith's subsequent intellectualization, were anchored for the Christian community in a compelling, holistic way via the embodiment of exemplary church leaders. Through their example, the activity of prayer and the work of theology coincided and were understood to be mutually informing.

40. Hans Urs von Balthasar, "Theology and Sanctity," in *Explorations in Theology*, vol. 1: *The Word Made Flesh* (San Francisco: Ignatius Press, 1989), 181–82.

As history unfolded, however, significant changes took place. The complexity of these changes is daunting; the symptoms are easier to point out than it is to list all the factors that contributed to them. Louth remarks that, by the time of Thomas à Kempis's *Imitation of Christ* (1418) and Cajetan's work on analogy (1506), the divide between theology and spirituality was evident: the former was primarily a work of devotion, whereas the latter was clearly one of the intellect. Louth goes on to say that the division was fixed by the time of the Renaissance. Others have argued that the transition occurred with the rise of modernity. Varying readings of Western intellectual history will pinpoint different culprits, privilege certain circumstances, and emphasize the significance of specific developments. The shift from a Ptolemaic worldview to a Copernican one, the gradual displacement of a Platonic perspective by the recovery and rise of a modern Aristotelianism, the questioning of institutional authorities, and the privileging of subjective experience (such as one's conscience, one's empirical senses, one's mental faculties and operations)—these and many other factors could be cited as contributing to the West's demythologization, disenchantment, and secularization. As complex and countless as the factors were, it is still widely understood and agreed upon that a transition did occur and a change in worldview did take place.

The Emphasis on Epistemology

In making sense of these developments for Christian theology, many writers have highlighted the significance of changes in epistemology and their concomitant effects on theological methodology. One figure who has undertaken such a narration is Ellen Charry, who notes in her fine study *By the Renewing of Your Minds* that, whereas in previous eras "a central theological task [was] to assist people to come to God," this work was contested in modern theology, "which has moved away from primary Christian beliefs and focused on theological method instead."[41] This point has rung true in what has taken place in present-day theology. Time and time again, we have been brought back to the question of theological method, largely because the contemporary intellectual climate, particularly the realm of academic theology, demands it. For many if not most academic

41. Ellen T. Charry, *By the Renewing of Your Minds: The Pastoral Function of Christian Doctrine* (Oxford: Oxford University Press, 1997), 5.

theologians, the principal challenge before them is to secure the basis by which theological claims can be made. We face this situation because of the deep problems and reservations at work in the realm of theological epistemology. Contemporary theology operates in the wake of a deep epistemological crisis, one that hinders its ability to speak confidently about God and God's present activity. Some have complained that this means theology is constantly in a process of "throat-clearing," and one can see the warrants for such an assessment in the current-day situation. But the present epistemological climate makes such work—as tedious and burdensome as it may be—necessary in some fashion.

For her part, Charry singles out three figures in particular who have contributed significantly to our present epistemological situation, which has in turn led to the theological crisis: John Locke (1632–1704), David Hume (1711–76), and Immanuel Kant (1724–1804). All three have been understood to press the faith-reason divide in such a way that the former was deprivileged and eclipsed by the latter, which meant that "theological reasoning" was increasingly delegitimated, if not altogether discounted. As for Locke, Charry believes that the result of his empiricism is that revelation is ultimately discredited if it goes beyond the purview of reason. [42] With Hume, Charry points to the questioning of both natural theology and divine revelation and in turn the privileging of knowledge secured on the model of experimental science, particularly with regard to its qualities as observer-independent, uniform, and repeatable. [43] Finally, Charry considers Kant and his critique of transcendent knowledge. She qualifies Kant's reception, admitting that perhaps his views are not so devastating to theology once they are related to some of the apophatic proposals (i.e., negative statements, affirming what God is not) from Christian antiquity. Using this particular selection of figures, Charry traces the roots of the epistemological crisis in theology to the modern period.

Certainly, modernity has a significant role to play in this crisis, but one can follow the intellectual narrative even further back. For instance,

---

42. Charry notes that Locke himself might not actually have held this view, but that this is the way he has been read by many over time (*By the Renewing of Your Minds*, 7). Charry does not make a direct reference to, but simply cites, *The Reasonableness of Christianity* (1695) as exhibiting the warrants for this comment. I would say that figures like John Toland (1670–1722, see his work *Christianity Not Mysterious*, 1696) and Matthew Tindal (1657–1733, see his work *Christianity as Old as the Creation*, 1730) illustrate the point better.

43. Charry, *By the Renewing of Your Minds*, 8–9.

given Louth's reading, the fateful divide between faith and reason, as well as between spirituality and theology, precedes even the Enlightenment. The Renaissance and even the period of Scholasticism show signs of the fissure. To begin the story with the Middle Ages helps to contextualize Locke, Hume, Kant, and others in the modern period, which allows us to see them as representing not so much breaks with a certain tradition as much as purveyors and maybe even developments of a process that long preceded them.

If we move to premodernity as a focus for the beginnings of this break, we see why some have elevated Scholasticism as a golden age in which reason and faith were brought together in a salutary way. The medieval period, after all, spawned the great "summas" of Christian antiquity—those massive tomes that synthesized the totality of life as *coram Deo*. Aquinas's *Summa theologiae* is often cited as exemplary of the genre with its vast, structural *exitus-reditus* scheme (all things come from God, and all things return to God), in which "grace perfects nature." Such a vision has repeatedly been found to be promising, as indicated by Leo XIII's encyclical *Aeterni Patris* (1879).

The genre of the summa (the first of which is sometimes associated with Hugh of St. Victor) is itself an intellectual expression of the time, and it alongside other developments (the rise of the Western university, the prominence of the "sentences" format usually associated with Peter Lombard, and others) made the medieval period especially fruitful intellectually. Perhaps one of the most important of these happenings was the retrieval of Aristotle. Of course, Aristotle was known to Western Europe in previous periods, largely due to the translations of Boethius, but that influence was curbed because of the number of writings available and possibly even because of developments in conciliar theology.[44] Nevertheless, an Aristotelian revival occurred in the twelfth century, which worked in tandem with the rising science and empiricism of the modern era. Pre-

---

44. Josef Pieper notes that a major factor for this neglect was the upsurge and repudiation of Nestorianism (*Scholasticism: Personalities and Problems of Medieval Philosophy* [New York: McGraw Hill, 1964], 102–3). Evidently, Nestorianism forged a strong alliance with Aristotelianism, given the intellectual similarities between the two; however, when the former was denounced at Ephesus, the latter suffered, leading to a departure of scholars in that tradition from the Roman Empire. This dynamic forms the background for the emergence of the figures most often associated with this revival of Aristotelianism from Arabic sources: Avicenna (980–1037), Averroës (1126–98), and Moses Maimonides (1138–1204).

viously, a "great tradition" had emerged, one in which Christianity and forms of Platonism worked hand in hand; however, that synthesis was extensively questioned in the twelfth century with the proliferation of Latin translations of Aristotle stemming from Arab sources. Simply put, Aristotelianism's turn to the immediate, to the particular, to nature, and, by implication, to reason was an exceedingly important development for the intellectual climate of the time.

With these developments, the notion that truth is available both from reason and from revelation became more and more pronounced. The desired outcome was a synthesis of sorts between the two so that reason and revelation could function constructively in their sustained interaction; with the passing of time, however, reason came to be understood as exercising a more determinate role. "Nature" as a source of knowledge also grew in importance, and, again, one can see how this outcome simply flowed out of these many contextual and intellectual factors.[45] Both nature and reason constituted a productive tandem that over time increased in their scope and significance. About this shift, Balthasar notes that postscholastic theology "confined itself to using a natural theology, antecedent to biblical theology as a basis for a rational exposition of the latter."[46] As a result, given the way the history of the Western intellectual tradition played out, one could say that the skepticism of Hume and Kant is a by-product of a certain approach to reason and nature that has its origins in the rise and flourishing of Scholasticism. Obviously, one could hypothesize that skepticism need not have been the result of this trajectory; nevertheless, one can trace a thread throughout these many figures and developments. In other words, a story with a modicum of traceable continuity can be identified along many of these—at points apparently disparate—threads. No doubt contrary to their wishes, the Scholastics may have planted certain seeds that subsequent generations cared for, modified, and pruned in such a way so as to topple—ironically—the great scholastic edifices of thought and with it the intellectual credibility within the West of a directed, confident form of God-knowledge.

45. Part of this development was due to a rediscovery of Lucretius's *De Rerum Natura* in the seventeenth century.
46. Balthasar, "Theology and Sanctity," 186.

One Transitional Example: Boethius

Where to begin, then, for the nascent traces of these tendencies? One possibility already alluded to is an exceedingly early figure, Boethius (ca. 480–ca. 524). As a Roman and member of a senatorial family, Boethius was part of the classical era of the Roman Empire, and yet he served in the court of Theodoric the Goth, who is symbolic of a new order following the fall of Rome. As such, Boethius was in his own life and situation a mediating figure, a reality that may have contributed to his lamentable end: He was charged with conspiracy against Theodoric, imprisoned, and executed. While in prison, he wrote his most famous work, *The Consolation of Philosophy*. Over the centuries, people have been quite puzzled by the *Consolation* because Boethius, in spite of this desperate time of need, does not mention Christ once in the work. Many have wondered how a pious Christian would fail to appeal to, and draw consolation from, Christ's life, particularly from his passion and crucifixion, during such an ordeal. Does this characteristic of the *Consolation* betray establishment Christianity, showing that, during times of duress, the default will always be wider cultural authorities rather than revelation?

Whatever one makes of the particular character of the *Consolation*, Boethius nevertheless displays in his five specifically theological tractates a particular methodology, one that is often considered the forerunner of the scholastic spirit, thereby leading many people to think of Boethius as the first of the Scholastics. This methodology explicitly involved the pursuit of Christian doctrines in as rational a way as possible. Of course, others had engaged in such work before, but in Josef Pieper's mind at least, "The newness [of Boethius's project in the theological tractates] lay in the explicitness of his program; that procedure [of taking reason as far as it will go] hitherto practiced *de facto* was consciously presented as a principle." Pieper goes on to reference a famous line from these works, one taken from a letter written to Pope John I: "As far as you are able, join faith to reason."[47]

Pieper's general assessment is worth quoting in full: "New and extraordinary, moreover, was the way in which Boethius carried out this

---

47. Pieper, *Scholasticism*, 37. The work in question is "Whether Father, Son, and Holy Spirit Are Substantially Predicated of the Divinity" ("Utrum Pater et Filius et Spiritus Sanctus de Divinitate Substantialiter Praedicentur"), and the line in question is "fidem si poterit rationemque coniunge."

principle of rational examination of dogma. He was wholly consistent; not a single Bible quotation is to be found in these tractates, even though they deal with virtually exclusively theological subjects. Logic and analysis is all. This was in fact an amazingly new element—which was to be imitated and continued in medieval scholasticism." Of course, medievals utilized and commented on Scripture, but this "conjunction of faith with knowledge, expressly proclaimed by Boethius for the first time, does constitute an earmark of scholasticism." In an exceedingly telling line, Pieper remarks that Scholasticism's "specific character is determined (or at least partly determined) by the weight that is ascribed to reason in proportion to faith."[48]

The "weight of reason" in relation to faith is very much the issue before us. What precisely is this weight, what shape does it take over time, and what is its source? These massive questions can be probed through further queries: Does the weight stem significantly from Western Constantinian arrangements? Does it increase with the fall of the Roman Empire? Does it shift considerably as both *fides* and *ratio* themselves vary in their place within Western intellectual history and culture? Again, the matters at play in these questions are so complex and significant that symptoms are often easier to come by than causes. The weight is already somewhat implicit in the questions being asked in relation to the *Consolation*; it becomes a matter of explicit methodological concern in Boethius's theological tractates. And it becomes overwhelming, I would argue, with Anselm, a later figure from the medieval period.

48. Pieper, *Scholasticism*, 37–38. In fairness to Boethius, one should also take into account the statement he makes in "The Trinity Is One God Not Three Gods" (*Trinitas unus Deus ac non tres Dii*): "If, the grace of God helping me, I have furnished some fitting support in argument *to an article which stands quite firmly by itself on the foundation of Faith*, the joy felt for the finished work will flow back to the source whence its effecting came" ("Quod si sententiae fidei fundamentis sponte firmissimae opitulante gratia divina idonea argumentorum adiumenta praestitimus, illuc perfecti operis laetitia remeabit unde venit effectus") (*Boethius: The Theological Tractates*, trans. H. F. Stewart, E. K. Rand, and S. J. Tester, Loeb Classical Library 74 [Cambridge, MA: Harvard University Press, 1973], 31 [emphasis added]).

Another Transitional Example: Anselm of Canterbury

Anselm of Canterbury (ca. 1033–1109) represents an interesting case, given that he has been variously interpreted over the years on a number of topics, including his theological epistemology. As mentioned above, Louth speaks of Anselm as maintaining the spirituality-theology interface. Balthasar, in contrast, is a bit more nuanced. Early in his already referenced chapter, Balthasar remarks, "The early medieval thinkers in the west, under the aegis of Augustine, did not depart from this basic concept. Anselm, himself abbot, bishop and doctor of the Church, knew no other canon of truth than the unity of knowledge and life." That claim certainly can stand, but Anselm's works betray a characteristic that Balthasar hints of only in passing as follows: "And this simply means that [the saints'] thought is a function of their faith; even though, as in Anselm's case, they may for the sake of understanding momentarily prescind from faith."[49] The admission is a curious one. If Balthasar's reading is accurate, why would Anselm feel compelled to withdraw momentarily from faith "for the sake of understanding"? How is this possible? Why was this strategy appealing? A further exploration of his writings is in order.

In the Prologue of his *Monologion*, from the mid-eleventh century, Anselm sets out the agenda of that work by explaining that some monks at the Abbey of Bec had asked him to offer them a model meditation on the essence of the divine. But they had a significant specification: They wanted "nothing whatsoever to be argued on the basis of the authority of Scripture, but the constraints of reason concisely to prove, and the clarity of truth clearly to show, in the plain style, with everyday arguments, and down-to-earth dialectic, the conclusions of distinct investigations."[50] Anselm goes on to oblige, leading him to open the *Monologion* in the following way: "Now, take someone who either has never heard of, or does not believe in, and so does not know, this—this, or indeed any of the numerous

49. Balthasar, "Theology and Sanctity," 184, 195–96.
50. Anselm of Canterbury, *The Major Works*, ed. Brian Davies and G. R. Evans (Oxford: Oxford University Press, 1998), 5. Citations of Anselm will also be followed by their Latin originals as found in *S. Anselmi Cantuariensis Archiepiscopi Opera Omnia*, 6 vols., ed. Franciscus Salesius Schmitt (Edinburgh: Thomas Nelson & Sons, 1946). In this case, "Quatenus auctoritate scripturae penitus nihil in ea persuaderetur, sed quidquid per singulas investigationes finis assereret, id ita esse plano stilo et vulgaribus argumentis simpliceque disputatione et rationis necessitas breviter cogeret et veritatis claritas patenter ostenderet" (1:7).

other things which we necessarily believe about God and his creation. I think that they can, even if of average ability, convince themselves to a large extent, of the truth of these beliefs, simply by reason alone."[51]

Several features of these opening remarks merit closer attention. First, the request itself is quite startling. It is remarkable that Anselm's fellow monks desired a meditation on the divine essence devoid of scriptural warrants but based strictly on rational considerations. What is the source of this desire? Second, Anselm met their request, thereby implicitly acknowledging that he saw such work as feasible and worthwhile. Quite astonishingly, he goes on to speak in a way that has been taken to suggest the self-sufficiency of reason for accessing the truth claims inherent to Christian beliefs about God and creation. Whether this is a faithful reading of Anselm, he certainly offered his proposals with a robust confidence in the adequacy and power of reason.[52] His response shows us that Enlightenment thinkers—those often decried for creating theological epistemological crises in modernity—simply represent one stage of a much broader cultural and intellectual climate in Europe, one in which reason was understood and appealed to in varying ways to secure and promote the truthfulness of Christian claims.

When Anselm subsequently writes the *Proslogion*, a greater methodological tension is detectable than one finds in his earlier work. Once again, Anselm gives the reader an orientation in this work's preface of what he is attempting to do. Anselm remarks that, after the *Monologion*, "I began to wonder if perhaps it might be possible to find one single argument that for its proof required no other save itself, and that by itself would suffice to prove that God really exists, that He is the supreme good needing no other and is He whom all things have need for their being and well-being, and also to prove whatever we believe about the Divine Be-

---

51. Anselm, *Major Works*, 11. Latin: "Aliaque perplura quae de deo sive de eius creatura necessarie credimus, aut non audiendo aut non credendo ignorat: puto quia ea ipsa ex magna parte, si vel mediocris ingenii est, potest ipse sibi saltem sola ratione persuadere" (1:13).

52. Etienne Gilson adamantly stresses that Anselm's context is one of faith, and readers of Anselm will come back to this point repeatedly. I am not questioning this feature of Anselm whatsoever. But I am wishing to highlight what Gilson also thinks appropriate to add: "Such being the rule, it remains to be known just how far reason can actually go, in the interpretation of faith." He adds, "It can be said that, practically, Saint Anselm's confidence in reason's power of interpretation is unlimited" (*History of Christian Philosophy in the Middle Ages* [New York: Random House, 1955], 129).

ing."[53] Anselm goes on to speak of how frustrating this search was for him, yet the notion came to him right before he was going to give up on the quest altogether, an event whose resolution provided him with significant relief. Anselm notes, "Judging, then, that what had given me such joy to discover would afford pleasure, if it were written down, to anyone who might read it, I have written the following short tract dealing with this question as well as several others, from the point of view of one trying to raise his mind to contemplate God and seeking to understand what he believes."[54] Once more, the intellectual desideratum is important to note. The result of Anselm's quest is not the key point here; rather, it is the sensed need and value of venturing on such a quest in the first place. Why, after all, would it be worthwhile to have a single argument that, by its own self-evident merit, would prove the reality of God?

The methodological tensions reach a peak when Anselm formally begins the work and includes words that could easily be present in writings such as Augustine's *Confessions* of several centuries before: "Come then, Lord my God, teach my heart where and how to seek You, where and how to find You."[55] An intellectual and spiritual tension is at work in Anselm, as evident in the form of the *Proslogion*; the heritage of *contemplatio* is detectable through addresses and prayers directed to God in the opening sections of this work. The quest, however, is framed in a certain sense as a kind of exercise in rational or philosophical theology, given its methodological leanings.

Such a comprehensive writing has generated a number of mutually contrasting interpretations both by Christians and by those outside the Christian faith. Karl Barth found Anselm's work in the *Proslogion* to have been largely misunderstood by subsequent readers; Barth, looking at the wider context, believed that Anselm's "proof for God's existence" (*Proslo-*

---

53. Anselm, *Major Works*, 82. Originally, "Coepi mecum quaerere, si forte posset inveniri unum argumentum, quod nullo alio ad se probandum quam se solo indigeret, et solum ad astruendum quia deus vere est, et quia est summum bonum nullo alio indigens, et quo omnia indigent ut sint et ut bene sint, et quaecumque de divina credimus substantia, sufficeret" (1:93).

54. Anselm, *Major Works*, 82–83. Originally, "Aestimans igitur quod me gaudebam invenisse, si scriptum esset, alicui legenti placiturum: de hoc ipso et de quibusdam aliis sub persona conantis erigere mentem suam ad contemplandum deum et quaerentis intelligere quod credit, subditum scripsi opusculum" (1:93–94).

55. Anselm, *Major Works*, 84–85. Originally, "Eia nunc ergo tu, domine deus meus, doce cor meum ubi et quomodo te quaerat, ubi et quomodo te inveniat" (1:98).

gion 2–5) should be understood as an effort made within the confines of Christian faith.[56] After all, Anselm originally subtitled this work *Fides quaerens intellectum* ("faith seeking understanding"). Some have even suggested that Anselm operates out of an implicit mysticism that makes what he says possible, even if with a rationalist tone.[57] Such readings are plausible and have been sustained occasionally, but there is no mistaking that Anselm has a penchant to grant reason a significant place of privilege methodologically, as evident in both the *Monologion* and the *Proslogion*. Anselm has shifted the weight to the prominence of reason, both by continuing Boethius's earlier inclinations but also by extending them even further so as to register "necessary reasons" for matters typically understood as being supported from beginning to end by revelation. His is a deductive kind of reasoning that allows him to argue for the rationality of such doctrines as the Trinity and the incarnation.

To return to Pieper's analysis of Scholasticism in general, the leading minds of the era—including Bonaventure and Aquinas—carried out the coordination "between believing acceptance of revealed and traditional truth on the one hand and rational argumentation on the other hand with unfailing resoluteness"; yet Pieper goes on to say that "they also knew just where to draw the line between the claims of reason and the claims of faith."[58] Such a remark raises further questions. How in fact did they know where to draw the line? And was this tension-laden balancing act unsustainable over time, especially as new realities presented themselves with the medieval era progressing and morphing into modernity? Again, symptomatically, it is clear that *fides* and *ratio* changed in their relation to one another and that the "weight of reason" became exceedingly overbearing in relation to matters of faith. After all, using reason in theological discourse is one thing, and the thought-world known simply as rationalism is another.[59] What emerged in the midst of this balancing act was a tipping of the scales to one side of the balance. Scholasticism always ran the risk of overestimating the power

56. See broadly Karl Barth, *Anselm: Fides Quaerens Intellectum* (London: SCM Press, 1960).

57. Pieper (*Scholasticism*, 70) draws attention to this reading, found in A. Stolz, "Zur Theologie Anselms im *Proslogion*," *Catholica* 2 (1933): 1–24.

58. Pieper, *Scholasticism*, 38.

59. Pieper defines the paradigm of "rationalism" as following from the assertion that "there cannot be anything which exceeds the power of human reason to comprehend" (*Scholasticism*, 45).

of reason in securing knowledge of God. As Pieper and many others have highlighted, William of Ockham (ca. 1287–1347) represents the consequence of this overestimation; in Pieper's words, one of Ockham's hypotheses was that "belief is one thing and knowledge an altogether different matter; and that a marriage of the two is neither meaningfully possible nor even desirable."[60] The perceived intellectual integrity of God-knowledge could not help but be affected as a result of reason's rising place of privilege.

The Resulting Privatization of Spirituality

With the rise of reason in particular as a guiding motif in philosophical and theological inquiry, spirituality and theology gradually became divided, and the ramifications of this separation were significant for both. As mentioned already, theology has had difficulties accounting for its proper subject matter: God-knowledge has been consistently questioned as to its availability and stability, given the increasing divide between *fides* and *ratio*. The brief survey above has aimed to show the highlights of these transitions. However, due attention should also be given to spirituality, for it too has morphed over time, and this process has not always been helpful in securing a kind of reliable form of God-knowledge.

McIntosh notes that around the twelfth century the term *spiritualitas* shifted from being concerned with "the power of God animating the Christian life" to characterizing a privatized quality, one referring to a "highly refined state of the soul, with the focus on how one achieves such states of inner purity and exaltation." McIntosh further adds that, by the time of the sixteenth and seventeenth centuries, the term "spirituality" in both Latin and the vernaculars came to signify inner dispositions and "interior states of the soul." Put another way, "spirituality" gradually became an anthropologically oriented category in the West, in the sense that human interiority and maybe even a "technology of the self" (even if treated through explicitly theological categories such as "sanctification," "moral theology," or even "mystagogy") became the focus. McIntosh concludes that "the mystical dimension of Christian spirituality, that transforming knowledge of God which early Christian writers often saw as the very foundation of theology, grew ever more estranged from theology" by

---

60. Pieper, *Scholasticism*, 39.

gradually focusing on the "mechanics of the spiritual quest."[61] Although not pursuing the matter extensively, he refers to Madame Guyon as a representative example of these shifts.

The case of Jeanne-Marie Bouvier de la Mothe Guyon (1648–1717) is a sad one in many respects. Not only did she have a tumultuous personal life, but she also appears to have been a victim of changing popular opinion and political mongering primarily in late-seventeenth-century France. Her tumultuous life was partly the result of her teachings on the spiritual life, which at some moments were favored and at others held with great suspicion. Sometimes the term used during her lifetime to designate her teachings was "Quietism," which apparently was used to signify what were deemed troublesome views of Miguel de Molinos at about the time of Guyon's own difficulties. Therefore, people used the charges against Molinos as a way of framing those directed to Guyon. Eventually, Guyon was imprisoned at the Bastille for several years, although the last years of her life turned out to be relatively peaceful, during which she cultivated relationships and became influential among many different kinds of groups through her writings. These included German Pietists, British Methodists, and American Quakers.[62]

McIntosh's selection of Guyon as exemplary of the transitions in spirituality is well-justified, as we can see by examining a number of her writings, including *A Short and Easy Method of Prayer*.[63] One notices straightaway a democratizing principle operative in this work. This feature is not altogether bad, but it is coupled with assurances of facility and availability that lend themselves to pivot on matters of technique and refinement. Early on, Guyon remarks, "Everyone is capable of inward contemplative prayer, and it is a terrible shame that almost all people have it in their heads not to do it."[64] In her view, "Contemplative prayer is nothing more than heartfelt affection and love. What is necessary is to love God and to focus on him";[65] therefore, it can be learned and undertaken at any time

---

61. McIntosh, *Mystical Theology*, 7, 8.

62. See "Introduction," in *Jeanne Guyon: Selected Writings*, ed. Dianne Guenin-Lelle and Ronney Mourad (New York: Paulist Press, 2012), 7, 13.

63. *Jeanne Guyon*, 55–98.

64. "A Short and Easy Method of Prayer," 57. French: "Tous sont propres pour l'Oraison; & c'est un malheur effroyable que presque tout le monde se mette dans l'esprit de n'être pas appellé à l'Oraison" (*Les Opuscules Spirituels de Madame J. M. B. de la Mothe-Guyon*, new ed. [Paris: Libraires Associés, 1790], 1:9).

65. "A Short and Easy Method of Prayer," 57. The French is simpler: "L'Oraison

without reference to a particular walk of life. Guyon states quite boldly, "Nothing is easier than experiencing God and tasting him. He is more a part of us than we are of ourselves. . . . The only way to look for him is as easy and natural as breathing the air and is no more than that."[66]

In Guyon's opinion, contemplative prayer is facilitated by either meditative reading or meditation itself. In terms of the former, "some strong truths about theory and practice" are to be "digested" (*digerer*) and "tasted" (*goûter*) slowly so that they can penetrate into one's self. Meditation involves a similar dynamic, with the end goal of focusing the spirit so as to cultivate the presence of God. These teachings all suppose that "the living faith, from the bottom of our hearts, in a present God impels us to focus on our inner being, bringing all of our focus inward rather than on external things. One important consideration from the very beginning is to liberate ourselves from a great many distractions or external stimuli in order to find God, who can only be found inside of us and in our depth, which is the inner sanctum where he lives." Guyon remarked slightly later, "Once we are centered within ourselves and are profoundly penetrated by God in our depths, once our senses are all gathered up and drawn inward from the circumference to the depths . . . once the soul is so gathered into itself, then it can focus gently and sweetly on the truth that is read."[67]

We can readily see the way Guyon has cast contemplative prayer and so spirituality generally in terms of a method that involves focus, intention, and interiority. Many of her remarks in this work are hortatory, urging her readers to press deeper and more inwardly, for there they can find God. All can engage in this activity, including those who cannot read, since Christ "is the great book, written on both the inside and the outside, which will teach all things." People may not know what the Our Father means, but according to Guyon's method, they are to dwell on parts of it in deep silence, waiting for God to show them God's will.[68]

Guyon's emphases, then, are quite distinct. Their populist character makes them theologically anemic, and the spiritual life is depicted by her

---

n'est autre chose que *l'Application du coeur à Dieu*, & l'exercice intérieur de l'amour" (9, emphasis original).

66. "A Short and Easy Method of Prayer," 59. French: "Rien n'est plus aisé que d'avoir Dieu & de le goûter. Il est plus en nous que nous-mêmes. . . . Il n'y a que la manière de le chercher, qui est si aisée & si naturelle, que l'air que l'on respire ne l'est pas davantage" (12).

67. "A Short and Easy Method of Prayer," 59, 60.

68. "A Short and Easy Method of Prayer," 61, 62.

as something to be intentionally refined through means focused on the interior life. In all of these qualities, Christian spirituality has become something quite different from previous accounts. The divide between theology and spirituality is all too evident from the side of the latter. "Spiritual masters" and "doctors of the church" are now separate categories, with few able to inhabit both spheres. Credibility and achievement in one domain could very well be understood to disqualify one from consideration in the other. In large measure, circumstances and developments emerging from early modernity forward have made the "pillars" alluded to in Balthasar's earlier cited remarks among the relics of a bygone age.

Prospects of Speaking of Pentecostalism as a Mystical Tradition

This contested context, in which the relationship between spirituality and theology is severed and each is pushed to extremes, is one Pentecostals have been bequeathed whenever they have sought to engage in the task of making sense of their own tradition theologically. As previously stated, Pentecostals have been ill-served by the academy's resources to account for their identity and faith-culture, and one of the culprits for this unhappy state is the way theological knowledge has been fractured over the last few centuries in the West. The act of making Pentecostalism "theologically respectable" has sometimes led to impoverished accounts of its own ethos, given that the terms assumed for doing so were themselves often limited and not fitting to the task.

The present argument has progressed by setting the stage for a Pentecostal use of Christian mystical themes for the purpose of clarifying Pentecostal identity. The strategy has been to take charge of this language and to recover it in a time-honored, tradition-conscious way so that it can be put to use by Pentecostals seeking to ground their identity in something broader and deeper than what many available options would have to offer. This strategy of moving beyond the present state of affairs is nothing new to Pentecostals, for the restorationist impulse by early Pentecostals had this much going for it: it indirectly, if not forthrightly, acknowledged that something on the theological and spiritual scene had gone awry. Obviously, the New Testament church could not and cannot be repristinated or repeated, but the restorationist impulse suggests, at least on the theological scene, that something may very well be in need of exhumation. I believe the call of Pentecostals for "New Testament Christianity" or even "the old-time religion" can mean something very particular in academic theological pursuits: spirituality and theology are in need of reconnection so that they can mutually inform and constitute one another as they are utilized to account for the God of Christian worship. The strategy presently envisioned for such a recovery is the claiming of the language and ethos of Christian mysticism for the Pentecostal movement as a whole.

Such a task, as it has been repeatedly stressed, is not easy. For instance, plenty of Pentecostals would most likely affirm the experience alluded to by Teresa of Ávila (1515–82) in her *Life*: "When picturing Christ in the way I have mentioned, and sometimes even when reading, I used unexpectedly to experience a consciousness of the presence of God, of such a kind that I could not possibly doubt that He was within me or that I was wholly engulfed in Him. This was in no sense a vision."[69] Such a claim could resonate well with the dynamic Smith alludes to as the epistemological commitment on display in Pentecostal testimony in which people remark that "they know that they know that they know" God is at work in their midst.[70]

Pentecostals would likely pause at the line that follows Teresa's quote above: "I believe [this experience] is called mystical theology."[71] For some, the potential terminological impasse would be sufficient to proceed no further; given the various connotations and uses of the language of mysticism, many would most likely immediately reject its applicability to Pentecostalism. This disinclination notwithstanding, the aim before us in this chapter is to qualify and nuance this language in such a way that it can be appropriated by Pentecostals specifically in their ongoing efforts at negotiating their identity.

Quite rightly, Pentecostals would most likely not see any value in the language of mysticism if it were simply of the variety found in religious studies discourses, particularly within the domain of religious phenomenology. Obviously, the Spirit "will blow where the Spirit wills," but Pen-

---

69. *The Life of Teresa of Jesus: The Autobiography of Teresa of Avila*, trans. and ed. E. Allison Peers (Garden City, NY: Doubleday Image Books, 1960), 119 (X). Spanish: "Acaecíame en esta representación que hacía de ponerme cabe Cristo, que he dicho, y aun algunas veces leyendo, venirme a deshora un sentimiento de la presencia de Dios, que en ninguna manera podía dudar que estaba dentro de mí, u yo toda engolfada en El. Esto no era manera de visión" (*Obras de Sta Teresa de Jesús*, ed. P. Silverio de Santa Teresa [Burgos, Spain: Monte Carmelo, 1915], 1:69).

70. Smith, *Thinking in Tongues*, 50.

71. *The Life of Teresa of Jesus*, 119 (X). Spanish: "Creo lo llaman mística Teología" (69).

PENTECOSTALISM AS A CHRISTIAN MYSTICAL TRADITION

tecostals typically do not wish to assume a discourse that suggests that all religious traditions and their adherents are, despite their utilization of different "doctrinal encasements," speaking of the same thing, which involves an anthropological dimension that can be labeled a *mysticus intuitus* or a framing of the common human condition as *homo religiosus*. Pentecostals generally are too theologically aware to embrace this epistemology.

As noted previously, Pentecostals want to see the spirituality-theology divide be lively and interactive, which is definitely not the case in the modern Western theological tradition. Therefore, whatever use they make of the language of mysticism, it would have to fit within a framework that would allow for this kind of interaction. They would want to avoid both a scholasticizing tendency within theology (in which it is abstracted from the very realities of lived Christian experience) and a privatizing tendency within spirituality (in which it is fostered through techniques and patterns that improve focus and push consciousness toward interiority so as to find God already present in the soul). It is no wonder, then, that scholars have from time to time noted that Pentecostals fit better within a premodern worldview, for within contemporary issues and debates, they at times exude a particular kind of eccentricity; on many registers they are simply out of step with several currents in Western theology. And yet, this kind of eccentricity has made them wildly relevant on other scores, particularly as the modern project has shown fissures in its conceptual and rational framework.[72]

Where does this description leave us? What are Pentecostals ultimately to do with the language of mysticism? Broadly, I believe a case indeed can be made for positing a "family resemblance" between Pentecostalism and Christian mysticism, as noted above by Cox and others. In this sense, Pentecostalism is not something entirely new on the Christian

---

72. A relevant case of this eccentricity is the movement toward theological interpretation in biblical studies. Joel Green notes that "in recent years, the tradition that has arguably examined this question [of one's theological commitments playing a role in interpretation] most seriously is the Pentecostal tradition" (*Practicing Theological Interpretation: Engaging Biblical Texts for Faith and Formation* [Grand Rapids: Baker Academic, 2011], 11). In Green's reading, because Pentecostals came relatively late to the field of biblical interpretation, they were able to critique some of the basic commitments of the Enlightenment project. Although I think this reading is true to some degree, I do not think timing is the only factor involved. Pentecostals were also able to see past the illusion of interpretive "neutrality" because of their particular theological-hermeneutical orientation, which allowed them to see precisely those limits.

scene. From a certain vantage point, Pentecostals in their speech, commitments, convictions, activities, and practices fall squarely within those forms of Christian existence that are sometimes marginalized by anti-supernaturalist theological tendencies. Pentecostals join a host of other Christians who believe in (among other things) exorcisms, miracles, and the active and present work of the Holy Spirit.

At the same time, if Pentecostalism is to be called a mystical tradition of the church catholic, it needs to be so within its own context and theology. In this sense, Pentecostalism is unique. For Pentecostalism appears to exhibit premodern characteristics, and yet it emerged in late modernity. How can we account for this combination? Broadly, the rise of Pentecostalism can be read (as Cox does in a certain way) as a kind of indictment of some of the most difficult happenings in the modern Christian West. The movement has also helped usher a global Christian revival, which few people could have anticipated a few decades ago. The Pentecostal ethos draws people from all walks of life with a message of God's presence in the mundane, God's power among the poor and the oppressed, and God's hope for a world suffering the stifling weight of its own self-destruction.

Specifically, how is Pentecostalism a unique mystical tradition in this contemporary context? For Pentecostals themselves, the following themes may not sound distinct or extraordinary, given that they are so germane to the way they experience and embody the Christian faith. To onlookers both in and out of the Christian fold, however, these themes may be anything but common and mundane. And for Pentecostals themselves, it may be useful to nuance further and clarify more carefully what may simply be assumed and operative in a typical Pentecostal setting. By way of organizing these themes, the schematization of purgation (*purgatio*), illumination (*illuminatio*), and union (*unio*) will be used. These categories are helpful in that they have a strong pedigree in the tradition of Christian mysticism (going back at least to Pseudo-Dionysius), but they also can highlight vital elements about the unique Pentecostal ethos as it emerged on the American scene in the early part of the twentieth century.

Purgation and Sanctification

Although Pentecostalism emerged in a number of contexts and via a variety of streams, there is something to be said for the strong links that exist between the Holiness movement of the nineteenth century and the emerging Pentecostal movement of the twentieth. Some of those links can be traced further back to American revivalist culture, which gained a definitive form with the First Great Awakening. In particular, happenings such as the tent meeting, altar activity, the promotion of universally accessible religious experiences, and others collectively form a particular culture of Christian embodiment on the American scene. Some might even take the narrative further back to such movements as Pietism and Methodism,[73] but the American signature is definitive in much of what became popular Pentecostal practices and phenomena.

At the same time, the intimate connection between Holiness and Pentecostal streams in particular needs to be emphasized, especially since some see a strong enough link to label the dynamics as constituting a single tradition or family.[74] Many of the earliest Pentecostal leaders had Holiness roots, whether informal (Richard Spurling) or formal (Charles Parham, William Seymour, and many others). This contextualizing observation is not incidental to what is being suggested about the ethos of Pentecostalism, for at a macro level, Pentecostalism as a movement of power emerged within a Holiness setting that emphasized purity. In fact, as Jacobsen notes of the Azusa ethos espoused by Seymour and his associates, the tendency was to think of the experience of Spirit-baptism *not* as a "crisis" or "work of grace" in that the two that bore the designation (justification/salvation and sanctification) had to do with making a "vessel" ready; these constituted the "double-cure" required to address sin in a person's life. Spirit-baptism in contrast was "a 'gift of power' to aid the fully saved and sanctified believer in the ministry of the gospel to others."[75] At this broad level, then, the movement did not find it possible to move to power before addressing in some sense the need for purity; otherwise, the emphasis on power could easily become unwieldy and maybe even become corrupting as a result.

One sees this logic also at work repeatedly at the micro, individual

---

73. David Martin, *Pentecostalism: The World Their Parish* (Oxford: Blackwell, 2002), 167.

74. As explicitly noted in Vinson Synan, *The Holiness-Pentecostal Tradition: Charismatic Movements in the Twentieth Century* (Grand Rapids: Eerdmans, 1997), and Henry H. Knight III, "The Wesleyan, Holiness, and Pentecostal Family," in *From Aldersgate to Azusa Street: Wesleyan, Holiness, and Pentecostal Visions of the New Creation*, ed. Knight (Eugene, OR: Pickwick Publications, 2010), 1–9.

75. Douglas Jacobsen, *Thinking in the Spirit* (Bloomington: Indiana University Press, 2003), 70.

level. The case of G. B. Cashwell well illustrates the point. Coming from North Carolina, Cashwell arrived at the Azusa Street Mission, only to be appalled at the sight of African-Americans taking leadership roles in the dynamics of corporate and public worship. He confesses that he returned to his lodging deeply disturbed, but with further prayer and tarrying, he came to recognize things that needed to be "crucified" in his own life.[76] Once that dynamic played out, he returned to the Azusa meetings, was prayed over by the African-American leaders, and went on to experience his personal Pentecost. In Cashwell's life, as well as in many others, the purity-power dynamic prevalent among movements between the nineteenth and twentieth centuries took on a personal note. At both the collective and individual levels, a period and a process of consecration and purgation were needed so that the ensuing power could come and take hold in a fitting way.

Illumination and Maturation

Many commentators on Pentecostalism have remarked that it promotes a different way of looking at and participating in reality. For a religious movement to provide this dynamic on such a massive and widespread scale is significant. Allusion has already been made to Cox on this score when he speaks of narrative and testimony functioning to relate an experience of God that exudes a "magical realism" that together "is so total it shatters the cognitive packaging."[77] And Smith makes much of "worldview" and "way of life" language so as to get to the heart of Pentecostalism. These observations and claims raise the following questions: How do Pentecostals come to see this alternative reality? How can one speak of this transition from one way of seeing to another, of having one's eyes opened so as to view the world as a God-drenched reality?

Some have simply referred generally to the category of "an experience" or particularly to "Spirit-baptism" to answer the query. Such responses are at a certain level misleading because they are too simplistic and reductive. The contribution of Land is pivotal here, who argues that

76. See his testimony in *Apostolic Faith* 1.4 (December 1906): 3; however, he does not mention that the issue involving his "death to many things" involved racial prejudice. For a fuller account, see Synan, *The Holiness-Pentecostal Tradition*, 113–14.

77. Cox, *Fire from Heaven*, 71.

Pentecostals come to embody their way of seeing and engaging the world through the sustaining of their collective spirituality. No single feature of this spirituality can account for the formative impact it has upon its practitioners; instead, in this case the sum is greater than its individual parts. Miracles play a role, but not solely. Tongues is an important sign, but not singularly. Prayer, the laying on of hands, speaking with anointing, prophecy—these all function vitally but not individually. All these many features of Pentecostal spirituality contribute to a process of forming and shaping a people in a vital way. The language of affections Land uses so prominently serves its purpose to relate this formational role. I on occasion have stressed the virtues in similar and complementary ways.[78] With both sets of terms, the focus is not on isolated incidents but on the way people are shaped and transformed by a collective, worshipful ethos.

Both Pentecostalism and features of the Christian mystical tradition emphasize dimensions of formation, growth, and maturation. In both of these currents, the spiritual life is cast as something lively and in need of attention and care. Rather than manipulation or construction, the favored actions in these schemes are attentiveness and devotion. Activities such as praising God through music, the sharing of testimony, responsive preaching, altar tarrying, laying on of hands, and "praying through," collectively contribute to a kind of modality of knowing and being that is both spiritually and theologically productive. In short, Pentecostal spirituality facilitates and inculcates a specific account and form of God-knowledge, one that is personal, demanding, humbling, and enriching. On the whole, participation is crucial, for the deepest registers of the self are engaged in this Christian tradition.

Union and Transformation

What primarily makes Pentecostalism a mystical tradition of the church catholic is its persistent, passionate, and widespread emphasis on encounter, which at some level is relatable through the language of union. The theme of encounter was highlighted above in the efforts to circumscribe the language of mysticism. From their end, Pentecostals believe that they encounter deeply and transformatively the God of their confession

---

78. See Castelo, *Revisioning Pentecostal Ethics—the Epicletic Community* (Cleveland, TN: CPT Press, 2012), chap. 3.

and adoration. This theme is central to Pentecostal identity.[79] Although Pentecostals may not frequently speak of transcendence or of mystery in referring to God, the implications of these terms are quite evident in Pentecostal testimonies. They typically lie in the background of the kinds of things Pentecostals associate with God's manifest presence and power. Much of that language and logic would fit within Boyer and Hall's designation of a "dimensional mystery." God presents Godself (or quaintly put, "God shows up"), and God goes on to establish a different kind of order, one in which God's glory and holiness alter and renarrate all else that is. In Louth's analogies, the encounter with God for Pentecostals can be understood relationally and perhaps, if they are prompted a certain way, aesthetically as well.[80] God's manifest presence, as witnessed in the encounter with this One, secures for Pentecostals the availability and veracity of God-knowledge. Encountering God, in other words, serves as the epistemological grounding for Pentecostal theological methodology. Beholding God, sensing God, feeling God (expressions that relate to Boyer and Hall's "facultative mystery") constitute the orienting epistemic framework for Pentecostal theology.

For Pentecostals, the theme of encounter involves an implicit theological realism. Rather than going deeper within, Pentecostals typically urge seekers to "get more of God" by pressing deeper into *God's* reality. Therefore, in their corporate worship settings, Pentecostals strive to create the space for people to encounter and (more fittingly stated) be encountered by the God of their worship. The assumption at work is that God is available and in turn can act and surprise through a kind of "event" in which one's creaturehood is overwhelmed by the sheer glory of the Creator. It is no wonder, then, that many Pentecostals fall prostrate, are "slain," shake, scream, or cry at such moments. Genuine cases of these experiences do not represent psychological contortions or expressions of pent-up frustration or despair; rather, these happenings are simply signs of a body overwhelmed by the "touch of the living God." If Pentecostals were familiar and comfortable with the language, they could join Teresa of Ávila in calling this sense of the divine "mystical theology."

79. Keith Warrington believes that the essence of Pentecostalism is the evident need for "a personal, experiential encounter of the Spirit of God" (*Pentecostal Theology: A Theology of Encounter* [London: T&T Clark, 2008], 20).

80. On a "Pentecostal aesthetics," see Smith, *Thinking in Tongues*, 80–85.

Conclusion

In this chapter I have sought to situate the language of mysticism within Christian theological discourse so that it could be of use for the narration of Pentecostal identity. Pentecostalism can be identified as a mystical tradition within the church catholic, but only if we recognize the mystical features of Christianity that hold the knowledge of God to be both intellectual and relational. Once we do so, we can recognize that Pentecostals implicitly operate out of mystical sensibilities in the ethos they sustain regarding worship and how it in turn reflects their belief that God engages and encounters those who thirst after God. The ultimate goal is a sense of the divine that is, in short, transformative. As Warrington remarks, "One experience with God can be more life changing than an encyclopedic knowledge of God. . . . Thus, Pentecostals value experience-based encounters with God because they have the potential to transform believers. They believe that if God initiates an experience, it must be in order to positively transform the individual concerned."[81] In this particular sense Pentecostals can be identified as modern-day mystics. The mystical dimensions of ancient Christianity are not dead for those who have "eyes to see" and "ears to hear" otherwise.

81. Warrington, *Pentecostal Theology*, 26.

CHAPTER 3

The Epistemological Form of Evangelical Theology

We move now to a third dimension of our overall argument, namely, how Pentecostalism relates to evangelicalism, particularly of the American variety. The present chapter is strategically placed, given that chapters 1 and 2 examined changes within the theological landscape, which in turn have influenced evangelicalism in important ways. This influence has to do, once again, with the theme of theological method.

In chapter 2 mention was made of Ellen Charry's reflection on the turn to method in theology during the modern era. At this time Christian doctrines largely lost their prescriptive quality and became more focused on abstraction and theorizing. In a footnote, Charry quotes an insightful claim by David Dawson, who draws connections between the transitions experienced in literary theory and in theology at the time: "Academic theology turned into theological method at about the same time that practical literary criticism turned into literary theory, and perhaps for much the same reason—as an apologetic or protectionist strategy by humanists who found themselves increasingly marginalized by the rising prestige of science and technology in the university."[1] Notice Dawson's mention of "an apologetic or protectionist strategy" pursued by those who were pushed to the edge of cultural relevance by a new scientific and technological order. This point should be kept in mind as we move to consider the particular epistemological traits of American evangelicalism. Why? Largely because of a very disturbing development. Whereas I have made

---

1. David Dawson, *Literary Theory: Guides to Theological Inquiry* (Minneapolis: Fortress, 1995), as quoted in Ellen T. Charry, *By the Renewing of Your Minds: The Pastoral Function of Christian Doctrine* (Oxford: Oxford University Press, 1997), 31n5.

the case here that the Christian life on the whole trades on holy mysteries, the American evangelical movement, although citing Scripture as its one true authority, has significantly failed to account for the mystery-laden qualities of this life. Much of this failure is attributable to epistemological matters. We have already seen indications of this difficulty even in such a promising work as Boyer and Hall's *The Mystery of God*. Despite their appeal to mystery, which they claim must transcend reason because of the superabundance of God's life, they nevertheless feel compelled to give reason some kind of prevailing acknowledgment, saying awkwardly that, even while transcended, reason still must operate. Of course, theological reflection is reason-oriented; we as creatures are rational and use our rational capacities in our theological efforts. The reference to reason in Boyer and Hall's presentation, however, is awkward by its inclusion as a postscript of sorts, as if its presence was necessary to register, even if in terms of an afterthought. Their implicit assumption is that whatever theology amounts to, even theology surrounding the mystery of God, it needs to be affirmed as rational in some sense. One could hypothesize that a fear is operative in Boyer and Hall in particular and within evangelicalism in general, one that has to do with avoiding certain methodological alternatives. If this hypothesis is true, then some options are simply to be avoided and others maintained at all costs.

In light of these and other details surrounding the epistemological and methodological forms evangelical theology has taken over the centuries, one could venture the following thesis: the story of American evangelicalism in particular can be told as the tale of how Christian theology was overdetermined by methodology. Of course, American evangelicalism can be narrated in a number of ways, but for purposes of this study, it is important to highlight just how significant epistemological and methodological issues have taken hold within the theological efforts of this strand of American Christianity. Perhaps out of both apologetic and protectionist concerns, American evangelicalism imbibed and adopted a very specific theological methodology, one that was particularly developed with ongoing reference to reason.

For purposes of perspective, Charry proves helpful once again in showing how reason changed from the Middle Ages to modernity in theological reflection (although what we have entertained thus far might nuance this claim further): "The use of reason in theology had started out as assistance to revelation by theologians like Anselm and Thomas. But in spite of their insistence that faith should seek understanding, reason as a tool of absolute knowledge took on a life of its own that bent in the direction of denying the intelligibility of Christian claims unless knowledge of God was empirically or rationally demonstrable."[2] American evangelicals embraced and promoted this usurpation of theological reflection by reason, and the signs of this capitulation were very much on display in the developments of the nineteenth- and twentieth-century forms of this Christian tradition. Rather than critically and creatively resisting the forces that promoted the marginalization of Christian theology, American evangelicals sought to employ those forces—consciously or subconsciously as a "plundering of the Egyptians"—in ways that lamentably have led to a kind of intellectual unraveling. That effort was largely methodological, driven as it was by an implicit account of reason that framed Scripture as an epistemological foundation that cohered on the basis of a given account of truth—one that was modern to its core.

Understanding the Term "Evangelical"

As noted in the opening pages of this work, "evangelicalism" is a contested term, one used to describe a number of constituencies in a myriad of contexts. As evidence of this dynamic, consider the 1970s, when a burgeoning industry within the field of American religious history was the work of specifying and delineating "evangelicalism" on the American scene—a trend no doubt motivated by a resurgence of evangelical influence in the political sphere (notably in the election of Jimmy Carter to the presidency and in the rise of the Moral Majority). In the heat of these academic debates, a number of possibilities were proposed and deliberated. Donald Dayton, for instance, wanted to drop the term "evangelical" altogether because, in his estimation, it was too often used as an umbrella category that aimed to account for too much diversity (which, according to some proposals, would include at least a dozen distinct traditions). On this reading, there is simply no way to use the term "evangelical" in such a sweeping way without diminishing and overlooking very important differences within the subsumed groups themselves.[3] If the term continued to be used, one rendering or one faction would necessarily seek to be primary and trump

---

2. Charry, *By the Renewing of Your Minds*, 10.
3. See Dayton's essays in Donald W. Dayton and Robert K. Johnston, eds., *The Variety of American Evangelicalism* (Downers Grove, IL: InterVarsity, 1991).

the others, which is what Dayton suspected to be the case with people like Bernard Ramm, who promoted what Dayton has called the "Presbyterian paradigm" in staking out evangelical identity.[4]

Despite Dayton's legitimate reservations, however, the term continues to maintain its prominence on the American scene today. Undoubtedly, reasons contributing to this usage include convenience and partisan formations coming out of its deployment. George Marsden's remarks continue to ring true, namely, that the word "evangelical" tends to solidify allegiances and demarcate boundaries in ways that not even denominational ties do.[5] There is simply too much political and cultural significance surrounding the term for it to be abandoned. But Dayton is right: its usage comes with significant costs, not the least of which is the blurring and avoidance of nuance. Therefore, people continue to retain and yet debate the category, adding subcategories and offering broad narratives to make the term do some kind of work.

One proposal along these lines is Timothy Weber's account of three significant historical groups that could be identified as forming the broad evangelical tradition. For a first category, Weber cites the Protestant Reformers and the general ethos that they cultivated in regards to sin, divine initiative, personal religious experience, the primacy of Scripture, and so on. Weber calls this branch *classical evangelicalism*. The second group he mentions is *pietistic evangelicalism*, which would involve the spiritual awakenings and revivals of the eighteenth and nineteenth centuries on both sides of the Atlantic, including Anabaptism, Puritanism, Methodism, and others. And finally, Weber mentions *fundamentalist evangelicalism*, which is those "primarily known for their rejection of liberal, critical, and evolutionary thinking and their strong defense of a few Christian 'fundamentals' in opposition to various modernisms."[6] This group was largely consolidated in the early 1900s and is associated in particular with a number of happenings during the 1920s.

---

4. See particularly Donald Dayton, "The Limits of Evangelicalism: The Pentecostal Tradition," in Dayton and Johnston, eds., *The Variety of American Evangelicalism*, 49. The work in question is Bernard L. Ramm, *The Evangelical Heritage* (Waco, TX: Word Books, 1973).

5. See George Marsden, "Introduction: The Evangelical Denomination," in *Evangelicalism and Modern America*, ed. Marsden (Grand Rapids: Eerdmans, 1984), ix.

6. Timothy P. Weber, "Fundamentalism Twice Removed: The Emergence and Shape of Progressive Evangelicalism," in *New Dimensions in American Religious History*, ed. Jay P. Dolan and James P. Wind (Grand Rapids: Eerdmans, 1993), 264–65.

For better or worse, on the American scene this third and last group continues to shape the term's associations among the masses. Again, no single group can claim the language exclusively, but this group in particular is often assumed to set the tone for what the term can mean in the wider public sphere. This last group is interesting in that it can be said to have arisen because of a particular crisis.

This reading has been espoused by many, including Stanley Grenz, who considered himself an evangelical but nevertheless wished to recast evangelicalism in ways different from this tradition. According to Grenz, the turn of the twentieth century in many ways constituted a collapse of the nineteenth-century "golden era" of evangelicalism in the United States, for the following reasons: "the failure of the revivalists to capture the mind of the era, the sociological disruption that followed the immigration of non-Protestant peoples and the intellectual ferment triggered by the evolutionary theories credited to Darwin."[7] The collapse was evident in the modernist-fundamentalist controversies of the 1920s, which overall was part of a wider division within American Protestantism, one that eventually led to "liberal" and "conservative" designations, which still operate today. Some are even more specific than Grenz's account and say that, between the 1870s and 1920s, evangelicalism in America lost its cultural footing.[8] Within a matter of decades, a significant shift occurred, leaving a group of conservative Christians to decry the culture with a "militant and separatistic spirit."[9]

After World War II there was a renewed sense of coalition-building among evangelical Protestants. Robert Webber's narrative picks up at this point, as he mentions three kinds of American evangelicals from the mid-twentieth century forward: the traditional (1950–75), pragmatic (1975–2000), and younger (2000–) evangelicals.[10] I summarize these in

7. Stanley J. Grenz, *Revisioning Evangelical Theology: A Fresh Agenda for the Twenty-First Century* (Downers Grove, IL: InterVarsity, 1993), 24. Mention should also be made of factors such as the rising prominence in America of historical-critical methodologies in biblical scholarship, rapid urbanization, increased secularization, and greater religious pluralism.

8. George M. Marsden, "From Fundamentalism to Evangelicalism: A Historical Analysis," in *The Evangelicals: What They Believe, Who They Are, Where They Are Changing*, ed. David F. Wells and John D. Woodbridge, rev. ed. (Grand Rapids: Baker, 1977), 143. Marsden has slightly varied the time-range elsewhere; see his *Reforming Fundamentalism: Fuller Seminary and the New Evangelicalism* (Grand Rapids: Eerdmans, 1987), 4, where he proposes the period between the 1890s and 1930s.

9. Weber, "Fundamentalism Twice Removed," 265.

10. Robert E. Webber, *The Younger Evangelicals* (Grand Rapids: Baker, 2002).

reverse order. In Webber's opinion, the third group is still emerging, and their overall shape and focus are in many ways yet to be determined. Webber's appeal to personal and anecdotal evidence for this group shows as much. The second group is "pragmatic" in that it was and continues to be focused on a market-driven, seeker-friendly, church-growth approach to Christian religiosity. Head pastors are functionally thought of in terms of managers, their megachurches are usually in suburban areas, and their goal is to provide meaningful experiences for their churchgoers. The first group, the "traditionalists," sought to be in line with fundamentalist commitments (particularly in their Reformed rendering and largely related to the topic of biblical inerrancy), yet—unlike the fundamentalists— they wished to be more engaged with society on ecumenical, political, and intellectual concerns.[11] This group has sometimes been labeled neo-evangelical or simply just evangelical, given that these designations were deemed more preferable at the time than the term "fundamentalism." This stream is responsible for the rise of an institutionalized evangelicalism seen most notably in the beginnings of the National Association of Evangelicals (1942), the founding of Fuller Seminary (1947), the establishment of the periodical *Christianity Today* (1949), and the long-revered ministry of Billy Graham.

Despite all the developments and diversity noted in many of the historical narratives surrounding American evangelicalism, the fundamentalist (per Timothy Weber's categories) and traditionalist or neo-evangelical (per Robert Webber's typology) groups will be the subject of what follows. Together, this fundamentalist and neo-evangelical trajectory has significantly shaped what the term "evangelicalism" means on the contemporary American scene. The justification for the link between these groups is that they partake of a common theological outlook, even if they are different on other counts. Both groups could affirm David Bebbington's often-cited description of the evangelical ethos as conversionism (the call for lives to be changed), activism (a desire to share the Christian faith), biblicism (the particular esteem of the Bible as uniquely authoritative), and crucicentrism (an emphasis on Christ's crucifixion in the work of salvation).[12]

11. The manifesto for this approach is Carl F. H. Henry, *The Uneasy Conscience of Modern Fundamentalism* (Grand Rapids: Eerdmans, 1947).

12. See David W. Bebbington, *Evangelicalism in Modern Britain: A History from the 1730s to the 1980s* (London: Unwin Hyman, 1989), 2–3 (elaborated more fully in 2–19). Interestingly, Bebbington is speaking about the British context, but these themes res-

But if one were to look more closely into this theological family, something more determinate binds them: a certain epistemological paradigm that secures truth in a very particular way. These groups share a scholasticizing tendency; they typically rationalize the Christian faith in such a manner that leaves little room for a mystical sensibility. The penchant to rationalization betrays itself usually in terms of how the Bible is conceptually viewed as authoritative and inspired. Both groups (and even subsequent evangelicals beyond this particular strand) find it appropriate to speak of the Bible as inerrant because it is assumed that only this kind of affirmation will secure its truthfulness over and against the modern pressures represented in historical-critical biblical scholarship, evolutionary theory, and debates surrounding cosmological and human origins. As many have lamented in the face of such pressures, without something as conceptually, morally, and practically demarcating as "inerrancy," one is left with the prospect of relativizing the biblical witness through appeals to metaphor, symbolism, literary genre, and so on. And once such a reinterpretation happens with topics such as, say, the historicity of Adam and Eve or the dating of Daniel, it is often assumed that the "slippery slope" effect will lead to questioning the legitimacy and truthfulness of the gospel itself.

The claim of the Bible's inerrancy has been defended on the American scene by many evangelicals in a manner that reveals a certain epistemological militancy, one that forces a person to take sides regarding the Bible's truthfulness, again with the latter being understood in a very particular, modern way. This militancy has emerged in a myriad of ways across a number of forms. One of the most popular cases occurred in the 1970s, when Harold Lindsell published his book *Battle for the Bible* (1976).[13] Soon thereafter the Chicago Statement on Biblical Inerrancy (1978) was formulated, a document repeatedly appealed to as a way of building broad consensus. Institutional purgings, denominational divisions, strategic initiatives, and similar efforts have collectively contributed to the sense shared by many that to be evangelical, one needs to subscribe to biblical inerrancy. Otherwise, one would be on precarious footing, slipping inevitably toward heresy and unorthodoxy—that is, caving in to the cultural

---

onate with major features of American evangelicalism as well and thus are often cited in terms of the latter.

13. Harold Lindsell, *The Battle for the Bible* (Grand Rapids: Zondervan, 1976); the sequel to this volume continued this kind of work; see *The Bible in the Balance* (Grand Rapids: Zondervan, 1979).

and worldly pressures to relinquish the fundamentals of the Christian faith.

In what follows, I wish to look more closely at this epistemological paradigm. It certainly is the case that many evangelicals have rejected it and so have looked to something else. Examples here include the "younger," "progressive" evangelicals Webber and others cite.[14] And yet I would argue that this modern epistemological paradigm continually haunts the evangelical ethos in varying ways up to the present day. Inerrancy is a shibboleth of evangelical culture; it perhaps may be claimed outright, privately and individually nuanced, or treated casually and thus conveniently put to the side, but all too often it is not debated or considered with the aim of examining its actual formulation and significance. It typically stands as a presupposition and as a badge for "insider-outsider" negotiation. As an unquestionable tenet for many believers in terms of evangelicalism's core identity, inerrancy continually resurfaces in the same tried and worn ways as a rallying cry to promote evangelical consolidation.[15] Therefore, what contributes to make the view of the Bible's inerrancy plausible—the epistemology at work—is rarely considered on its own terms. Without doing so, it is difficult if not impossible to understand its context, which is necessary in order to evaluate it properly.

This situation has lamentably taken its toll on the Pentecostal ethos, both historically and at present. Without the conceptual resources to contextualize evangelicalism's reliance on modern epistemological sensibili-

14. For another account of this group, see Richard Quebedeaux, *The Young Evangelicals: The Story of the Emergence of a New Generation of Evangelicals* (San Francisco: Harper & Row, 1974). Interestingly, the role Fuller Theological Seminary has played in these dynamics is considerable. Whereas Fuller is directly and repeatedly vilified by Lindsell, it is gushingly praised by Quebedeaux.

15. Given this history of a continually resurrected form of "traditional evangelicalism," Webber may be a bit too optimistic about where he thinks things currently stand. Speaking of a cultural evangelicalism that bound itself to modern thought-forms, he remarks, "The current dilemma of twentieth-century modern evangelicalism is that the twentieth-century cultural paradigm in which the evangelical faith was explained, proclaimed, and defended has come to an end" (Webber, *The Younger Evangelicals*, 15). Certainly, this paradigm has been questioned and thus destabilized as a result, but the current situation does not represent a pronounced, transitional shift. Rather, the contemporary setting is a liminal one, showing signs of vitality with regard to all three of his categories. In a time like ours in which uncertainty, terrorism, and globalization are rampant concerns, many have found the oldest of the three paradigms a comfort of sorts, an anchor so as to maintain some sense of security and stability in a continually changing world.

ties, Pentecostals have often assumed that there is only one way to secure the truthfulness of the Bible—the evangelical way—before the modernist-fundamentalist controversies. As difficult as it was to accommodate the evangelicals in a certain sense, Pentecostals certainly saw them as allies over and against Protestant liberals. Given the apparent options available, Pentecostals—despite how they have traditionally read and engaged Scripture in their worship practices—have repeatedly found themselves espousing a doctrine of Scripture (and an epistemology that grounded it) that ultimately is in tension with the instincts and intuitions present in their spirituality.

I wish to argue that the theological methodology at work in the fundamentalist/neo-evangelical lineage is precisely one that cannot be accommodated to Pentecostal identity when it is significantly marked by its mystical orientation. The burden of this chapter is to show why this is particularly the case for specified theological positions expressed by representatives from the nineteenth, twentieth, and twenty-first centuries. The chapter concludes with some pertinent matters of historical and theological concern for Pentecostals as they seek to claim an identity consonant with the kind of epistemology that undergirds their mystical impulses.

"Old Princeton"

So-called Old Princeton was a theological phenomenon that embodied in many ways a number of evangelical tendencies in theology that were associated with the nineteenth century and that would go on to be carried into the twentieth. The name refers to several significant figures associated with Princeton Theological Seminary from its founding in 1812 to the latter part of the nineteenth century. These scholars include Archibald Alexander (1772–1851), Charles Hodge (1797–1878), Archibald Alexander Hodge (1823–86), and Benjamin Breckinridge Warfield (1851–1921).

One of the most prominent characteristics of Old Princeton was its reliance on the Scottish Enlightenment for its epistemological and methodological grounding. Such an intertwining is not surprising: both the Scottish Enlightenment and significant features of American culture thrived in a context influenced in varying degrees by Calvinism. But even with this admission, more details are worth noting regarding the specifics of how this branch of the Enlightenment was so influential. In speaking of the Enlightenment as a whole, Henry May has proposed four different

stages and discusses the influence of each on the American scene.[16] His
stages are:

Moderate/Rational (marked by figures such as Newton and Locke and
  dominant in England until the mid-eighteenth century)
Skeptical (characterized by wit, present both in Britain and in France,
  represented by Voltaire, Hume, and Holback)
Revolutionary (exemplified by Rousseau, Paine, and Godwin, who
  represent a tendency to establish a new realm by getting rid of
  the old)
Didactic (the point at which a certain part of the Scottish Enlightenment became so popular in America).

The Didactic Enlightenment figured so prominently in America because it helped address two desiderata held by the emergent nation coming
out of its revolutionary period. According to May, "Americans wanted to
believe at once in social and even scientific progress and in unchanging
moral principles." With these felt needs by "the early builders of nineteenth century American official culture," the only suitable European
teachers to be found "were the Common Sense philosophers of Scotland."[17]
A strong confluence of factors was thus operating.

Scottish common-sense philosophy, or simply common-sense realism, was spearheaded by Thomas Reid (1710–96), a Presbyterian cler-
gyman who sometime held the chairs of moral philosophy at the Uni-
versities of Aberdeen and Glasgow. Reid reacted to Bishop Berkeley and
David Hume (a personal friend) by pursuing an even more skeptical line
of thought: Reid held that the doubt that was introduced by these skeptics
should itself also be questioned; in other words, their doubt should also
be doubted on its own terms, thereby leading to a philosophical conun-
drum and leading Reid to believe that a way forward was to look not at the
particular, idiosyncratic problems of philosophers but to the assumptions
held by everyday people. The latter operated and assumed correspondence, causality, predictability, and a host of other things questioned by
the skeptics, and given both the popularity and relative success of these
assumptions "on the ground," Reid believed this dose of "common sense"

16. See broadly Henry F. May, *The Enlightenment in America* (New York: Oxford
University Press, 1976).
17. May, *The Enlightenment in America*, 342.

should chasten philosophical proposals as they tend toward abstraction and irrelevance at the hands of professional philosophers. The assumption was that "normal people, using responsibly the information provided by their senses, actually grasped . . . the real world," and in turn they could make judgments on the basis of that knowledge.[18] Dugald Stewart (1753–1828), a student of Reid who held a similar post to Reid's at the University of Edinburgh from 1785 to 1809, followed this line of thinking and was quite influential, both in his native context as well as in the United States.

On the American scene, this joining of faith, morality, and education under the umbrella of common-sense realism was occurring already in antebellum America. Francis Bacon (1561–1626) was being repeatedly appealed to in this context, so much so that one scholar has referred to the "beatification of Bacon" in the consciousness of the burgeoning nation at this time.[19] This is a most curious development, given that Bacon, although often lauded as the founder of scientific method, was rarely referenced by the intelligentsia in the period immediately following his death. Newton and Locke, as well as Hume, Smith, and Paley, did not often refer to Bacon, despite being some of the most important English-speaking intellectuals in the centuries following Bacon. And yet during the early decades of the nineteenth century, reference was being made to "the Baconian philosophy" with a tone of awe and reverence.[20] This development was no doubt because of the intellectual and cultural influence of various Scottish thinkers (esp. Reid and Stewart, but also George Campbell, James Beattie, and Thomas Brown).[21]

The influence this school of thought had on the American consciousness was largely methodological. The belief sustained in the wake of this Scottish influence was that "God's truth was a single unified order and that all persons of common sense were capable of knowing that truth."[22] With

18. Mark A. Noll, "Introduction," in *The Princeton Theology, 1812–1921*, ed. Noll (Grand Rapids: Baker, 1983), 31.

19. Theodore Dwight Bozeman, *Protestants in an Age of Science: The Baconian Ideal and Antebellum American Religious Thought* (Chapel Hill: University of North Carolina Press, 1977), 72–74. As Bozeman notes, part of this task involved portraying Bacon and Newton as exemplars of Protestant piety so as to offer a vision in which the sciences and Christianity could be harmonized.

20. For a condensed summary of this view, see Bozeman, *Protestants in an Age of Science*, 21.

21. For more on this relationship, see Douglas Sloan, *The Scottish Enlightenment and the American College Ideal* (New York: Teachers College Press, 1971).

22. George M. Marsden, *Fundamentalism and American Culture*, 2nd ed. (Oxford: Oxford University Press, 2006), 14.

such an account of truth in place, early American educators endorsed common-sense realism to such a degree that it became the dominant school of philosophical thought being taught in American colleges during much of the nineteenth century. Part of this prominence was because many of the colleges at the time were led by moderate Calvinists. Presidents of these schools were usually clergymen, and they typically taught a number of classes, including moral philosophy.[23] These factors contributed to a set of conditions in which "in spite of competition from various forms of Romantic Idealism, Common Sense Realism remained unquestionably *the* American philosophy" during the time period.[24]

With this methodological outlook in place, Christians often used it in apologetics to make the case for the truthfulness and reasonableness of their faith. Marsden remarks, "Especially in the eighteenth and the nineteenth centuries, defenders of Christianity assiduously collected evidences from natural sciences to confirm truths revealed in Scripture. Nineteenth-century American apologists . . . typically based their apologetics on explicitly Baconian principles."[25] In these efforts, hypotheses and metaphysical speculations were vilified, and observation and objective certainties were privileged. The moral order (as well as political economy, aesthetics, and a host of other topics) could be understood this way, since the physical universe operated as such, and ultimately, it was confessed, God is the source of both. Therefore, when Christians during the era spoke of God's revealed truth, they were inclined to use this "one-size-fits-all" epistemological approach. Truth is one—whether scriptural, moral, or scientific—and so methods to ascertain truth should consequently be united as well.

Relating this school to Princeton, Noll believes the Scottish philosophy came from Scotland to America in its fullest form via John Witherspoon, who became the president of Princeton College in 1768. Other names to be included here are William Graham, Ashbel Green (who became president of Princeton in 1812), and the "last great defender of the Scottish Philosophy," James McCosh (called to the presidency of Princeton in 1868).[26] As these many names demonstrate, a culture developed at Princeton in which this philosophical orientation was primary. In many

23. May, *The Enlightenment in America*, 346–48.
24. Marsden, *Fundamentalism and American Culture*, 14.
25. George M. Marsden, *Understanding Fundamentalism and Evangelicalism* (Grand Rapids: Eerdmans, 1991), 162.
26. Noll, "Introduction," 31–32.

ways, Princeton represented the bastion of common-sense realism on the American scene, and the movement was perpetuated intergenerationally and across institutions (i.e., between the college and the seminary). Many examples from this context could be given to illustrate the point, but here I explore one: the *Systematic Theology* of Charles Hodge, one of the stalwarts of the Old Princeton school of thought.

Early on in this work, Hodge clarifies his methodological views, beginning (not unsurprisingly) with an analogy to the hard sciences such as astronomy and chemistry. The first words of his multivolume systematics are the following: "In every science there are two factors: facts and ideas; or facts and the mind. Science is more than knowledge. Knowledge is the persuasion of what is true on adequate evidence. But the facts of astronomy, chemistry, or history do not constitute the science of those departments of knowledge." Hodge goes on to specify what must be involved with a science, taking theology as the example: "If . . . theology be a science, it must include something more than a mere knowledge of the facts. It must embrace an exhibition of the internal relation of those facts, one to another, and each to all. It must be able to show that if one be admitted, others cannot be denied."[27] With this understanding in mind, Hodge believes that the Bible presents the "facts" or "truths" of faith,[28] which "the theologian has to collect, authenticate, arrange, and exhibit in their internal relation to each other." In short, the theologian—like the scientist—has "to ascertain the laws by which [the facts] are determined."[29]

This approach has all the merits of a Baconian system of thought. It casts the Bible in a very specific way, as indicated by the following quote: "The Bible is to the theologian what nature is to the man of science. It is his store-house of facts; and his method of ascertaining what the Bible teaches, is the same as that which the natural philosopher adopts to ascertain what nature teaches."[30] Without due attention to the problematic nature of such a casting, Hodge simply assumes that Scripture presents the "facts" of faith and that theologians are to detect the "laws," or principles, that hold them together.[31] This last activity is necessary by the very struc-

27. Charles Hodge, *Systematic Theology*, 3 vols. (Peabody, MA: Hendrickson, 2003; orig. pub., 1872–73), 1:1.

28. Hodge uses this language to account for the Bible's claims; see *Systematic Theology*, 1:2.

29. Hodge, *Systematic Theology*, 1:1.

30. Hodge, *Systematic Theology*, 1:10.

31. A quote from Arthur Pierson is apropos here: "A Baconian system . . . first gath-

ture of human knowing. As Hodge remarks in a way befitting a systematic theologian, "Such is the constitution of the human mind that it cannot help endeavoring to systematize and reconcile the facts which it admits to be true." Therefore, not only is this kind of reflection a necessity, given the ways humans process and interpret knowledge, but Hodge also goes on to say that such work helps people reach higher planes of knowledge, is in line with pastoral and teaching functions, and ultimately is the will of God, the latter point emphasized once more in terms drawn from the natural sciences: "As the facts of nature are all related and determined by physical laws, so the facts of the Bible are all related and determined by the nature of God and of his creatures. And as He wills that men should study his works and discover their wonderful organic relation and harmonious combination, so it is his will that we should study his Word, and learn that, like the stars, its truths are not isolated points, but systems, cycles, and epicycles, in unending harmony and grandeur."[32] With these many points, one can say that the "beatification of Bacon" had indeed taken place via the Scottish influence at Princeton.

As such, the door was opened for the most important word to describe Scripture's authority coming out of this Baconian framework: *inerrancy*. This language is not exclusive to Old Princeton, but this school helped the cause. B. B. Warfield in particular went to great lengths to speak of the Bible's authority in terms of inspiration, which for him would include inerrancy.[33] Hodge for his part makes the point explicit: "If what [the scriptural writers] assert, God asserts, which, as has been shown, is the Scriptural idea of inspiration, their assertions must be free from error."[34]

---

ers the teachings of the word of God, and then seeks to deduce some general law upon which the facts can be arranged" (as quoted in Marsden, *Fundamentalism and American Culture*, 56).

32. Hodge, *Systematic Theology*, 1:2, 3.

33. See the article "Inspiration" (*Presbyterian Review* 2, no. 6 [1881]: 225–60) by A. A. Hodge and B. B. Warfield as a late example of an "Old Princeton" perspective addressing views of the Bible, including inerrancy.

34. Hodge, *Systematic Theology*, 1:163. On the one hand, Hodge did not hold to inerrancy as rigidly as some figures subsequently did (see *Systematic Theology*, 1:169–70). On the other hand, he is also willing to tackle head-on objections that Scripture be without error. In short, Hodge believes that the affirmation that Scripture contains errors would be due to two factors: the authors contradicting themselves or their witness being inconsonant with what history and science show us to be true. On the first score, Hodge believes that these tensions are generally of little consequence and can be due to a number of reasons, including faults of transcription. As to the latter point, Hodge

In Hodge's mind, when Christ remarked that "Scripture cannot be broken" (John 10:35), he was implying that it was without error.[35] Such is the possible consequence of a Baconian framework when applied to the understanding of Scripture's inspiration and authority.

This Baconian strategy aids theologians not only in ascertaining what is true but also in distinguishing what is false. False theories in the sciences as well as false theologies have gone astray because they have made "mistakes as to matters of fact."[36] If investigators would simply be attuned to the facts and would reason in a fitting way (i.e., inductively) regarding them, then they could develop appropriate laws concerning the way things are. Presumably, the logic would hold for things like gravity, light, and thermodynamics, as well as sin, happiness, and God's will. It is important that this kind of methodology, when applied to theology, should secure itself against all kinds of threats by assuming a baseline, or stable authority, in the midst of rapid change. Higher criticism of the Bible, Darwinism, the culturally deprivileging effects of immigration, and so on—these all can be questioned and resisted, since they fail to take account of the facts of Scripture. These alternative and highly erroneous views seek to renarrate, explain away, or simply ignore what is plainly available in the Bible; they allow the theories to determine the facts, but this is simply wrongheaded faith, just as it would be wrongheaded science if such practices were extended to the natural sciences.

Excursus: Hodge on Mysticism

Given the topic of this book, it will be helpful to explore Hodge's views on mysticism, which he expresses in an entire chapter within his *Systematic Theology*. Hodge immediately recognizes the difficulty of determining what mysticism refers to. He is aware (although he does not use these terms) that the notion can be utilized in the field of religious studies to

---

believes that what Scripture proposes and what science indicates is that the universe was created by an intelligent designer; the Christian may not be able to account for a number of things, but on this score, the point is indisputably rational. See Hodge, *Systematic Theology*, 1:169–70.

35. Hodge, *Systematic Theology*, 1:163.

36. Hodge, *Systematic Theology*, 1:11. Hodge makes this claim in relation to the need for scientists and theologians to demonstrate diligence and care as they pursue their work.

talk about phenomena within varying religious traditions. He settles on the following broad understanding: "In a wide sense of the word, a Mystic is one who claims to see or know what is hidden from other men, whether this knowledge be attained by immediate intuition, or by inward revelation."[37] Hodge notes a number of exemplars of the term in Christianity, including the Alexandrian school and Quakerism, all the while nuancing and qualifying in what ways this broad term can and cannot be applied to such cases.

To his credit, Hodge depicts the Christian life very much as a pneumatological reality as he talks about mysticism. He notes, "Evangelical Christians admit a supernatural influence of the Spirit of God upon the soul, and recognize a higher form of knowledge, holiness, and fellowship with God, as the effects of that influence." And yet he wishes to distinguish these points from the term "mysticism," despite their association by certain Christian authors who believe such pneumatological grounding would make of each true Christian believer a proper mystic. What we come back to in these delineations is precisely the way mysticism is to be understood. Hodge believes that, on Christian terms, the work of the Spirit to illuminate, teach, and guide believers is *not* properly considered as features of mysticism. In one sense, a mystical framework can be understood as any system that assigns "more importance to the feelings than to the intellect,"[38] and if such a framework were to be admitted for Christian theology, then its chief exemplification would be Friedrich Schleiermacher. But Hodge is quite clear that this view ultimately cannot hold for elaborating the Christian way of life.

For Hodge, mystics "are those who claim an immediate communication of divine knowledge and of divine life from God to the soul, independently of the Scriptures and the use of the ordinary means of grace."[39] Put another way, mysticism is excessively subjective and thus not attentive to the objectivity of revelation. Mysticism is not "scientific," given that it is bound to the hiddenness of the individual's self and experience. Hodge takes great pains to sustain this kind of understanding, despite the problems that it yields. For instance, Hodge distinguishes mystical experience from the illumination of the Spirit. At one point he says that God "does hold immediate intercourse with the souls of men," thereby justifying the

37. Hodge, *Systematic Theology*, 1:61.
38. Hodge, *Systematic Theology*, 1:64.
39. Hodge, *Systematic Theology*, 1:66.

notion that Christians are "spiritual"; however, in Hodge's mind illumination and mysticism are different on at least three points.

The first difference is in terms of the purpose of such experience. For Christians, the illumination of the Spirit is for the sake of enabling the discernment of truth one finds "objectively revealed" in the Bible, whereas mystical experience "communicates truth independently of its objective revelation. It is not intended to enable us to appreciate what we already know, but to communicate new knowledge."[40]

Second, the two differ in the manner of achieving such experiences. Christians would seek the Spirit properly through prayer and diligent use of proper means (one assumes here the spiritual disciplines); the mystic, in contrast, seeks his or her intuitions through the neglect of all means and the "suppression of all activity inward and outward." In this last case a kind of passivity is at work, one that involves simply "waiting for the influx of God into the soul."[41]

Finally, both differ as to effects. For the Christian, the effect of illumination is that the Word dwells in us in terms of wisdom and understanding; for the mystic, the effect is a kind of self-absorption: "What dwells in the mind of the Mystic are his own imaginings, the character of which depends on his own subjective state; and whatever they are, they are of man and not of God."[42]

This last quote, as denunciatory as it is (and the Old Princetonians were often keen to express their views in a biting polemical style), suggests precisely the issue for Hodge in the way he has set up this contrastive. Mysticism for Hodge is ultimately an anthropological category; it has to do with subjective personalization and privatization, neglecting in turn any resources (including Scripture) beyond itself to shape or substantiate it. Hodge's chapter is remarkable in that he goes on to include quite a number of exemplars of the mystical tendency in historic Christianity, but the contrastive framework is set: What these people did and continue to do is to look introspectively and to deny what God has revealed objectively for all to see. At times, they have caused great evil because their foundation was not the Word of God but private fancy; they have neglected what God has shown and in turn have been the authors of new revelations. Tellingly, Hodge remarks that maybe the authors and characters of Scripture expe-

---

40. Hodge, *Systematic Theology*, 1:68.
41. Hodge, *Systematic Theology*, 1:68.
42. Hodge, *Systematic Theology*, 1:68.

rienced proper Christian mystical dynamics; these, however, should be understood as miracles, and just as the latter have ceased (so he asserts), so has the former. In other words, Hodge's rejection of Christian mysticism also works out of a cessationist paradigm.[43]

One recognizes that Hodge has set up his contrastive quite conveniently. He has depicted mysticism in the most insular way possible, very much as a strategy to preserve his methodological and epistemological commitments about how revelation works. In many ways, his presentation comes off as quite inconsistent, for whereas he wishes at times to stress how fanciful and anthropological mystical experience is, he at other points is willing to consider authentic Christian experiences of mystical encounter with God in the Bible's formulation.[44] The source of this tension is that he is ultimately interested in safeguarding the objectivity and scientific character of the Bible as he has established such matters at the beginning of his work. He is unwilling to allow for a pneumatological recalibration of that system.[45] It is this framework that cannot be questioned, and it must be protected at all costs, even if it means the unfair characterization of several Christian thinkers and movements, as well as an appeal to a cessationist paradigm that will at once say that the mystical logic of the Christian life worked in a previous era but no longer applies in this present, miracle-less dispensation. To conclude, Hodge finds mysticism as a threat to the task of attending to what God has revealed and done across time. His epistemological and hermeneutical orientation prevents him from seeing Christian mysticism (as I have defined it in chap. 2) as a feature of that work in the present.

43. Hodge, *Systematic Theology*, 1:97–98.

44. Interestingly, he also lauds certain figures from Christian history, calling them "evangelical Mystics" and affirming them as being "great blessings to the Church" (Hodge, *Systematic Theology*, 1:79); these include Bernard of Clairvaux, Hugh and Richard of St. Victor, Gerson, and Thomas à Kempis.

45. As Ernest R. Sandeen notes, "This attempt to adapt theology to the methodology of Newtonian science produced a wooden, mechanical discipline as well as a rigorously logical one. The witness of the Spirit, though not overlooked, cannot be said to play any important role in Princeton thought" (*The Roots of Fundamentalism: British and American Millenarianism, 1800–1930* [Grand Rapids: Baker, 1978], 118).

Fundamentalism

Old Princeton represents a stage of development in American Protestant-ism in which it was facing a number of cultural tests and challenges, which reached a fever pitch at the turn of the century. As such, the battle lines became more entrenched, and the passing of generations led to differ-ent transitions and coalitions. A representative figure of this dynamic is J. Gresham Machen (1881–1937), who eventually left Princeton Seminary because it had become more moderate on these questions with the passing of the Old Princeton guard. Machen established Westminster Seminary in Philadelphia in 1929 so as to promote the spirit of Old Princeton in an effort to face the threat of "theological liberalism" from what had become a fundamentalist posture. In fact, it was largely the common threat of Prot-estant liberalism that created a coalition of many different figures of vari-ous theological persuasions who facilitated the collective rise of American fundamentalism.

The term "fundamentalism" is typically traced to a series of books published as *The Fundamentals* (1910–15), which had as its aim the pro-motion of orthodox Christian doctrine in the face of the encroachments of liberalism. Those who promoted this series came out of the millenar-ian movement, one that had roots throughout the nineteenth century. Therefore, when one wishes to think of the roots of fundamentalism, one must delve into this millenarian tradition and not merely the controver-sies in the early 1900s. As Sandeen has pointed out, one should distinguish between a fundamentalist *movement* and a fundamentalist *controversy*.[46] Nevertheless, amalgamating efforts were undertaken at the turn of the twentieth century with their shared common-sense proclivities, as well as their common foe of liberalism/modernism. The way fundamentalists found to secure the faith against the problematic and discrediting effects of this liberal tradition was to recall the "fundamental" beliefs of the Chris-tian faith, which included a robust assertion of the Bible's authority. After all, it was contended, theological liberalism moved to the anthropological register of affections and experiences because it had discounted the verac-ity and reliability of the Bible through higher criticism. The fundamental-ists saw this move as deleterious, one that would destroy the very founda-tion of Christian faith as a revealed—and thus objectively true—religion.

On this last point, the fundamentalists made use of the Old Princeton

---

46. Sandeen, *The Roots of Fundamentalism*, xvii.

witness to good effect. These two camps cannot be equivocated: they are distinguishable both in terms of time and theological-denominational orientations (Princeton was Reformed, whereas the fundamentalists were composed of a number of groups, including Baptists), and yet they share a connection in that the later fundamentalists were all too ready to employ the aid of the well-esteemed Princeton legacy and its wider Presbyterian base for their purposes. As a case in point, the Presbyterian General Assembly of 1910 devised a statement of five essential doctrines—inerrancy of Scripture, the virgin birth of Christ, Christ's substitutionary atonement, Christ's bodily resurrection, and the authenticity of past miracles—that were deemed crucial in the changing times; this statement (with modification to the fifth point) was picked up by fundamentalists and known with time among some as the "five points of fundamentalism."[47]

In the midst of the modernist-fundamentalist controversies, the first of these points—the Bible's inerrancy—continued in its preeminence as a distinguishing marker or test of membership only in conservative camps. Appeals, for instance, to the fabricated concept of "the original autographs" were sustained at this time, drawing on a heritage that arose from both Princeton and millenarian camps. The Fundamentals as a series was lauded, in part because of its defense of the Bible against biblical criticism. And the founding of the World's Christian Fundamentals Association in 1919 and its associated creed (with its first article on the Bible's verbal inspiration and inerrancy) aimed to consolidate these various tendencies in an organizational manner. The language of fundamentalism was largely secured at this time, and its running theme was a devotion to a particular conception of the Bible as a way of resisting the tendencies of modernity and liberalism. Throughout these many efforts, the Baconian/common-sense approach to theological methodology and epistemology prevailed. Rather than adapting to the times by espousing a different philosophical and hermeneutical outlook, this system's supporters just entrenched themselves deeper into its logic, only to weaken it by pressing up against its limits.[48]

47. Marsden, *Fundamentalism and American Culture*, 117. Fundamentalists had a number of documents and statements, but early on, this association was made, even though there are some historiographical mistakes associated with it. See Sandeen, *The Roots of Fundamentalism*, xviii–xix.

48. This weakness certainly comes through with the appeal to the "original autographs." The system was maintained at the cost of requiring tangible—but irretrievable—artifacts deemed necessary to support it.

Yet, however appealing this kind of Baconian/common-sense methodology may be for the present, it certainly generated not only a stance representative of a school of thought but also a posture of a broad evangelical alliance against what were deemed attacks to the consistency of the Christian faith across time. At the heart of this approach was that "God could not, would not, convey truth through an errant document." As Sandeen continues, "Both Princeton and the millenarians [and so the emerging fundamentalists] had staked their entire conception of Christianity upon a particular view of the Bible based ultimately upon eighteenth-century standards of rationality."[49] Their view of truth was a particular one, but they universalized it as a way to secure conceptually its objectivity. In altering our earlier quote, one could say this methodology has repeatedly been picked up even up to the present "as an apologetic or protectionist strategy [by American evangelical Christians] who [find] themselves increasingly marginalized" on their home soil. The source of their marginalization could be any number of things, including science, the university, a secularizing culture, and an increasingly complex and interconnected world. Whatever the challenges might be in terms of the hot-button issues of a given era, upsurges of the Old Princeton orientation and its Baconian/ common-sense methodology can continually be noted across a variety of Christian networks, associations, institutions, and churches on the American scene. Evangelical Christianity in America has yet to fully recover from the loss of cultural relevance it endured at the turn of the twentieth century, and a major sign of this ongoing defeat and despair is the continual appeal to Scripture in terms of this quite particularly modern epistemological framework.

Neo-Evangelicalism and Carl F. H. Henry

With the passing of decades, fundamentalist theology waned to the extent that it was associated with a certain militancy that was anticultural and in tension with much of the intellectual tide increasingly marking the American scene, especially after World War I. Carl F. H. Henry (1913–2003), a capable and ambitious intellectual within the fundamentalist tradition, found this set of affairs unpalatable. Harold John Ockenga (1905–85), another leading voice during the ferment of this midcentury consoli-

---

49. Sandeen, *The Roots of Fundamentalism*, 130, 131.

dation, lamented the situation in one of Henry's early works by quoting a comment made to him by a soldier: "Why must the church be on the wrong side of every major social issue?" Ockenga's response? "If the Bible-believing Christian is on the wrong side of social problems such as war, race, class, labor, liquor, imperialism, etc., it is time to get over the fence to the right side. The church needs a progressive Fundamentalism with a social message."[50] In the body of the work, Henry himself expressed that he was troubled by the insularity of his fundamentalist kin and called them out to be more engaged with the wider world's ills. The shift he wished to see was a kind of evangelicalism that was more attuned and responsive to the difficult problems facing the lot of humanity during midcentury.

As helpful and necessary as this call was for evangelicalism to change its approach toward the wider world, remnants akin to the Old Princeton methodology continued to be perpetuated at midcentury. Put another way, to be a "Bible-believing Christian" (as Ockenga remarked) was a slogan continually understood by these neo-evangelicals in a very particular way: One should take the Bible on good faith to mean what it says, and the way this dynamic was understood (both in terms of "meaning" and "saying") had the resonance of the Baconian/Scottish common-sense philosophical outlook. Interestingly enough, a strategy for engaging the wider culture was to deepen the commitment to this outlook by stressing the Christian faith as a revealed and rational religion. If objectively true, God's revelation in Scripture should appeal to all those who exercise their reasoning faculties most fully. If Christianity was anything, they would say, it was rational, for it came from a rational God who revealed himself in propositional, verbal, and thus rational ways.

This approach to theology is on display in Henry's six-volume magnum opus, *God, Revelation, and Authority* (1976). The first volume is largely methodological and will attract most of our attention in what follows. Rather than beginning with an analogy to the hard sciences, Henry starts his work with a remark that sets the tone for all that follows: "No fact of contemporary Western life is more evident than its growing distrust of final truth and its implacable questioning of any sure word."[51] Despite obvious differences, both Hodge and Henry begin their works with the

---

50. Harold John Ockenga, "Introduction" to Carl F. H. Henry, *The Uneasy Conscience of Modern Fundamentalism* (Grand Rapids: Eerdmans, 1947), 13.

51. Carl F. H. Henry, *God, Revelation, and Authority*, vol. 1 (Waco, TX: Word, 1976), 17.

challenge of establishing credible theological knowledge in ways that resonate within their broader cultural contexts. Each in his own way is tackling
the question of truth. For both, revelation is truth, and because it is so,
revelation is also rational.

In typical fundamentalist-evangelical fashion, Henry stresses the dire
situation of the times. Part of this condition involves a global distrust of
all kinds of influences. Henry mentions a growing skepticism regarding
claims and agendas in the wake of such things as the Watergate scandal and
the rising power of the media and marketing. He repeatedly calls this the
"crisis of word and truth." At one point Henry says that "the modern crisis
of truth and word is not something historically or culturally unique," yet
a few pages later, he remarks, "Few times in history has revealed religion
been forced to contend with such serious problems of truth and word,
and never in the past have the role of words and the nature of truth been
as misty and undefined as now." Within such an environment, Christianity suffers more than other religions, given that it is a "religion of verbal
revelation."[52]

Henry is concerned about how, in his opinion, religion has devolved
into a matter of personal preference "rather than a truth-commitment
universally valid for one and all." In morphing to such a shape, religion
necessarily loses public credibility; it becomes a matter of choice and taste
rather than something that can call and shape the self and society. And
Henry believes that the only way to secure this last point is to have revelation and truth that are timeless and transcendent. It is not enough to deal
with the data of revelation; the more significant question Henry believes
the wider culture is asking is, How does one proceed from these data to
conclusions that commend themselves to rational reflection? This casting
of God's truth within rational reflection makes it both publicly accessible
and relevant. In being testable, verifiable, and capable of being judged,
truth has a character that can affect the public—it can be credible and thus
demanding and authoritative beyond its private ecclesial confines. "Only
by restoring human speech to the Word of God," Henry notes, "can the
present futility of words be canceled and contemporary idiom [with such
words as 'free,' 'good,' 'true,' 'holy,' and 'love'] be rejoined to truth and reality."[53] Henry's account of Christian truth, then, is for him ultimate truth,
and Christian engagement with the wider society can be such as to order

52. Henry, *God, Revelation, and Authority*, 21, 24, 26.
53. Henry, *God, Revelation, and Authority*, 13, 14, 28.

the world to such an account. The prospect of not doing so is for the church to abdicate its responsibility to render a credible and relevant Christian witness, thereby allowing the world to fall ever deeper into the abyss of relativism, pessimism, and nihilism.

Henry considers a wide array of figures and movements, so much so that it is often difficult to determine his own views, but at least the following points are clear. First, access to truth rests on God disclosing it. Unlike modern theologians, who in his opinion have replaced theology with anthropology, Henry affirms that God-knowledge is available from God's very self. In his reflections he assumes the logic of Romans 1—all have some knowledge of God's existence and character, but this kind of "natural" revelation has been clouded by sin. A surer foundation is the special revelation of God's Word, which goes on to republish "objectively" this natural revelation in a way that resists human misusage or reduction. This last category, the Bible, serves as a universally valid criterion of truth, something that Henry sees as logically necessary to avoid individual fancy. With such a criterion in place, truth-negotiation can be secured as a rational kind of undertaking, since what God reveals is in the form of rational concepts. A general definition Henry offers early is the following: "Revelational theism provides cognitive information about God and the true nature of reality and it supplies categories of thought and definitions of reality that require the replacement of philosophical conjecture." This lodging of revelation in rational form sustains its universal character: "Christians must indicate their conviction that Christianity is distinguished above all by its objective truth and must adduce the method of knowing and the manner of verification by which every man can become personally persuaded." In other words, Henry manifests a strong penchant toward intellectualizing and rationalizing the Christian faith. In one of his guiding summary statements, he remarks, "Divine revelation is the source of all truth, the truth of Christianity included; reason is the instrument for recognizing it; Scripture is its verifying principle; logical consistency is a negative test for truth and coherence a subordinate test." All of this holds because Henry believes that the truth of the gospel not only can but must be cast in propositional, axiomatic, and theoretical forms. In what can only be taken to be an exceedingly strong claim for theology's essential rationalist character, Henry states, "Yet the content of revelation does indeed lend itself to systematic exposition, and the more orderly and logical that exposition is, the nearer the expositor will be to the mind of God in his revelation." To summarize, as Henry does in one of his critical chapters: "Christianity is a rational religion because it is grounded in the rational living God and his meaningful revelation."[54]

Before moving to a consideration of Henry's treatment of mysticism, a concluding set of remarks is in order by way of relating Hodge and Henry. They both represent a rationalistic and scholastic tendency in evangelical theology in that they have a realist account of truth that is objectively available in the Bible, which ultimately represents for them a collection of facts, axioms, and propositions that in turn need to be ordered and "systematized" by the theologian. I believe that such an approach not only miscasts the role and place of Scripture in a worshiping community, but it also has a way of neglecting the role of tradition and culture in the Bible's formulation and reception.[55] In other words, the privileging of this rationalist model does away with the significant challenges of contextualization, which would involve not only geographic and cultural considerations but hermeneutical, philosophical, and social-scientific considerations as well.

Excursus: Henry on Mysticism

Like Hodge, Henry also takes the opportunity to talk about mysticism, and he does so in intuitionist terms. Unlike Hodge's qualifications and nuancing, Henry seems to be quite clear in what he believes is at work with this perspective: "Mystics claim that direct insight into the invisible world is available through personal illumination as a means of access to the Divine allegedly transcending all ordinary levels of human experience." Mystics, Henry says, talk of the divine as ineffable, so their God-talk is self-contradictory or paradoxical and so "beyond the criterion of truth and falsehood." Henry sees this as a problem in that, without such a criterion, there is no way to judge mystical claims; furthermore, these qualities make speech related to mystical experience impossible, since ineffability is privileged over rationality. Therefore, the mystic participates in commitments that, at the end of the day, make such intuitions private

---

54. Henry, *God, Revelation, and Authority*, 223, 201, 213, 215, 240–41, 244.

55. Although I chose Hodge and Henry as symptomatic of this scholastic tendency prior to reading their work, I found it assuring that Stanley J. Grenz and John R. Franke also chose these particular individuals to illustrate the scholasticizing tendency in evangelical theology (see *Beyond Foundationalism: Shaping Theology in a Postmodern Context* [Louisville: Westminster John Knox, 2001], 13–15). As part of their reflections, they note that both Hodge and Henry are prone to neglect factors related to contextualization.

and subjective, devoid of any kind of evaluation. Henry argues, "But if one claims universal validity for any affirmations about the Divine, he must introduce criteria for judging between alternative views; simply to claim that one pursues a private epistemology no more entitles him to a sympathetic hearing than a pyromaniac is due exoneration because he acts on his own unique moral code."[56]

Like Hodge, Henry too talks of Friedrich Schleiermacher as an exemplification of this problematic tendency. He groups Schleiermacher with Jacobi and Schelling to say, "These men wrote not of God as the Religious Object, but of their own religious sentiments," further adding of Schleiermacher that he "in effect substituted the psychology of religious experience for theology, or the science of God."[57] Relatedly, Henry believes that mysticism is implicitly pantheistic and that it involves a degree of manipulation from the human side through various techniques. For these and other reasons, Henry finds the phrase "Christian mysticism" unviable.

Lamentably, Henry's treatment of mysticism is less nuanced and extensive than Hodge's. Henry does not go into great detail about the definitional possibilities for mysticism, assuming instead a very specific account and in turn generalizing it to the whole. Undoubtedly, one significant reason why Henry can do this is that he does not speak of the Spirit much, if at all, in his considerations of mysticism. And this critique could be extended even more so to the whole of Henry's project in *God, Revelation, and Authority*: the work is pneumatologically anemic, especially in the way it sets up methodological concerns. Henry's project is first and foremost a theology of the Word, or Logos. Without recourse to a pneumatological idiom at critical points along the way, Henry has constructed a theological epistemology that all too easily defaults to a modern, rationalist paradigm. No wonder, then, that mysticism cannot fit within such a program; the agenda has been constructed so as to exclude it from the very beginning.

Pentecostalism, Evangelicalism, and Institutionalization

These surveys might make it seem that Pentecostalism is clearly not in the evangelical camp, and yet in one of the early public treatments of the Pentecostal movement, John Nichol maintains that Pentecostalism has a

56. Henry, *God, Revelation, and Authority*, 70–71, 72.
57. Henry, *God, Revelation, and Authority*, 72.

Protestant ethos.[58] He does so initially at two levels. First, he argues that Pentecostals subscribe to "Reformation principles," such as salvation being a free gift of divine grace and the Word of God requiring interpretation according to an individual's conscience. Second, he locates the movement within the Anabaptist tradition, the radical/left wing of the Reformation, because of the general support by Pentecostals of believer's baptism and their emphasis on the Spirit. After making these points, he adds, "In matters of doctrine, Pentecostals can be described as Evangelicals whose theology is akin to Fundamentalism, and their writings on both sides of the Atlantic seem to support such a generalization."[59] Nichol mentions some quotes from leading Pentecostal scholars, but perhaps his most convincing bit of evidence is the Statement of Truth adopted by the Pentecostal Fellowship of North America. Founded in 1948, this group codified its beliefs in eight articles, all but the fifth article following verbatim the statement of faith of the National Association of Evangelicals.

Of course Pentecostalism did not emerge in a vacuum. As many historians have shown, Pentecostalism in America took off as it did largely because it was a renewal movement among Holiness ministers who flocked to various centers of revival (Azusa being the most prominent) for their "personal Pentecost," only to go back to their areas of service or to new missionary realms preaching their newfound beliefs and experiences. Naturally, these ministers could not abandon their previous convictions, even after their recent "Pentecost" experiences. When the time came to formulate what they were expecting and had experienced, they necessarily used the categories and concepts available to them as a result of their own formation, experiences, and associations. Donald Dayton in particular has highlighted this contextualization of Pentecostal beliefs and theology, particularly as represented in his emphasis on the fourfold pattern for the "full-gospel" understanding. With the exception of initial-evidence thinking (in which tongues is seen as the initial evidence of Spirit-baptism), all the other major features of Pentecostal theology had been highlighted previously by the Holiness movement and other religious currents in the nineteenth century.[60]

58. See broadly John Thomas Nichol, *Pentecostalism* (New York: Harper & Row, 1966).

59. Nichol, *Pentecostalism*, 3.

60. Donald W. Dayton, *Theological Roots of Pentecostalism* (Peabody, MA: Hendrickson, 1987), 22. Dayton here cites A. B. Simpson, founder of the Christian and Missionary Alliance, but Simpson represents a convenient representation of the grouping itself. As

As Pentecostalism emerged, it relied on this evangelical heritage, despite the embarrassment this association provided for fundamentalists and evangelicals of various stripes. Pentecostals appealed to Simpson but also to Reuben Torrey and A. J. Gordon; they relied on dispensationalist schemes of the Scofield variety, even though such frameworks were often cessationist in nature; and in the heat of the modernist-fundamentalist debates, Pentecostals quite clearly identified with the fundamentalists—they "read fundamentalist literature and adopted anti-Modernist and anti-evolution rhetoric." Interestingly enough, the favor was not returned; "the influence . . . was largely in only one direction, from fundamentalism to pentecostalism."[61] Both historically and prospectively, Pentecostalism's emergence relied upon fundamentalist and evangelical constituencies.

This reliance may have been intentional, but was it theologically warranted? Once we have contextualized the American Pentecostal movement in its wider setting and have recognized that Pentecostals sought alignments and alliances with fundamentalists and evangelicals, could we go on to say that theologically they are ultimately in the same family of traditions? Given the way that so much of the fundamentalist-evangelical ethos relies epistemologically on Baconian thinking (i.e., common-sense realism) and its strong rationalizing tendencies in theology, we could ask whether Pentecostals have typically read Scripture from a common-sense perspective. Are their methodological (i.e., epistemological and hermeneutical) inclinations and their accounts of truth and meaning based on the approach of the Scottish Enlightenment? Have they typically considered theology as a rational enterprise that involves, to use one of Henry's terms, "axiomatization"?[62] As Pentecostalism has gradually identified more clearly its philosophical grounding and engaged in the difficult work of formulating its theological identity, the answer of much recent scholarship has been mixed.[63]

Dayton notes, "All the elements of this four-fold pattern occur separately or in various combinations in other Christian traditions" (22).

61. Marsden, *Fundamentalism and American Culture*, 94.

62. Henry, *God, Revelation, and Authority*, 239–40.

63. The most sustained expression in the direction of denial is Kenneth J. Archer, *A Pentecostal Hermeneutic: Spirit, Scripture, and Community* (Cleveland, TN: CPT Press, 2009). Of course, exceptions exist on this score. Archer mentions the cases of William and Robert Menzies, as well as Gordon Fee, as those who have seen alignment with evangelical hermeneutical tendencies as a boon and aid to Pentecostal scholarship (see 189–90). I tend to sympathize with Archer's instincts regarding all of what is involved

Contemporary scholars have carried on a lively debate on these topics, and studies have addressed the hermeneutical sensibilities of Pentecostals in their various historical stages. Relying in part on a schema proposed by Veli-Matti Kärkkäinen, L. William Oliverio Jr. has proposed an extensive typological treatment of hermeneutical approaches in Pentecostalism.[64] He employs four categories:

1. original, classical Pentecostal
2. Evangelical-Pentecostal
3. contextual-Pentecostal
4. ecumenical-Pentecostal.

Part of the importance of Oliverio's study is the manner in which he expands and nuances the first type. He recognizes that Pentecostals held to the authority of Scripture in what can be deemed a "Protestant way"—that is, in considering it primarily authoritative for matters of faith and practice—yet a major feature of this approach was to see Scripture as providing "normative exemplars for Christian experience."[65] That is, Scripture can be considered a primary authority in various ways; the Pentecostal view of scriptural authority was both similar to and different from Protestants generally and evangelicals in particular. The similarities are often on display in the tendencies by early Pentecostals to believe that Scripture can be taken "at face value" and that the "plain sense" is available to those who have a proper spiritual disposition.[66] In this, they sounded exceedingly close to a Baconian/common-sense paradigm, which would not necessarily be surprising, given the Christian subcultures out of which Pentecostalism emerged.[67]

---

within the Pentecostal theological ethos, which includes a unique character that has a bearing on hermeneutics and epistemology.

64. See L. William Oliverio Jr., *Theological Hermeneutics in the Classical Pentecostal Tradition: A Typological Account* (Leiden: Brill, 2012), and Veli-Matti Kärkkäinen, *Toward a Pneumatological Theology: Pentecostal and Ecumenical Perspectives on Ecclesiology, Soteriology, and Theology of Mission*, ed. Amos Yong (Lanham, MD: University Press of America, 2002), chap. 1.

65. Oliverio, *Theological Hermeneutics in the Classical Pentecostal Tradition*, 31.

66. See Grant Wacker's elaboration of the notion "plenary relevance" in *Heaven Below: Early Pentecostals and American Culture* (Cambridge, MA: Harvard University Press, 2001), chap. 4.

67. It is also not surprising that, by promoting such a hermeneutic, early Pentecostals were primed to experience doctrinal divisions, which actually occurred early, and at an alarming rate.

But there are differences as well as similarities in the hermeneutics of early Pentecostals and evangelicals. Oliverio insightfully remarks that the willingness of Pentecostals to allow their theology to be interpreted by charismatic experience made for an interactive dynamic between theology and experience. This openness represents "an attempt to resolve the modern Protestant divide on the matter of theological method. The authority of the Bible (orthodoxy) is interwoven with the primacy of religious experience (both in orthopraxis and orthopathos). This is a movement, then, though not a consciously theoretical one, toward a way beyond the divide between the biblical propositionalism of conservative Protestantism and the placing of the locus of divine revelation on religious experience as in liberal Protestantism."[68] So while the views of early Pentecostals on the perspicuity of Scripture might make them sound Protestant in their orientation, the way they integrated their experience with their vision of "the apostolic faith" in order to live it out practically makes their approach unique. This orientation allows for a different kind of nuance, one that opens up mystical dimensions to the spiritual reading of Sacred Writ.

It is thus no surprise that some Pentecostal scholars have opted to emphasize hermeneutical continuity with evangelicalism, while others have stressed discontinuity. Much depends on the sources one uses. The second of Oliverio's types, the Evangelical-Pentecostal hermeneutic, also supports those who stress continuity between the groups, for they would be inclined to see the second type as a further development of the first type. All these efforts to contextualize and describe Pentecostalism within broader traditions might help weaken the argument that the Pentecostal movement simply "fell out of the sky," but they also have the concomitant effect of blurring the distinctive features of this unique group.

Pneumatic Interpretation

Broadly, one could say that Pentecostals read Scripture not so much to encounter the facts or truths of the Christian faith as to encounter the living God of Christian confession. That is, the Pentecostal hermeneutical orientation is relational and experiential to its core, especially when on display within the broader gamut of their practiced spirituality. Pentecostals op-

68. Oliverio, *Theological Hermeneutics*, 34.

erate out of an epistemology that in many ways would be complicated by the rationalism at work in the form of evangelicalism surveyed above.[69] In the Pentecostal dynamic, Scripture comes alive in a unique way. Encountering the living God who inspired these texts is not so much a spiritually solipsistic or nebulous form of engagement but rather one that illuminates and grants greater clarity to the reading of the texts themselves.[70] Rickie Moore well summarizes the point:

> Thus we know that [in the Pentecostal reading of the Bible] there is a vital place for emotion as well as reason, for imagination as well as logic, for mystery as well as certainty, and for that which is narrative and dramatic as well as that which is propositional and systematic. Consequently, we appreciate Scripture not just as an object which we interpret but as a living Word which interprets us and through which the Spirit flows in ways that we cannot dictate, calculate, or program. This means that our Bible study must be open to surprises and even times of waiting or tarrying before the Lord.[71]

This kind of activity works from its own logic, its own rationality—in short, its own account of truth. In this approach to Scripture, Pentecostals are much closer to those of the ancient church, which practiced *lectio divina*, than they are to their fundamentalist and evangelical counterparts. Their similarity is their view that the ultimate end of reading Scripture is not "accounting for the facts" so much as it is hearing from God.[72] This kind of activity would posit its own form of "objectivity," one anchored in the matrix of communal worship. Given this orientation, one could say

69. An early article that makes this point is Jackie David Johns and Cheryl Bridges Johns, "Yielding to the Spirit: A Pentecostal Approach to Group Bible Study," *Journal of Pentecostal Theology* 1 (1992): 109–34.

70. See John McKay, "When the Veil Is Taken Away: The Impact of Prophetic Experience on Biblical Interpretation," *Journal of Pentecostal Theology* 2, no. 5 (1994): 17–40, as well as Jackie David Johns, "Pentecostalism and the Postmodern Worldview," *Journal of Pentecostal Theology* 3, no. 7 (1995): 73–96, and Scott Ellington, "Pentecostalism and the Authority of Scripture," *Journal of Pentecostal Theology* 4, no. 9 (1996): 16–38.

71. Rickie D. Moore, "A Pentecostal Approach to Scripture," in *Pentecostal Hermeneutics: A Reader*, ed. Lee Roy Martin (Leiden: Brill, 2013), 11.

72. The distinction is made by Jack S. Deere (*Surprised by the Power of the Spirit* [Grand Rapids: Zondervan, 1993], 187), quoted by James K. A. Smith in "The Closing of the Book: Pentecostals, Evangelicals, and the Sacred Writings," *Journal of Pentecostal Theology* 5, no. 11 (1997): 49–50.

that Pentecostals read the Bible as a mystical text; they repeatedly seek to encounter God through this book, making this spiritual discipline a significant feature of their mystical outlook within their wider spirituality.

A person who appreciated this last concern profoundly is Howard M. Ervin, who in 1981 wrote an article on Pentecostal hermeneutics that was widely discussed.[73] In suggestive form, Ervin proposes what he calls a "pneumatic epistemology," one that can overcome some of the stalemates in theological hermeneutics. He gives quite a bit of attention to Bultmann's demythologization project, but many of his points apply to our current concerns with the evangelical ethos. He affirms Scripture as bearing witness to the Word of God, which at the end of the day is "beyond all human words, for it is spoken by God. . . . It is indeed the word that contradicts all human words. . . . It is both an eschatological and an apocalyptic word that judges all human *gnosis*. It is a word for which *there are no categories endemic to human understanding*. It is a word for which, in fact, there is no hermeneutic unless and until the divine *hermēneutēs* (the Holy Spirit) mediates an understanding."[74] In Ervin's account of Pentecostal practice, reading the Bible involves a transformational component: "The biblical precondition for understanding that Word is man's ontological re-creation by the Holy Spirit (the new birth)."[75] Put another way, reading Scripture qua Scripture is a pneumatologically dependent activity.

A pneumatic epistemology understands that "rationality by itself is inadequate for the task of interpreting the words of Scripture. It is only as human rationality *joined* in ontological union with 'the mind of Christ' (1 Cor 2:16) is *quickened* by the Holy Spirit that the divine mystery is understood by man."[76] Ervin is not averse to using the language of mysticism; in fact, he goes on to quote Georges Florovsky to that effect when speaking of Pentecostal biblical hermeneutics: "What is the inspiration [of the Bible] can never be properly defined—there is a mystery therein. It is a mystery of the divine-human encounter. We cannot fully understand in what manner 'God's holy men' heard the Word of their Lord and how they could articulate it in the words of their own dialect. Yet, even in their

---

73. Howard M. Ervin, "Hermeneutics: A Pentecostal Option," *Pneuma* 3, no. 2 (1981): 11–25. Interestingly, this work was originally a dialogue paper in the Catholic-Pentecostal dialogue (Second Quinquennium, 1978–82). For a review of this paper's reception, see Kärkkäinen, *Toward a Pneumatological Theology*, 9–15.

74. Ervin, "Hermeneutics: A Pentecostal Option," 16 (emphasis original).

75. Ervin, "Hermeneutics: A Pentecostal Option," 17.

76. Ervin, "Hermeneutics: A Pentecostal Option," 18 (emphasis original).

human transmission, it was the voice of God. Therein lies the miracle and the mystery of the Bible, that it is the Word of God in human idiom."[77]

The implications of this pneumatic epistemology for a doctrine of inerrancy are significant. Pentecostals cannot hold to inerrancy without compromising their distinct hermeneutical vantage point and all that such a move would entail for their understanding of God-knowledge. In the words of Smith, "I think it is precisely this one vestige of Princeton [i.e., inerrancy] . . . which frustrates any Pentecostal theology which attempts to be evangelical. It is not simply that Pentecostalism precludes the doctrine of inerrancy—that is, it is not an issue of errors in the Bible. The doctrine of inerrancy signals a more fundamental relationship to texts—one of textualization."[78] In this article, Smith pits certain accounts of orality and textuality in contrast to one another. In his opinion, the kind of textualization at work in evangelical accounts of inerrancy runs counter to other revelational themes within Pentecostal spirituality, including orality, continuing revelation (in terms of prophecy, illumination), receptivity, and the like. In other words, it is contrary to a pneumatic epistemology as outlined above. This kind of textualization runs akin to Henry's notion of axiomatization, and in both cases, there is a rationalistic closure involved in the reading and engagement of Holy Scripture.

Two Distinct Traditions

In discussing these two traditions, Pentecostalism and evangelicalism, we must remember that each is in the midst of incredible and hard-to-categorize change. Pentecostalism itself, through its distinct "waves" and global representations, has become a behemoth to account for. Nevertheless, over the last few decades, it has been coming into its own within the theological academy. As for evangelicalism, it too is experiencing significant change. As referenced above, one of the important contributions stemming from Robert Webber's work is his set of categories, which put into perspective the many transitions and forms American evangelical Christianity has taken recently. He notes many past developments in terms of

---

77. Ervin, "Hermeneutics: A Pentecostal Option," 17–18, quoting Georges Florovsky, *Bible, Church, Tradition: An Eastern Orthodox View* (Belmont, MA: Nordland Publishing, 1972), 27.

78. Smith, "The Closing of the Book," 62.

"traditionalist" and "pragmatic" groups, but he also has an eye to the present and future with his "younger" evangelicals. A sector of this group has a number of characteristics, including a tendency to value community, the ancient traditions and practices of the church, the category of narrative, and the embodiment of relational missions. In these and other ways, "younger" evangelicals often tend to resist and find unhelpful (if maybe even downright unworkable or wrongheaded) the kind of epistemic commitments on display in their evangelical antecedents (and in some cases their contemporaries). In holding such views, implicitly or explicitly, they destabilize and as a result open up the possibilities for the label "evangelical."

Several authors have written from this broad persuasion. For example, Dave Tomlinson, in *The Post-Evangelical* (1995), describes the pervasive influence of modernity on conceptions of what it means to be evangelical, particularly in the British context.[79] Hans Boersma, J. I. Packer Professor of Theology at Regent College, has been active in promoting evangelical interactions with Roman Catholics, which is clear in his works on the *nouvelle théologie* and sacramentology.[80] But perhaps the person whose work most consistently conveys the kind of alternative vision for evangelicalism that coalesces at points with the claims being made in the present volume is the late Stanley Grenz. In his manifesto *Revisioning Evangelical Theology* and in the expansion of its agenda in *Renewing the Center,* Grenz wishes to push beyond evangelical entrenchment within doctrinal disputes (particularly ones related to Scripture) by offering a broad and generous vision and orientation of what evangelicalism is at its heart. Grenz prefers the language of "sensibility," writing that evangelicalism is best understood as a "distinctive spirituality." As he further adds, "The genius of the movement . . . is a shared religious experience, which . . . is couched in a shared theological language."[81]

Grenz highlights a number of convictions that flesh out this spirituality in traditionally evangelical ways, including the centering of life on the Bible, a vibrant and personal faith, the important role of prayer and

---

79. A version of this book with the American context in its purview was eventually released; see Dave Tomlinson, *The Post-Evangelical*, rev. North American ed. (Grand Rapids: Zondervan, 2003).

80. Hans Boersma, *Nouvelle Théologie and Sacramental Ontology: A Return to Mystery* (Oxford: Oxford University Press, 2013) and *Heavenly Participation: The Weaving of a Sacramental Tapestry* (Grand Rapids: Eerdmans, 2011).

81. Stanley J. Grenz, *Renewing the Center: Evangelical Theology in a Post-Theological Era*, 2nd ed. (Grand Rapids: Baker Academic, 2006), 31, 37.

personal devotions, the understanding of church life as one of fellowship, and the prominence of worship and music. He also uses the first two categories of Ernst Troeltsch's *The Social Teaching of the Christian Churches* to show that evangelical spirituality is caught between outward and inward, as well as individual and corporate, aspects of holiness. He appeals to the traditions of "heart-religion" and the religious affections, incorporating Puritan, Pietist, and other strands of Christian expression that emphasize the importance of experience. But his broader goal is to recalibrate a sense of what it means to be evangelical. Rather than an identity registered primarily in terms of adherence to certain doctrinal formulations, evangelicalism for Grenz is best understood as a way of life. As a theologian, Grenz obviously values doctrine, but he believes that evangelical distinctives are not only doctrinal in nature. Like Webber, Grenz is optimistic about the future of such a vision: "This understanding of the nature of evangelicalism is showing signs of increased acceptance within the contemporary postfundamentalist coalition. In fact, a fundamental shift in self-consciousness may be under way, a move from a creed-based to a spirituality-based identity. Attendant to this change may be the pending passing of the dominance of the older neo-evangelical establishment."[82]

Ongoing Challenges to a Strict Identification

Despite these developments and changes, ongoing challenges seem to prevent any strict identification between Pentecostalism and evangelicalism. It is difficult to assess, for instance, the degree to which both Webber and Grenz are accurate in depicting a transition for the movement. Certainly developments on those fronts are at work, as Webber and Grenz point out in their reflections, but it is not clear to what degree their vision has caught on. For instance, institutional representations of the neo-evangelical establishment continue to exist and to exert their influence, including *Christianity Today*, the National Association of Evangelicals, and the Evangelical Theological Society.

Of course, aspects of this alternative vision are quite appealing to Pentecostals. Grenz wishes to push even beyond the early evangelicals to the witness of the church fathers, all with an eye to the contemporary church's postmodern situation. In doing so, he wishes to contextualize the mod-

82. Grenz, *Revisioning Evangelical Theology*, 44, 37.

ernist foothold upon the evangelical establishment. He is also inclined to think of spirituality and theology as mutually conditioning activities,[83] which is a hallmark of the orientation of the present study. Furthermore, his emphasis on community for the theological task represents an interest in contextualization (as opposed to the excessive abstraction and propositionalism he sees in many evangelical voices); he is aware that, by making this move to contextualization, epistemological matters are necessarily brought into the picture, since theology is always undertaken by particular people in particular circumstances.[84]

Nevertheless, as promising as these directions are, concerns still remain in Grenz's project that make a strict identification between evangelicalism and Pentecostalism impossible. Of course, Grenz is just one representative, but he will be used here to illustrate the need for the groups to remain distinct, despite the promising agenda he promotes. Put another way, even a project like Grenz's, which is highly aware of evangelicalism's theological shortcomings from the past, still retains enough of that heritage to make the harmonization between evangelicalism and Pentecostalism impossible.

The first difficulty concerns verbalization and textualization. For all that Grenz wishes to make of the importance of spirituality in his efforts toward revisioning what evangelicalism can be, the centrality of the Bible in his proposals functions on some counts as it did for his forebears. Admittedly, for Grenz a particular view of Scripture is not a litmus test for determining who are "in" or "out" of the evangelical fold; he does not rationalize, propositionalize, or axiomatize Scripture in the manner of the neo-evangelicals. He puts the claims made about Scripture in the Westminster Confession to good effect by affirming that it is the Spirit who addresses a Scripture-reading community. With reference to speech-act theory, Grenz says, "The Bible is the instrumentality of the Spirit in that the Spirit appropriates the biblical text so as to speak to us today. Through Scripture the Spirit performs the illocutionary act of addressing us."[85]

---

83. Grenz, *Revisioning Evangelical Theology*, 58.

84. Grenz quotes Michael Goldberg to good effect when the latter talks of Augustine: "Though a propositional theology may have its place, that place is limited by life itself, for as its propositions are abstracted and drawn from life, so too, in the end, they must return to life and have meaning for life in order to be theologically significant" (Michael Goldberg, *Theology and Narrative* [Nashville: Abingdon, 1982], 95, as quoted in Grenz, *Revisioning Evangelical Theology*, 85).

85. Grenz, *Renewing the Center*, 215.

Nevertheless, in Grenz's program Scripture continues to serve as an objective anchor of God's self-disclosure—the first and foremost place to look to see who God is and what God is like. In repeatedly elaborating the claim that the Spirit works and speaks "through Scripture," he functionally curtails the Spirit's breadth and operations to textuality, or verbalization. Of course, Pentecostals agree that reading Scripture is a pneumatic activity, and it is indeed significant that Grenz argues as he does on this point. However, Pentecostals also wish to say that the Spirit is not limited to working only "through Scripture." The Spirit's work of healing, sanctifying, convicting, and empowering takes place in a myriad of ways in addition to the reading and proclamation of Scripture.

Perhaps Grenz's goal in connecting the Spirit's work to Scripture is to allay fears of privatization and self-projection in theology. If so, then Grenz has only perpetuated (albeit in a different way) the same mentality of his forebears, namely that Scripture functions as the content-generating, meaning-securing, and subjectivity-countering means of God revealing Godself in a stable, long-lasting way. For instance, as he considers the cultural dynamics of hermeneutics, saying at one point that "evangelical theologians should listen intently for the voice of the Spirit, who is present in all life and therefore precedes us into the world, bubbling to the surface through the artifacts and symbols humans construct," Grenz nevertheless expresses a subsequent cautionary note: "Whatever speaking that occurs through other media does not come as a speaking against the text. To pit the Spirit's voice in culture against the Spirit speaking through Scripture would be to fall prey to the foundationalist trap . . . [elevating] some dimension of contemporary thought or experience as a human universal that forms the criterion for determining what in the Bible is or is not acceptable."[86] Grenz is rightly concerned when elements of a culture are elevated as foundational. Joining a long list of conservative Protestants, Grenz is also afraid of the outcomes associated with liberal Protestantism. At the same time, one wonders whether Grenz has worried sufficiently about making Scripture a specific kind of foundation, not one that is universal and timeless to be sure (as the neo-evangelicals would have it, but as Grenz has tried to avoid) but one that is local to the community of faith.

Grenz believes he has avoided this tendency because of his call for evangelical theology to be more conversational. He wants to see evangelical theology proceed as an interplay of Scripture, tradition, and culture rather

---

86. Grenz, *Renewing the Center*, 218.

than in the form of a foundationalist project he sees in Wayne Grudem and others, who, by setting up a proper foundation (i.e., the Bible's inerrancy), can construct an edifice of theological thought in a piecemeal kind of way.[87] Grenz actively seeks to avoid the foundationalism of Grudem because of a commitment to a coherentist philosophical paradigm, but his call for the construction of "webs of belief" or "belief-mosaics" continues to be driven and constrained by modern methodological patterns.[88] In a comment that recalls themes mentioned above in chapter 1, Grenz says, "In short, theology is a second-order conversation that seeks to serve the mission of the church, which is understood as a people who proclaim and live out the biblical narrative of God's saving action in Christ through the Spirit." Once again, we are faced with the prospect of theology being thought of largely as an intellective affair, a second-order form of cognitive effort that takes place distinct from the life of practiced faith. Grenz remarks that "nonfoundationalist approaches see Christian theology as an activity of the community that gathers around Jesus the Christ."[89] Such a claim is definitely helpful, but it is nevertheless exceedingly abstract. Despite his intuitions being well-directed, Grenz promotes a project that is very closely tied to the evangelical heritage by way of intellectualizing the Christian faith.

A second way Grenz's approach cannot fully reconcile evangelicalism and Pentecostalism involves the topic of embodiment. Consider, for instance, Grenz's *Theology for the Community of God*. This textbook (one used in my own education at a Pentecostal seminary) is a helpful resource in that it grants a communitarian motif for organizing "systematics." With such a motif, one would think that matters of contextualization would be important to Grenz; after all, he does say that theology is contextual, that it always happens somewhere, and that the particular locality of a particular form of theology is significant for the shape it takes and the concerns it

---

87. Grenz, *Renewing the Center*, 212–13.

88. Take one of the lines from the end of *Renewing the Center* as illustrating the point: "Doctrine, then, is the set of propositions that together comprise the Christian belief-mosaic. But the task of formulating, explicating, and understanding doctrine must always be vitally connected to the Bible, or more particularly, to the biblical narrative" (353). Notice that propositional thinking here is not directed to Scripture (as in the fundamentalist/neo-evangelical trajectory), *but it is nevertheless retained* and directed to doctrine. Such a vision is more similar to Grenz's forebears than he might have cared to admit.

89. Grenz, *Renewing the Center*, 214, 209.

considers. He refers to Paul Tillich's "method of correlation," as well as to the Wesleyan Quadrilateral as examples that attempt to take the reality of human experience seriously in the theological task.[90]

But this presentation implies a telling contrast present in previous evangelical proposals: biblical faith vs. elements of a specific culture. Notice, for example, the following statement: "Even though Scripture must remain the primary norm for theological statements, contextualization demands that we take seriously the thought-forms and mindset of the culture in which our theologizing transpires. Only then can we explicate the biblical message in language understandable in our specific setting."[91] Grenz grants that there is something that can be called "biblical faith," as distinct from cultural thought-forms and mind-sets, and that the task of the theologian is to communicate the former in a way that takes seriously the latter. Through such a presentation, one is distinct from the other, and to some degree the theologian *transcends both* by being able to shape one in ways that can appeal in the other.

Frankly, this project is simply unworkable. As proof, note that Grenz's *Theology for the Community of God* contains few remarks regarding race or gender and how these factors are significant for the theological task, or how this task can reconfigure and reimagine these factors.[92] These themes, of course, are significant for any exercise geared toward the "community of God," and yet these matters are generally passed by. Why? Perhaps because sometimes contextualization among evangelicals is assumed to be important and to be "taken seriously" strictly in terms of communicating the gospel—in other words, in relation to mission and evangelism. But perhaps another point is worth making in the case of Grenz. He is very well aware that the neo-evangelical camp and its penchant to rationalize the Christian faith are products of a particular context. As a result, Grenz wishes to make a postmodern turn at this point by referencing the reality of God's community in theological efforts. Nevertheless, Grenz never gets

90. Stanley J. Grenz, *Theology for the Community of God* (Grand Rapids: Eerdmans, 2000), 15–16.

91. Grenz, *Theology for the Community of God*, 15.

92. The closest Grenz comes to considering these matters is in his presentation of Jesus as the "universal human" (286–93). In this section, Grenz addresses issues of marginalization and sexuality. In this treatment, Grenz is much more able to nuance issues on sexuality than on privilege (as a rough page count indicates—two pages to marginalization compared to four on sexuality—both nevertheless troubling, given a work of approximately 700 pages).

around to specifying particular features of a Christian community's identity and how those might significantly influence the theological task. That Grenz forgoes significant discussion of such matters as race and gender when he speaks about anthropology as theologically understood is more than simply an oversight; it is one further indicator that evangelicalism, even in its newer, more hopeful forms, continues to struggle with accounting for the body in particular and embodiment generally as theologically relevant. In this setting, "biblical faith" continues to be intellectualized and content-driven, whether that content be understood propositionally or narratively, foundationally or postfoundationally. Simply put, contextualization continues to be a challenge for evangelical theology moving forward. Despite calls to "take context seriously" in the theological task, it is difficult to imagine this happening apart from a robust account of the role of the human body and person in theological efforts.

Pentecostals, in contrast, are implicit endorsers of the merits of embodied theology. This point comes through quite immediately in the way they typically use their bodies in worship, whether in the raising and clapping of hands, swaying with music, shouting and crying, or anointing of the sick. But the recognition and potential reimagining of the human body go further still. Observers often point out that, in terms of both race and gender, Pentecostals have been generally more successful than their evangelical counterparts in integrating and recognizing a multitude of gifts across the divides that stratify society. Admittedly, Pentecostals have a number of difficulties to face on both scores, but it is true that, on the American scene, both women and people from various racial and ethnic backgrounds have played significant roles in the Pentecostal movement as a whole. Such developments are not due to any kind of prescience by Pentecostals that led them to be more inclusive and open to nonmajority voices; such a reading would be blatantly anachronistic. On the contrary, something deep within Pentecostal identity and existence has made these developments possible. One of these constituent factors, I believe, is Pentecostalism's character as a mystical tradition. With the affirmation of such things as worship, the affections, spiritual practices, "the anointing," and others, Pentecostalism has created a space in its contexts for other dynamics besides intellectualization and abstraction, which in turn have allowed for a disruption of the status quo and the true participation of God's one people in the economy of grace.

A third point to raise as to why evangelicals and Pentecostals continue to have an uneasy relationship concerns the realm of desire. As courageous as Grenz's revisioning project is, it nevertheless falls short of rendering a suitable account of Christian spirituality as Pentecostals understand and pursue it. To be sure, certain comments and recognitions are present in Grenz's account toward this end, but more are needed. On the positive side, Grenz recalls the Puritan and Pietist strands of evangelicalism to make the case that, going forward, the movement needs to take up the centrality of experience. He stresses the need for an evangelical spirituality to avoid extremes so as to retain a balance between "the inward versus the outward and the individual versus the corporate dimensions of holiness." In terms of the first set, Grenz emphasizes "heart religion," stating quite directly, "A nonnegotiable principle of evangelicalism is that religion is a matter of the heart." He pays homage to Augustine and Edwards, while citing the importance of such language as the "affections" and "convictions." As a summarizing set of claims, Grenz continues, "The proper heart affections of the believer include the personal desire to engage in the Christian life and to enjoy fellowship with the people of God. But above all, heart-religion entails a commitment to Jesus Christ. . . . [This commitment] includes a personal attachment to a risen and living Person, with whom the believer experiences 'a personal relationship.' This inner life, in turn, both constitutes and is foundational for spirituality." In ways that easily coincide with the claims of the present work, Grenz remarks that the pursuit of understanding God "does not require the severing of intellectual from spiritual theology. On the contrary, so-called speculative theology is actually best served when theologians keep the quest for holiness in clear focus as the ultimate purpose of their task. All theological work must be directed toward the goal of fostering the spirituality of the believing community and of those engaging in the theological enterprise."[93] In all these points, Grenz posits a very suggestive framework, one that Pentecostals could easily endorse.

The difficulty comes with the particulars at work within the framework itself. First of all, it is simply astonishing how pneumatologically deficient Grenz's proposals are. For a program that aims to revitalize a spirituality, it is unfortunately hyper-Christocentric. "The spiritual life," Grenz says, "is above all the imitation of Christ. Discipleship means seeking to follow the model set forth by Jesus himself, for true Christians will reflect in their lives the character of Jesus."[94] Such affirmations in them-

---

93. Grenz, *Revisioning Evangelical Theology*, 44, 45, 57–58.
94. Grenz, *Revisioning Evangelical Theology*, 48.

selves of course raise no red flags. The lingering question is, however, How are Christians to do so? In what ways and categories can Christians fully live this kind of life?

On this point, Grenz resorts to a worrisome anthropological focus. He notes that, when contrasting his views from the outward conformity he sees in more high liturgical traditions, "spirituality is generated from within the individual"; ultimately, "becoming Christlike is an individual matter." When speaking of church attendance, he says that evangelicals "long to be at the gathering because we are committed to the Lord and therefore the body of believers. . . . We are inwardly motivated, rather than outwardly compelled, to attend church services." One must be vigilant in monitoring the warmth of one's heart, and all should be admonished to "take charge" of their lives and apply themselves "to the task of spiritual growth." In what sounds exceedingly draconian, Grenz states, "If a believer comes to the point where he or she senses that stagnation has set in, evangelical counsel is to redouble one's efforts in the task of exercising the disciplines." Later, he wishes to add a corporate dimension to spirituality alongside its primary, individualist orientation, but in doing so, he speaks of spirituality as a "project."[95]

What is blatantly missing throughout is a thoroughgoing, well-developed Spirit-logic that grounds the Christian life overall. Grenz does mention the Spirit a handful of times, but only in passing and with little to no effect in altering or substantiating his proposals significantly. But as the many references above show, without a Spirit-logic infusing an account of Christian spirituality, one is left with a call for human striving. Without ongoing attention to the Spirit's presence and work, proposals in Christian spirituality teeter on woefully inadequate strategies of self-improvement or self-construction. Obviously, Grenz would wish to denounce these tendencies, but what resources does he employ to avoid these undesirable outcomes? When on a single page Grenz remarks that Christians ought to take seriously "their own responsibility to become spiritual," that spirituality needs to be understood "in terms of a balanced life," that "Christian spirituality is an individual project in the process of which we must dedicate all our personal resources," what work can a single reference to hearts being warmed "by the regenerating power of the Spirit" actually do?[96] Once again, for all the promise Grenz shows in his work, his call for an evangelical

95. Grenz, *Revisioning Evangelical Theology*, 46, 47, 51.
96. Grenz, *Revisioning Evangelical Theology*, 56.

spirituality betrays the lonely Christocentrism of previous generations of evangelicals. The pneumatology that is present is simply not robust enough for his program to lift off the ground in a theologically salutary way.

When Pentecostals live out their spirituality and then reflect on it, they simply must frame the results in terms of pneumatology. Their first inclinations are not to think of vigilance, exertion, self-monitoring, and the like; rather, Pentecostals are inclined to speak of how they delight in and enjoy the presence of God. For Pentecostals, spirituality is not a project; on the contrary, it involves an ongoing paradox between resting in God and desiring earnestly after God. As Steven Land suggested in the very subtitle of his book, Pentecostals are genuinely passionate for God and God's kingdom. And these flames of holy desire are fanned by the power, beauty, and goodness of God's manifest presence, God's Holy Spirit, who is experienced within the corporate modality of worship. Pentecostals pursue and live out their spirituality not from obligation but because of the sweetness that is the Holy Spirit's touch. Over time, they often learn to hear the Spirit's voice, recognize the Spirit's presence, join the Spirit's work, and yearn restlessly for the Spirit's reign. Quite simply, from the Pentecostal viewpoint, Christian spirituality is a Spirit matter. It requires a Spirit-logic (alongside a Christ-logic, to be sure) for making sense of growth and maturation in the Christian life.

Conclusion

Whatever becomes of evangelicalism and Pentecostalism, their long trajectories have distinguished them as movements that are both overlapping and distinct. Many scholars and laypeople have wished to emphasize the continuity and affinity between them, but at present very good reasons exist for their explicit and ongoing demarcation. In particular, Pentecostalism cannot subscribe to the deep-seated methodological and epistemological impulses inherent in American evangelicalism. Even with calls to reform, evangelicalism is continually haunted by a particular methodological heritage. It is exceedingly difficult to imagine American evangelicalism apart from its scholasticizing and rationalizing tendencies, and these features stand opposed to what Pentecostals most value about their own tradition. To consider but one example, Pentecostals cast biblical authority and practices of Bible reading in ways very different from those of evangelicals, especially when they try to explain the logic of how Scripture functions in their practiced spirituality.

CHAPTER 4

Expanding the Pentecostal Understanding of Spirit-Baptism

Chapter 3 explored the rationalism at work in contemporary and past expressions of evangelicalism on the American scene so as to show its fundamental incompatibility with Pentecostal assumptions and commitments surrounding theological knowledge. Among the many factors within this exploration, evangelicalism's rationalism was highlighted as a significant hurdle for a strong identification between the two groups. Evangelicalism's tendencies toward abstraction and rationalization frame an account of God-knowledge that is at its core pneumatologically deficient. Even with the overtures toward spirituality and renewal an author like Grenz is willing to make, difficulties still present themselves. Grenz and others continue to privilege "the contribution of modernist foundationalism," even if undertaken at a more local level (in the case of Grenz, the community of faith). Within such conditions, Scripture continues to be the revelational authority par excellence. The Spirit as such becomes primarily—and in some sense, reductively—an enabling and capacitating mechanism by which to see, interpret, and apply faithfully that which is fundamentally available in Scripture.

This chapter and the next are analytic (chap. 4) and constructive (chap. 5) in nature; they seek to create further links between Pentecostalism and Christian mysticism so as to provide ways beyond the limitations of past evangelical proposals. Such work may not be at first apparent or amenable to rank-and-file Pentecostals, but the goal in what follows is an ongoing effort at tradition-negotiation, which involves not simply rehearsing the past for an ignorant present but capturing anew the spirit of the movement through multiple strategies and points of contact, all for the sake of deepening an abiding appreciation for that which Pentecostals view as their task to guard—a vital and ongoing witness to the power of God's Spirit to transform and heal a broken world.

Pentecostals assume a Spirit-drenched world so that what may appear as textualized in Scripture is in some sense anticipated and realized—and thus witnessed—in their worship settings. Miracles are recorded in Scripture, *and* they are available now. Theophanies, visions, and dreams are running themes in Scripture, *and* they can be features of current-day testimonies as well. In terms of the most discussed of Pentecostal expressions, people spoke in other tongues on the Day of Pentecost, *and* people can and do so now as part of Pentecostal spirituality. These commitments suggest that, whereas American evangelicalism imbibed significantly from the wells of modernity, in some sense Pentecostalism is also "transmodern." Yes, certain features of Pentecostal expression betray modern thought-forms, but others most certainly do not. Some observers refer to the latter as premodern concepts; others prefer to speak of postmodern categories. James K. A. Smith's account of a Pentecostal worldview or way of life seems fitting to the task of describing and conceptually demarcating the Pentecostal ethos, since he typically refers to both premodern and postmodern characteristics. More significantly, he sees the importance of framing Pentecostalism in terms of worship and "lived liturgy," a point that he bolsters with aid from Land's account of Pentecostal spirituality.[1]

As helpful as these phrases are, one is still left with challenges, not simply descriptive but also methodological. If Pentecostalism is a worldview or a way of life and the notion is understood in terms of tenets constituting a vital spirituality, does not this proposal run the risk similar to those in the presentation of, say, the "five fundamentals" touted by certain evangelical Christians? In other words, can the conceptual demarcation of Pentecostalism still fall prey to the excesses of rationalization and abstraction? Can Pentecostals resist the tendency to overrationalize or hyperconceptualize as they go about making sense of their own ethos and tradition, or do they necessarily have to follow evangelical tendencies on this score simply because that is all that can be done?

Arguably, Pentecostals have often not resisted this tendency, given the way they have often presented their distinctives. Especially with regard to American Pentecostal denominations, one could say they have fallen prey

---

1. See James K. A. Smith, *Thinking in Tongues* (Grand Rapids: Eerdmans, 2010), 12, for a brief summary of this proposed worldview; his second chapter in the volume is an extended development of the idea.

to these inclinations as they have gone on to talk about baptism in the Holy Spirit in particular. This topic increased in importance as Pentecostalism became established over the decades, and as both insiders and outsiders have joined in the call to identify what makes Pentecostalism theologically distinctive. It was assumed in such an exercise that a single practice or understanding could identify the key to Pentecostalism as compared with other Christian alternatives. And repeatedly the phenomenon of tongues was highlighted for such purposes. Pentecostals were thus seen and identified primarily as Christians who speak in tongues. Ironically, that kind of reduction paved the way for Pentecostalism to drift further toward evangelicalism, for many simply assumed that Pentecostalism shared with evangelicalism just about everything else except this one feature; it came to be understood by many as "evangelicalism with tongues." As the present argument has gone to this point, such a reading of the Pentecostal movement is exceedingly problematic, in terms not only of Pentecostalism's past theological characteristics but also of its prospects for the future. Nevertheless, the "evangelicalism with tongues" understanding is popular and widespread among partisans and nonpartisans alike.

I believe that ways forward out of this quagmire of a simplistic characterization of Pentecostalism do exist, but they need to be presented carefully. The task does not simply involve the use of different categories per se; rather, the process of delineation must be of another kind. The work involves questioning conceptualization itself—a pointing out of the inadequacy of words, concepts, and ideas so as to indicate the necessary role of embodiment and experience for getting at what makes Pentecostalism what it is. Smith's proposals are a step in the right direction: to speak of Pentecostalism as a "way of life" helps to indicate the primacy of lived reality. His additional work in emphasizing phenomenology and the limits of intellectualist thought-forms are all welcome on this score. However, further work along this trajectory is still needed because the sensibility is long overdue for formal development within Pentecostal theology. Pentecostals are in need of conceptually suggesting the limits of what can be said and categorized in the theological task, for their spirituality demands the development of that kind of orientation.

Pentecostalism can be aided on this front when it is thought of as a mystical tradition of the church catholic, given that Christian mysticism has a long history of cultivating an apophatic sensibility in the theological task, one that points precisely to expressing the limits of speech and thought so as to point to dimensions beyond them. The topic of apophaticism has received increased attention lately, especially in postmodern theological proposals. One of its uses has been as a mechanism to secure deconstruction, but this use is not the only one possible. Given its many definitions and uses, apophaticism should be understood as a contested notion; the matter needs further demarcation if it is to be put to use for a specific end.[2]

In terms of the present volume, we will consider apophaticism as a belief within the Christian tradition that assumes a "doxological realism" and that leads to a kind of linguistic and conceptual humility. Apophaticism in this sense can point to many things, including the inadequacy of words, forms of silence, and different ways of engagement so as to form a collective response that signifies human limits and (more significantly) to give expression to a kind of God-directedness that is worshipful at its core. In contrast, Pentecostals, of course, are not typically known for their silent worship experiences or their participation in contemplative, meditative prayer.[3] Quite the contrary! Pentecostals are typically loud in the expression of their spirituality and are often prone to chide Christians who are not. A certain pride can set in among those who are willing to "shout unto the Lord"; their zeal can represent their spiritual gusto, and it can function as a badge of honor. These dynamics do not seem to fit with what typically is associated with the apophatic dimensions of Christian existence. In any case, apophaticism can serve a crucial role in countering logo-centricity. Therefore, links and interconnections are possible, since both apophaticism and Pentecostalism are at odds with the kinds of evangelicalism surveyed previously—ones that assume that revelation needs to be rational, and that which is rational in this particular sense is inextricably bound to an understanding that words can adequately and fittingly account for the mysteries of the faith. Broadly, apophaticism and Pentecostalism (when each is cast a certain way) share a number of affinities and concerns. Interestingly enough, these can be brought to light when considering tongues, or glossolalia.

2. One helpful survey article is Martin Laird, "'Whereof We Speak': Gregory of Nyssa, Jean-Luc Marion, and the Current Apophatic Rage," *Heythrop Journal* 42 (2001): 1–12.

3. This is not to say that there is no place for silence in Pentecostal corporate worship settings. Moments of silence do emerge from time to time in these contexts, and when they do, the situation is both eerie and quite disarming, given the "loud norm." See Daniel Castelo, "An Apologia for Divine Impassibility: Toward Pentecostal Prolegomena," *Journal of Pentecostal Theology* 19, no. 1 (2010): 118–26.

Mention was made above that glossolalia has been privileged when talk of Pentecostal theological identity has been undertaken. The literature devoted to tongues-speech is massive now, and perspectives from a variety of disciplines have been employed to illuminate its character and significance.[4] The glaring difficulty with this focus on tongues for describing Pentecostalism is that it is not the most important feature of Pentecostal identity once we consider a "thick" description of the movement historically and theologically. Some scholars who have contributed significantly to Pentecostal studies in the academy have helped offer these broader and deeper accounts. Plenty of disciplinary lenses, historical themes, and theological emphases have been proposed to generate a sense of Pentecostalism's character. Therefore, given the bevy of proposals on this front, it is difficult to continue this tack of privileging tongues for Pentecostal identity; for those who do, they simply neglect the important contributions that have been achieved by scholarly developments of the last few decades.

But many Pentecostals do continue to sustain this privileging of tongues for the establishment of Pentecostal identity. They understand tongues to be intricately tied to Spirit-baptism, and the two in tandem can function as a general account of what true and authentic Pentecostal experience is. In this vein, they take Acts 2 to be the biblical pattern for the present day, and they see it repeated in Acts 8 (by implication), 10, and 19. As Gary McGee notes, "Leadership opportunities in many Pentecostal denominations and local congregations are frequently offered only to those who have experienced glossolalia, perhaps marking the only time in Christian history when this type of charismatic experience has been institutionalized on such a large scale."[5] Those kinds of discriminations arise from an emphasis that has in turn been tied to institutional identity. Put another way, the interrelationship between tongues and Spirit-baptism has been denominationally politicized, thereby privileging tongues as the central identity marker of Pentecostalism.

This emphasis, however, is difficult to sustain beyond theoretical or ideological domains, for the reality on the ground via documented re-

---

4. For a sample of the research, see Watson E. Mills, ed., *Speaking in Tongues: A Guide to Research on Glossolalia* (Grand Rapids: Eerdmans, 1986), and Mark J. Cartledge, ed., *Speaking in Tongues: Multi-disciplinary Perspectives* (Milton Keynes, UK: Paternoster, 2006).

5. Gary McGee, "Editor's Introduction," in *Initial Evidence: Historical and Biblical Perspectives on the Pentecostal Doctrine of Spirit Baptism*, ed. McGee (Peabody, MA: Hendrickson, 1991), xv.

search is that most self-identified Pentecostals do *not* speak in tongues.[6] This fact seems to threaten Pentecostal identity, for something that is often mentioned as the hallmark of Pentecostal identity is in fact not widespread among those who claim the identity itself. In light of this tension, we have to ask, At what point does Pentecostal identity break down? What, actually, is sustaining or defining the identity? These are difficult questions, and their poignancy is a direct result of this privileging of glossolalia in efforts to identify the core of the Pentecostal movement.

The language used by the classical Pentecostal establishment—the denominations, institutions, and official documents that depict the identity publicly—to indicate this privileging is that tongues is the initial (and sometimes added here is "physical") evidence of the baptism in the Holy Spirit.[7] Some speak of this evidentialist logic as the distinct Pentecostal doctrine; they would say that other traditions may employ the language

6. In their article "Global Statistics," David Barrett and Todd Johnson comment on the "First Wave" of the Pentecostal movement (in other words, the classic forms being considered here): "Most Pentecostal denominations teach that tongues-speaking is mandatory for all members, but in practice today *only between 5% and 35% of all members have practiced this gift,* either initially or as an ongoing experience" (in *New International Dictionary of Pentecostal and Charismatic Movements,* ed. Stanley M. Burgess, rev. and exp. ed. [Grand Rapids: Zondervan, 2003], 291 [emphasis added]). The point has not been lost on various constituencies, for among other examples, it became an issue of discussion at the fourth quinquennium of the International Catholic-Pentecostal Dialogue (as reported by Steve Overman in the foreword to Aaron T. Friesen, *Norming the Abnormal: The Development and Function of the Doctrine of Initial Evidence in Classical Pentecostalism* [Eugene: Pickwick Publications, 2013], xi).

7. A sample of denominational belief statements suggests as much. For example, the Church of God in Christ states that "tongue-speaking is the consequence of the baptism in the Holy Ghost." Although this church ties this experience with the fruit of the Spirit, it goes on to say: "When one receives a baptismal Holy Ghost experience, we believe one will speak with a tongue unknown to oneself according to the sovereign will of Christ" (www.cogic.org/our-foundation/what-we-believe). The Church of God (Cleveland) believes in "speaking with other tongues as the Spirit gives utterance and that it is the initial evidence of the baptism of the Holy Ghost" (www.churchofgod.org/beliefs/declaration-of-faith). The International Pentecostal Holiness Church holds that "the initial evidence of the reception of [Pentecostal baptism of the Holy Ghost and fire] is speaking with other tongues as the Spirit gives utterance" (www.iphc.org/beliefs/). Finally, the Foursquare Church proclaims the following on this theme: "We believe that those who experience Holy Spirit baptism today will experience it in the same manner that believers experienced it in the early church; in other words, we believe that they will speak in tongues—languages that are not known to them" (see, for example, www .opendoorcc.org/page/our_beliefs).

of "baptism in the Spirit," but classical Pentecostals have made the move to distinguish their understanding from rivals by adding this evidentialist qualification.[8] As a result, it has garnered significant weight, sometimes in the midst of controversy,[9] for purposes of Pentecostal self-identification. In such a context, it is not surprising that tongues are exorbitantly highlighted.

What follows is an exploration of how this understanding emerged in terms of its warrants and logic, which can provide a basis for reappraisal. In particular, the language and epistemology behind the logic of "evidences" will be exposed as a modern thought-paradigm, one similar to the evangelical scholasticizing tendency elaborated previously. Below, I survey three Pentecostal theologians who have similar concerns as those raised in this chapter, which will prepare for the constructive work in chapter 5.

The Background to a Peculiar "Doctrine"

If such recasting work is to take place, we first need to review some background. For those who have some historical knowledge of the Pentecostal

8. In this vein, Stanley Burgess comments: "The expectation of a baptism in the Spirit actually has been rather common in Christian history, although for most Christians it early became institutionalized into sacramental form. Instead, it seems to me that the real historical distinctive of modern Pentecostalism is its insistence that tongues be viewed as the 'initial physical evidence' for Spirit baptism" ("Evidence of the Spirit: The Ancient and Eastern Churches," in Gary McGee, *Initial Evidence*, 3). This reading is challenged to some degree within this volume itself because of an emphasis on the teaching of Edward Irving. For more on the Irvingite movement, see McGee, *Initial Evidence*, 35–36, as well as chap. 3.

9. One of the most famous cases of this kind was Fred F. Bosworth, who, despite being associated with the Assemblies of God at its founding in 1914, eventually left the denomination in 1918 because of his disagreement with this evidentialist logic, which became pronounced for the denomination when it drafted its Statement of Fundamental Truths in 1916. In the original draft, tongues were spoken of as an "initial sign" of "baptism in the Holy Ghost," but with the controversy with Bosworth, the matter was further nuanced. McGee notes of the changes, "When [article 6 of the Statement of Fundamental Truths] was amended two years later in the controversy raised by Bosworth, the doctrine was identified [by the Assemblies of God] as 'our distinctive testimony' and the article was changed to read 'the initial physical sign of speaking with other tongues'" (McGee, *Initial Evidence*, 110). For some general considerations of this controversy, see Carl Brumback, *Suddenly . . . from Heaven: A History of the Assemblies of God* (Springfield, MO: Gospel Publishing House, 1961), chap. 18.

movement, mention of the doctrine of Spirit-baptism with the evidence of speaking in tongues will bring to mind Charles Parham, sometimes referred to as the father of American Pentecostalism.[10] Parham originally began his ministry as a faith-healer and preacher in Kansas, and he was influenced by a number of Holiness revivalists during the last years of the nineteenth century. The message of divine healing was dear to him personally, since all his life he faced a number of physical infirmities, most notably rheumatic fever. As he emerged as an itinerant minister, he drew inspiration from such people as John Alexander Dowie, Dwight L. Moody, A. J. Gordon, A. B. Simpson, R. A. Torrey, Benjamin H. Irwin, and Frank W. Sandford. Collectively, these figures provided a theological (and to some extent ideological) world for Parham. Healing was an important theme in this context, as was a millenarian eschatological framework that assumed Christ's imminent return. Because of this belief, an empowering experience that would aid in evangelistic efforts was often expected as necessary. This experience, sometimes deemed by this wider culture as "baptism in the Holy Spirit," and the logic at play were significantly shaped by the messages preached at a number of revivals, including those famously associated with the town of Keswick in England. This message involved the charge to lead a "higher life" with God that would in turn contribute to more sustained service and evangelistic activity. In this milieu, "baptism in the Holy Spirit" was an experience of empowerment.[11]

These many influences were crucial for Parham. He maintained a tri-

10. For the details of Parham's life and evolution, I am indebted to the work of James R. Goff Jr. See his *Fields White unto Harvest* (Fayetteville: University of Arkansas, 1988). For personal features of the narrative, I am relying on Sarah E. Parham, *The Life of Charles F. Parham: Founder of the Apostolic Faith Movement* (repr., New York: Garland, 1985). The prominence Parham has enjoyed in terms of being the "founder" or "father" of the movement, despite the difficult features of his life and theology, is largely the result of key Pentecostal presentations. One of the first works to reclaim Parham for Pentecostal historiography after the fallout between Parham and the movement is Frank J. Ewart, *The Phenomenon of Pentecost* (Houston: Herald Publishing, 1947). Following this effort was Klaude Kendrick, *The Promise Fulfilled: A History of the Modern Pentecostal Movement* (Springfield, MO: Gospel Publishing House, 1961); in this work, Kendrick views Parham as patriarch, as well as emphasizes the phenomenon of tongues as key to the identity of the movement. Furthermore, the role of Seymour and Azusa for Pentecostal origins is significantly downplayed in this volume.

11. Many examples of this approach could be cited, but R. A. Torrey's work is important to note; see his *The Baptism with the Holy Spirit* (New York: Fleming H. Revell, 1897) and *The Holy Spirit: Who He Is and What He Does* (Old Tappan, NJ: Fleming H. Revell, 1927).

partite experiential stance—in part due to Irwin—by thinking that a Christian was to experience both sanctification and Spirit-baptism subsequent to conversion,[12] all the while thinking of Spirit-baptism along broadly Keswickian lines (i.e., as an experience of empowerment). When Parham visited Sandford in Maine during the summer of 1900, his conviction grew that the experience of Spirit-baptism was for worldwide evangelism. He returned to Topeka, Kansas, from his East Coast trip and in October 1900 began a missionary school he named Bethel Bible College, modeled after Sandford's Shiloh community. As December approached, Parham and his students reached a "problem." As he recounts the matter,

> What about the 2nd Chapter of Acts? I had felt for years that any missionary going to the foreign field should preach in the language of the natives. That if God had ever equipped His ministers in that way He could do it today. . . . Having heard so many different religious bodies claim different proofs as the evidence of their having the Pentecostal baptism, I set the students at work studying out diligently what was the Bible evidence of the baptism of the Holy Ghost, that we might go before the world with something that was indisputable because it tallied absolutely with the Word.[13]

Parham left for a few days on an evangelistic trip to Kansas City, and when he returned, his account portrays the students affirming that they had agreed that the one prevalent scriptural evidence of Spirit-baptism was speaking in other tongues. "To my astonishment," Parham relays, "they all had the same story, that while there were different things occured [sic] when the Pentecostal blessing fell, that the indisputable proof on each occasion was, that they spake with other tongues."[14] Parham assumed that

---

12. In fact, Parham had some inflammatory comments to make about the "finished work" theology, which is ironic, since this branch of Pentecostalism has done the most to retrieve Parham as the founder of the movement. As for Parham's views, the following is one of the most difficult remarks in his corpus: "The diabolical end and purpose of his Satanic majesty, in perpetrating Durhamism on the world, in repudiating sanctification as a definite work of grace, has now clearly been revealed. By seeking to destroy the grace of sanctification he is seeking to efface the only grace of God to make us overcomers, and thereby hinder necessary preparation for Redemption" (Parham, *The Everlasting Gospel* [Pentecostal Books.com, 2013; orig. pub., 1911], 134).

13. Parham, *The Life of Charles Parham*, 51–52.

14. Parham, *The Life of Charles Parham*, 52.

these tongues were missionary in nature, making them "xenoglossa," or "xenolalia"—that is, they were actual human languages unknown to their speakers. This kind of impartation, following what was deemed the model of Acts 2, would make people instant missionaries who could facilitate worldwide evangelism during these "last days."

The community at Bethel in turn prayed and searched for "the blessing," and on January 1, 1901, a certain aspiring missionary by the name of Agnes Ozman was prayed over, since she felt the need for an experience of the Holy Spirit to help her fulfill her call. After a time of travailing, she began to speak in other tongues (a phenomenon that, on her account, she had experienced several weeks prior).[15] Parham himself labeled Ozman's speech Chinese, and subsequently on January 3, others within the school (including Parham himself) went on to experience similar phenomena to what Ozman had, doing so in an "upper room." Parham believed he spoke in a number of human languages during this period, including Swedish, and Ozman was said immediately after the New Year's Day events to have spoken in Bohemian (as allegedly verified by a native speaker).

As Goff notes, strong tensions exist between Parham's and Ozman's accounts of the particulars leading to and culminating in the New Year's Day revival.[16] Whereas Ozman's account is less climactic, Parham's narration presents this incident and others as forming a collective witness that the sign of Spirit-baptism was making its appearance at a crucial moment in world history, similar to how it had taken place in Acts 2. As noted above, Parham was "astonished" at the consensus reached by the students. And in the events following, Parham is further buoyed: "One Government interpreter claimed to have heard twenty Chinese dialects distinctly spoken in one night. All agree that the students of the college were speaking in the languages of the world, and that with proper accent and intonation."[17] In these accounts, Parham exaggerates the role of the student body in the formula's rise and development, as well as emphasizing the providential nature of the happenings. Ozman, in contrast, depicts her role as one of pedagogue, teaching the students this understanding of Spirit-baptism post factum to the events transpiring on New Year's Day. However the events took place, Parham had a direct stake in downplaying his involvement, despite having "pieced the theological puzzle of Pentecostalism to-

15. See Goff, *Fields White unto Harvest*, 71.
16. See generally Goff, *Fields White unto Harvest*, 69–72.
17. Parham, *The Life of Charles Parham*, 54–55.

gether sometime during the fall of 1900," when he "predicted the revival that would ultimately confirm his conjectures."[18]

The most significant features of this "puzzle" involve the development and framing by Parham of the logic of Spirit-baptism in full anticipation of the events that have gained legendary status in Pentecostal historiography. According to Goff, Parham was first exposed to the notion of missionary tongues via a Holiness periodical he read in 1899 that featured a story about a person named Jennie Glassey. Glassey was associated with Sandford's Shiloh group and was said to have miraculously learned various African dialects that would aid her missionary work to the continent.[19] The phenomenon of missionary tongues was appealing to Parham, and it no doubt helped propel him to visit Sandford during that summer. Returning home from his trip to Maine, Parham had crystallized the understanding in his mind: Spirit-baptism was evidenced by missionary tongues and was an experience of power for end-times world evangelization. When he had students search Acts 2 for the sign of Spirit-baptism, he had already formulated in his mind what they would find. The experiences that followed on New Year's Day and the days after confirmed Parham's unique account of how one identifies cases of Spirit-baptism and what its purposes are within God's lordship over history. Despite narratives to the contrary, this incident suggests that Pentecostals indeed have taken their doctrine to the altar so as to frame what they would eventually find there.

Some might criticize these developments by saying that Parham set up his students to find what he wanted them to find, but this evaluation does not take into account the way doctrines generally tend to be formulated and developed over time. Of course, Parham in a manner of speaking, "set up" his students, for everybody is "set up" a certain way as they come to Scripture and try to make sense of the Christian faith. Doctrinal formulations do not simply fall out of the sky in divine splendor, ready formulated with the technicalities and sophistication that often constitute them. Quite the contrary, for human discernment, reasoning, and articulation play vital roles throughout. As such, doctrine and experience go hand in hand, mutually influencing one another throughout a significant and lengthy process. This is not simply a Lindbeckian point, but one appreciated sometimes by Pentecostals as well.[20] A time of testing and devel-

18. Goff, *Fields White unto Harvest*, 71, 72.
19. Goff, *Fields White unto Harvest*, 72–73.
20. Note Lindbeck's famous line: "We cannot identify, describe, or recognize ex-

opment necessarily accompanies doctrinal understandings so that what was first suspected or understood can be abandoned, tested, refined, or significantly altered, given the passing of time, the pressing needs of communities, what comes to be learned or prioritized, and so on. Speaking of Parham's case, Jacobsen notes that people could look at Parham's prompts as "instrumental" (paving the way) or "causal" (in some sense creative) of the experience that was said to confirm the understanding.[21] The problem with both categories is that they are too agent-oriented. Parham was most likely not attempting to be intentionally deceitful or manipulative. He derived a conviction and believed it made good sense in relation to other convictions he held, and those in his midst shared enough affinity with these convictions to be in community with him and to learn from him as an authority figure. Therefore, if the question Parham raised to his students is taken seriously in its form—namely, "What is the Bible evidence of the Baptism of the Holy Ghost?"—and if their principal place to look was Acts 2, then a specific answer indeed presents itself.[22] All their other commitments, including the understanding that they were at the cusp of a worldwide revival that would usher the second coming of Christ, simply worked in tandem with it.

The problem is not with the students being set up per se; the difficulty resides in how this understanding was or was not challenged in due course, given a testing and discernment process. Once Parham and his community had the experience of tongues, was the theological framework confirmed or in need of modification in light of it? Plenty of effort—one might say too much effort—was expended by Parham and his colleagues to say that it was confirmed. Jacobsen detects such a reflex among Parham's students, noting that they "were convinced that they had spoken in 'foreign' tongues

---

perience qua experience without the use of signs and symbols" (George Lindbeck, *The Nature of Doctrine* [Philadelphia: Westminster, 1984], 36). Jacobsen quotes Myer Pearlman to good effect on this point: "Certainly it is more important to live the Christian life than to merely know Christian doctrine, but there would be no Christian experience if there were no Christian doctrine" (Douglas Jacobsen, *Thinking in the Spirit* [Bloomington: Indiana University Press, 2003], 5, quoting Myer Pearlman, *Knowing the Doctrines of the Bible* [Springfield, MO: Gospel Publishing House, 1937], 10).

21. Jacobsen, *Thinking in the Spirit*, 4.

22. For the sake of perspective, note that Torrey also raised the question of the evidence of Spirit-baptism in light of Acts 2, but he answered in the negative—that tongues were not the evidence—because he also took into consideration other biblical passages (particularly 1 Cor 12:30), as well as believers he knew whom he deemed to have had the experience but who had not spoken in tongues. See *The Baptism with the Holy Spirit*, 18.

because they knew that that was what was supposed to happen. They were so convinced of the truth of Parham's view that they lost all awareness of the fact that they were actually interpreting their experience to make it fit Parham's predefined theological ideal."[23] Parham's students could not help but interpret their experience through their leader's theological framework, for that is what they were subconsciously inclined to do. But they could be faulted for extending that framework if their subsequent experience directly challenged it in decisive ways. With the advantage of hindsight, we can see that these matters reached a crossroads, and institutional Pentecostalism recognized the point. The recognition, however, was only—and unfortunately—partial.

Over time, institutional Pentecostalism dropped the idea that evidential tongues for Spirit-baptism were necessarily missionary tongues. Repeated testing and evaluation over time could not sustain this commitment. Certainly in Acts 2 and perhaps even in other scenarios from time to time the phenomenon of xenolalia has occurred, but Parham's interpretation that it represents the biblical *pattern* for the experience could not hold up, given the weight of communal reflection and evaluation.[24] Interestingly, Parham for the rest of his life held to this belief of missionary tongues being the biblical evidence of Spirit-baptism, and he decried the movement he helped establish for abandoning this central commitment. From one angle, it is surprising he would so tenaciously hold the view, but from another, his unflappable commitment makes sense. If missionary tongues were not on the table and instead were replaced with unknown tongues (i.e., glossolalia), Parham's theological system would be severely damaged, since xenoglossa served a "utilitarian link" between Holy Ghost power and evangelism.[25] Such a modification would threaten what Parham had come to believe about his ministry and the role of Pentecostalism in God's providential ordering of cosmic history.

Institutional Pentecostalism of the American variety made the modification of largely replacing xenolalia with glossolalia as the initial evidence of Spirit-baptism; in doing so, it retained broadly Parham's formu-

---

23. Jacobsen, *Thinking in the Spirit*, 5.

24. One of the earliest examples of this understanding is A. G. Garr, who mistakenly believed he would be able to speak Bengali when he arrived as an early Pentecostal missionary to India, though he had never previously studied the language. Garr would go on to have an important ministry throughout Asia and in America, but his early experiences required a reassessment of Parham's logic.

25. Goff, *Fields White unto Harvest*, 75.

laic structure.[26] Doing so has put this branch of Pentecostalism at odds with other Pentecostal constituencies across the globe, ones for whom initial-evidence logic is *not* compelling or mandated.[27] In proceeding in such a way, institutional Pentecostalism took a path that was both more sensible but also more problematic than Parham's. Now with this modification, the pressure was relieved of figuring out which language each instance of tongues was, since the precise identification would indicate a missionary call to a region where that language was spoken. Furthermore, the distinctive marker of classical Pentecostalism—the experience of Spirit-baptism—avoided being discredited, since the falsifying of tongues as known human languages could have that concomitant result. For these and other reasons, the change was important. But even with this change, institutional Pentecostalism has continued to privilege tongues (now glossolalia) as the initial evidence of Spirit-baptism, and in doing so, it has exposed even more dramatically the weaknesses of Parham's original vision.

Perpetual Challenges with the Understanding

Before considering further these weaknesses, we should ask, Why did institutional Pentecostalism fall short in overhauling its doctrine? It is hard to answer this question with certainty, but one suspects at least two factors were at play. One is that a wide variety of people in a midst of fluctuating circumstances continued to narrate testimonies consistent with the contours of the formula; they continued to utilize it (albeit in this altered, glossolalic form) to describe their own experiences. And as the movement grew and extended itself intergenerationally, these testimonies became

26. Parham seems to have preferred the language of "Bible evidence," and his work assumes that it was the *sole* evidence. Although occasionally used by Parham, the modifier "initial" rose to prominence as Pentecostals aimed to define more clearly and rigidly their distinctives. This reading is more in line with Friesen (*Norming the Abnormal*, 46) than with Goff (*Fields White unto Harvest*, 173).

27. This point should not be understated, for it represents another layer of instability to the claim that tongues as the initial physical evidence of Spirit-baptism is at the heart of Pentecostal identity. Not only is this not true in terms of the reality "on the ground" of these fellowships, but as hinted above, it is also not true of various Pentecostal fellowships outside the American denominational orbit. Constituencies in this category would include Pentecostals in India, Chile, Germany, the United Kingdom, and Scandinavia.

conceptually and definitionally calcified. They formed a logic that was imparted and picked up by those who joined the fold.

One exemplar of this tendency is G. F. Taylor. In his *The Spirit and the Bride*, Taylor talks about how he was told by a Christian brother that it was his belief that those who received baptism in the Holy Ghost would speak in tongues. Taylor confesses, "This was a surprise to me, as it was the first time that I had ever thought on this line. I replied that I had had the Baptism of the Spirit for years, but this was Pentecostal power. He told me that I had had the witness to my sanctification, but had not had the Baptism of the Spirit." In Taylor's case, he eventually appealed to the witness of the Spirit and to scriptural grounds: "So I decided that I would find out, and at once began to pray God to teach me. The Spirit seemed to confirm what the brother had told me. But fearing lest I should be mistaken, I took my Bible, and, with my heart open to God, I began to search the Word; and to the surprise of my heart I found it [*sic*] the teaching of the Word that all who receive the Baptism of the Holy Ghost speak with other tongues as the Spirit gives utterance."[28]

Another and quite decisive example is Daniel W. Kerr. He took an active stance in 1918 to solidify this understanding in light of the Assemblies of God controversy that erupted with the contrarian views of Fred F. Bosworth. Kerr represents the move to consolidate and further refine this logic in light of competing and internal alternatives. Years later, Kerr would say that "a Baptism which cannot be seen and heard is not according to the pattern [*sic*] Baptism on the day of Pentecost, at Caesaria, at Ephesus and at Damascus." (The mention of Damascus assumes that Paul experienced Spirit-baptism with tongues in his Damascus road experience, which is what he referred to when he later professed to speak in tongues; see 1 Cor 14:18.) To start this article, Kerr makes a wide-ranging claim that indicates this consolidating effort: "As a Pentecostal people, we hold that the Bible evidence of the Baptism with the Holy Ghost . . . is speaking in other tongues as the Spirit gives utterance. We have found that whenever we . . . begin to let down on this particular point, the fire dies out, the ardor and fervor begin to wane, the glory departs. We have found where this position is held and wherever it is proclaimed, the Lord is working."[29]

---

28. G. F. Taylor, *The Spirit and the Bride* (no location, 1907), 40, as reproduced in facsimile form in *Three Early Pentecostal Tracts* (New York: Garland, 1985).

29. D. W. Kerr, "The Bible Evidence of the Baptism with the Holy Ghost," *Pentecostal Evangel*, August 11, 1923, 2.

On this last point, note that tongues as the "Bible evidence" is now put to service as a barometer of authentic Pentecostal vitality.

In many of these cases, a "this is that" kind of reasoning is employed, one that involves making connections between the biblical testimony and lived experience.[30] Pentecostals value very much this kind of hermeneutic in that it creates expectation for the possibilities available in the Christian life. This strategy is one of their main arguments against dispensationalist cessationism, and Pentecostals therefore find it important to uphold. At the same time, the hermeneutic is difficult to question when it takes on very particular forms that are simply "given" without further possibilities for debate or revision. For instance, Acts 2 is simply assumed by many Pentecostals to set the biblical pattern for how Spirit-baptism takes place today. This reading is taken to be unquestionable, even if problematic features or inconclusive evidence comes to the fore in light of it. Such privileging means that destabilizing details may be conveniently ignored for the sake of maintaining consistency. One sees such moves when the language of Spirit-baptism is deemed functionally equivalent to many other Spirit-related terms ("receiving the Spirit," "being filled with the Spirit," and the like), as well as when tongues is assumed to be at work in Spirit-encounters when the biblical passages do not specifically say so (e.g., in Acts 8 and, as seen in Kerr's elaboration above, Paul's conversion).[31]

A second factor that was most likely at work in the resistance to thoroughly reformulate Parham's logic was epistemic convenience and appeal. Tongues will always play a role in forms of Pentecostal and charismatic spirituality, but classical Pentecostals found it important to register tongues as an evidence and a sign, as well as labeling it "initial" and "physical." These terms together created a formula, one that allowed a person to know with relative ease if someone had the Pentecostal expe-

30. The phrase "this is that" is popular among Pentecostals; it comes from the wording of Acts 2:16 in the King James Version, where Peter makes the connection between Joel 2 and the happenings he was witnessing. The phrase also serves as the title of a collection of works by Aimee Semple McPherson (Los Angeles: Echo Park Evangelistic Association, 1923).

31. Taylor is especially guilty of coming to questionable conclusions. In addressing the observation that Scripture never records Jesus as speaking in tongues, Taylor says that Scripture implies it, given that Jesus must have spoken to the Samaritan woman and to the Syrophoenician woman in their own languages, yet he presumably did not properly learn these languages; the conclusion Taylor draws is that Jesus must have spoken to them in tongues granted by the Spirit (*The Spirit and the Bride*, 48).

rience of Spirit-baptism. The quote by Kerr above suggests as much—Spirit-baptism must be seen and heard for it to be authentic. Jean-Daniel Plüss has stated that the formulators of initial-evidence logic "might just as well have called it 'basic empirical proof,'" in that it satisfied the epistemic needs of knowing if and when people had the experience.[32] This epistemic need may reflect the American context in particular. As noted previously, researchers and commentators (esp. those from around the globe or who at least are aware of global Pentecostalism) have often commented that initial-evidence logic is especially characteristic of American Pentecostal denominations. What is the tie, if any, between initial-evidence logic and American intellectual sensibilities? One answer is that the desideratum of empirically verifying instances of Spirit-baptism is very much in line with the intellectual climate of the nineteenth century, surveyed above in chapter 3. Remarkably, evangelicalism went one direction with this intellectual heritage, and Pentecostalism did not entirely escape the ramifications of this decision. In their reading practices and understanding of plausibility, Pentecostals have also appealed to a common-sense tradition. In particular, initial-evidence logic reflects a kind of philosophical positivism in which the dynamics of the spiritual life are open to scientific/empirical verification. The terms "initial," "physical," "sign," "proof," and especially "evidence" collectively indicate very clearly this mind-set. For a revivalist movement getting off the ground, this kind of epistemic framing surrounding its key experiential distinctive was crucial so as to establish internal and external credibility. If this experience could be attested, using the prized standards for knowing in its given context, how could this understanding not be compelling to the masses?

This strategy of picking up Parham's logic with only the modification of substituting glossolalia for xenolalia has proven to be difficult, particularly as institutional Pentecostalism has faced the challenge over the generations of drawing people into its identity. The difficulty largely revolves around the shape and purpose of Spirit-baptism itself. The prioritization of a mechanism for identifying Spirit-baptism—what I have called initial-evidence logic—has often overshadowed what can be termed the ontological and teleological dimensions of the experience itself. These are highlighted via the following questions: What is Spirit-baptism, and

---

32. Jean-Daniel Plüss, "Azusa and Other Myths: The Long and Winding Road from Experience to Stated Belief and Back Again," *Pneuma* 15, no. 2 (1993): 191.

what is its purpose?[33] Parham's paradigm could answer these questions quite readily: Spirit-baptism is an experience of empowerment evidenced by missionary tongues so that people could be expeditiously equipped for worldwide evangelism during this period of the "latter rain." One may not agree with Parham's logic, but it is tight and compelling on its own terms.[34] It gives purpose and character to Spirit-baptism by locating it within God's economy of redemptive activity. In critiquing other Pentecostals, Parham elaborates in *The Everlasting Gospel* the notion of Pentecost as being a "pouring forth" and stresses that God "wants our experiences to be a benefit to other people and not for mere gratifications of our own feelings."[35] But with the shift from xenolalia to glossolalia, the sign of tongues as initial evidence becomes less about missionary work and more about identifying authentic Pentecostal experience. A "dissociation of speaking in tongues and Spirit Baptism from its original setting" occurs with this move,[36] and Parham's logic breaks down as a result. As such, a kind of theology-vacuum presents itself, for we lack a broader, contextualizing theological account in which to fit the experience. The phrase "glossolalia is the initial physical evidence of baptism in the Holy Spirit" becomes not so much a doctrinal claim as an epistemic criterion.

Given that the language of "evidence" was retained for identifying Spirit-baptism while it was divorced from a theological narrative that could keep it grounded in something beyond itself, institutional Pentecostalism reflected and perpetuated through official declarations a philosophical

33. I find it particularly interesting that Torrey raises these questions at the very beginning of *The Baptism with the Holy Spirit*, thereby suggesting just how crucial these questions are regarding any discussion of Spirit-baptism and further highlighting how their centrality has been overshadowed in Pentecostal theology, given the preoccupation with tongues as the distinctive marker of Pentecostal spirituality and doctrine.

34. In fact, one could say that the role tongues plays in Parham's framework is quite different from the role it plays in institutional Pentecostalism. The similarities are there, to be sure, but Parham's focus is largely in terms of a theology of history. In both *A Voice Crying in the Wilderness* and *The Everlasting Gospel*, there is little focus on Spirit-baptism and tongues. Interestingly, Parham at times critiques Pentecostals for overemphasizing tongues. For instance, he says, "We have reached a fanatical state where we make the speaking of tongues a basis, or test, of fellowship, or of spiritual activity" (*The Everlasting Gospel*, 79). Yes, Parham believed his understanding of tongues to be a biblical standard, but he did so on the way to affirming a particular role for it in something broader and ultimately more important that included the end times, witnessing, "the sealing," "the anointing that abideth," and so on.

35. Parham, *The Everlasting Gospel*, 80.

36. Plüss, "Azusa and Other Myths," 191.

framework that was modern to its core. Yes, Parham contributed this language, and one could say that he reflected this philosophical paradigm in his original proposals, but his alternative was also theologically grounded in assumptions about both what God was doing in these end times and the role Pentecostals had in this work. The modification by institutional Pentecostalism from xenolalia to glossolalia weakened this connection, leaving bare the philosophical commitments, which were in turn further calcified through tedious qualification and refinement. To cite Plüss once more, "By following this route Pentecostals began to conceptualize, to narrow and to pin down what they meant by 'speaking in tongues' and 'baptism in the Spirit.' As a result, what began as 'speaking about an experience' ended in a 'formalization' devoid of much substance."[37]

The Institutionalized Limits of Spirit-Baptism

Part of the difficulty with clarifying Pentecostal approaches to the language of Spirit-baptism is the various uses of the phrase, both on its own terms and in its Pentecostal appropriation. As to the first point, the New Testament does not employ the language of Spirit-baptism per se; the instances in which this notion is alluded to in the New Testament reflect the verbal form "to baptize," and those altogether number only seven cases (Acts 2 *not* being one of them).[38] Second, it is a bit peculiar that, within the New Testament witness, being baptized in the Holy Spirit is a significant feature of John the Baptist's portrayal of the work of the One who is to come, as recorded in all four canonical gospels, yet such language is used by Jesus only once, and this in his postresurrection appearances. As the language has been picked up by ecclesial traditions, the resonances of meaning available vary considerably. In addition to the Pentecostal options, there are also the sacramental or high-liturgical views, as well as broadly evangelical ones, and all of these are mutually exclusive, given that their points of differentiation rest on particular theological and ecclesial orientations.[39]

As for the Pentecostal option in particular, layers of consideration

37. Plüss, "Azusa and Other Myths," 192.

38. The seven places are Matthew 3:11, Mark 1:8, Luke 3:16, John 1:33, Acts 1:5 and 11:16, and 1 Corinthians 12:13.

39. For more on this point, see Daniel Castelo, *Pneumatology: A Guide for the Perplexed* (London: Bloomsbury T&T Clark, 2015), chap. 6.

must be noted. At the first level would be the constructed *biblical trope* on the basis of the seven passages already noted. In terms of Pentecostal usage, it is generalized to other passages as well, so that phrases with "filling" are assumed by some Pentecostals to be the functional equivalent to "baptizing." At a second level would be the symbiotic dynamic between the *doctrine* of Spirit-baptism and that which people call the *experience* of Spirit-baptism. As we have remarked, these are properly distinguishable at the conceptual level, but popularly in terms of testimonies and usage, they often are not. People simply say "Spirit-baptism," and a variety of matters, including doctrinal and experiential ones, are implied as part of the mix. These conflations, however, contribute to the challenge of recasting the theme. We have already elaborated extensively the doctrine in terms of Parham's orienting vision. As for the experience, testimonies often include a variety of images and themes to describe what at times come across as defying words and expression.

In the midst of these references to the ineffable, the experience of Spirit-baptism is often narrated in terms of a set of assumptions surrounding religious experience. These assumptions may seem obvious to Pentecostals themselves, but they are not necessarily so to others in and out of the Christian fold. Spirit-baptism is often talked about by Pentecostals in terms of a distinct "work of grace" or a "crisis experience." This tendency would put it in the company of conversion and sanctification. Although discriminations are often made among them, these "crises" are talked about in very similar ways. This similarity stems from a heritage not only in the Holiness movement of the nineteenth century but even in the Great Awakening of the eighteenth century. This American revivalist framework is perhaps relatable through the expression "objective experiential realism," and the idea runs something like the following: all Christians have the potential to undergo particular spiritual experiences that are broadly uniform in nature and normative for the Christian life. These are in a sense "out there" to be experienced by the earnest, God-seeking person in the context of revivalist worship. The doctrinal formulations both help set up the anticipation of this experience on the front end and provide a way to narrate its larger significance for the Christian life on the back end, yet the experience itself is left to stand as something distinctly and reliably noteworthy. Experiences undergone in terms of "crises" or "works of grace" in this paradigm are not ones that are assumed to arise from a deep anthropological core; rather, they are seen by the earnest worshiper as a participation beyond himself or herself; they are available to any sincere seeker. Therefore, whether the experience was salvation, sanctification (in certain cases), or Spirit-baptism, early Pentecostals assumed that these could be experienced by everybody at some point.

These distinctions germane to the notion of crisis experiences have become difficult to sustain over time for a number of reasons. Such has been the case for both the Holiness movement (in relation to sanctification) and the Pentecostal movement that followed it (as pertaining to Spirit-baptism and sanctification for some). Part of the challenge involves how considerably it relies on individual narration. Some people might find it fitting to describe their experiences via the logic provided. The testimony "I was saved, sanctified, and baptized with the Holy Ghost" simply rolls off some people's tongues as a tight, multifaceted dynamic. Others, like Benjamin Irwin and David Wesley Myland (and perhaps even Parham himself), find it appealing to add further experiences or nuances to the language.[40] Some might find such accretions helpful, but all these different wordings challenge and threaten institutional reliance on a particular construct. Furthermore, the waning of revivalist culture on the American scene inevitably impacts this way of reflecting on religious experience. People must be taught how to use this language, and they have to see it on display among others and encouraged to use it themselves in order for the language to be perpetuated. With fewer testimonies and instances of its usage, the language tends to weaken and fall out of use. In summary, a symbiotic relationship exists between the language of "crisis experience" and revivalist culture; they feed off each other in important ways, so that if one suffers, the other does as well.

40. Benjamin H. Irwin is notoriously remembered for introducing a whole bevy of experiences that were to follow Spirit-baptism, including baptisms of dynamite, lyddite, and oxidite. D. Wesley Myland sometimes spoke of the "Pentecostal fulness" (see *The Latter Rain Covenant and Pentecostal Power*, 107–10, as found in *Three Early Pentecostal Tracts*). And as for Parham, he made a distinction between the "anointing that abideth" and Spirit-baptism. The former is traceable to what the disciples experienced when they were breathed upon by Jesus in John 20. In this experience, one's eyes are opened, the Scriptures are illuminated, and the Spirit is received as Anointer and Teacher, whereas in Spirit-baptism a person is strictly empowered for witness. See Parham, *A Voice Crying in the Wilderness*, chap. 3. These varying dynamics put their descriptions on the edge of assumed logics, which sometimes resulted in possibilities that moved beyond them. For instance, Jacobsen can speak of Myland's theology as follows: "Myland's theology bears a closer resemblance to some of the mystical writers of the Orthodox and Catholic traditions than it does to the logical religious treatises of reformational Protestantism" (*Thinking in the Spirit*, 113).

Questions about the classical Pentecostal understanding of Spirit-baptism have also surfaced on biblical-hermeneutical grounds. One of the most important figures on this score is Gordon Fee.[41] Given Fee's work, one can see that it is difficult to say that Acts 2 constitutes a "biblical pattern," when various factors are considered. One factor would be the challenge of reconciling the events in Acts 2, 8, 10, and 19. Another matter would be how myopic this focus is on Luke's testimony, which is a point important to Fee not simply because he was a Pauline scholar but, more important, given the significance of Paul overall for the formulation of Christian pneumatology. Finally, it is always a challenge to draw a normative pattern from historical occurrences. Whereas there may be some justification for seeking a norm in matters of growth and maturity in the Christian life, the same is not true for the crisis-orientation at work in initial-evidence logic. How, then, can we talk about a norm for classical Pentecostal spirituality?

Perhaps the most damaging consequence of this way of speaking of religious experience is the way it goes about commodifying Christian spirituality. By speaking of distinct, available, uniform experiences in the Christian life that are simply "there for the taking," revivalists of various stripes essentially cast the goal of spirituality as "obtaining" or "having" these discrete experiences. The danger is in portraying these experiences as commodities that people obtain or consume, just as they do other things. Furthermore, when traditions discriminate on the basis of the "haves" and the "have-nots" of these experiences, political dynamics are introduced, including power-laden structures of those who are and who are not entitled to carry on the Pentecostal identity in formal capacities. For those who do not fit this narration, they can be dismissed, marginalized, and patronized as a result. Through the commodification of religious experience, the Christian life is depicted as a ladder of achievement or as a status-filled dynamic. Most Christians, including Pentecostals, would formally object to these outcomes. The difficulty for Pentecostals is that the logic and the language they tend to prefer in handling Spirit-baptism point in this direction.

Despite this bleak assessment, alternative proposals for recasting ini-

---

41. See Fee's *Gospel and Spirit: Issues in New Testament Hermeneutics* (Peabody, MA: Hendrickson, 1991), chap. 7, as well as "Hermeneutics and Historical Precedent—a Major Problem in Pentecostal Hermeneutics," in *Perspectives on the New Pentecostalism*, ed. Russell P. Spittler (Grand Rapids: Baker, 1976), 118–32.

tial-evidence logic have presented themselves recently among Pentecostal scholars, and these are promising in that they move beyond the empirical and "scientific" logic at work with the formulaic language traditionally used. Three of these accounts will be surveyed below so as to show the kind of nuancing possible in the treatment of Spirit-baptism within the Pentecostal fold. Interestingly, many of the points these scholars raise are relatable to the Christian mystical tradition. I would argue that such affinities are not coincidental, for if Pentecostalism is a mystical tradition within the church catholic, then those features have the potential to emerge in discussions related to something as central and defining to the Pentecostal movement as Spirit-baptism. They may also prove helpful when the movement comes to recognize the limits of an evangelical tradition that is in many ways at odds with its fundamental character.

Promising Reassessments: Edith Blumhofer

In the introduction to a volume devoted to offering profiles of Assemblies of God leaders, historian Edith Blumhofer offers a running account of Spirit-baptism that is important to consider in that it goes against the trend of dominant offerings. She affirms that the experience of early Pentecostals was one of "divine encounter," which in turn "introduced meaning, certainty, and mission into even the most humble existence." Blumhofer admits that, with time, Pentecostals came to be associated with an experience that was "always accompanied by speaking in tongues" and that tongues speech "became known as the 'uniform initial evidence' of the baptism with the Holy Spirit," but she argues that this "dogmatic description" failed to capture dominant features of the experience for early Pentecostals.[42]

One of those features was the process of spiritual growth and transformation that was involved with the experience of Spirit-baptism. These early Pentecostal seekers alternated "between ecstasy and conviction as they pursued their 'personal Pentecosts.'"[43] They sought and fostered the presence of God by renouncing worldliness and attending countless

42. Edith L. Blumhofer, "Pentecost in My Soul": Explorations in the Meaning of Pentecostal Experience in the Early Assemblies of God (Springfield, MO: Gospel Publishing House, 1989), 16.
43. Blumhofer, "Pentecost in My Soul," 17.

worship services and events. In other words, they actively sought a lived spirituality. Although tongues speech was associated with initial-evidence logic, Blumhofer also points to accounts that suggest that, in tongues-speech, the body is given up to God's control. Tongues here functions as a sign of self-renunciation unto a God who should reign supremely in one's life.

According to Blumhofer, another of the features unaccounted for by the "dogmatic description" of initial-evidence logic has to do with the results coming out of Spirit-baptism, ones particularly related to identity.[44] Blumhofer is fully aware that, from Parham's vision (and this relying on other Holiness accounts), Spirit-baptism was often affirmed in terms of empowerment for service. Blumhofer in no way denies the importance of this reading, but she believes another major factor is often dismissed. This factor is not so much related to activity (doing) but to identity (being). This emphasis on identity raises several points. First, one finds a running tension between fulfillment and expectation as part of Pentecostal identity. Blumhofer remarks, "The Spirit-baptized believer was assumed to have attained fullness yet was admonished to pursue fullness: The believer had begun to drink from a fountain that both quenched thirst and created it, and that would 'never run dry.'" This paradoxical framing works against an overrealized eschatology, which is an important danger to avoid in Pentecostal spirituality. Second, one sees on occasion imagery in the elaboration of this identity that has resonances with a kind of Christ-centered devotion that has characterized Christianity's mystical traditions. Blumhofer says of the Spirit-filled life: "It was described as 'feasting with the Lord'; it made people 'happy and free'; its fruits were 'peace' and 'rest.' In short, the experience made life a foretaste of heaven." Blumhofer mentions *The Apostolic Faith* paper of Azusa to make her point: "Those seeking Spirit baptism were instructed not to pray for tongues, but rather to desire to know and experience Christ."[45]

In these elaborations, Blumhofer is essentially showing that Spirit-baptism was sought and took shape in terms of varying dynamics that are lost in the formulaic and dogmatic treatments inherent to initial-evidence logic. Spirit-baptism did involve empowerment of believers to witness,

---

44. Blumhofer mentions a third theme that will not be surveyed here, one having to do with the dispensational significance of Spirit-baptism, which in turn created "a climate of anticipation and intensity" (*"Pentecost in My Soul,"* 17).

45. Blumhofer, *"Pentecost in My Soul,"* 19, 20.

but she also wishes to stress the formational aspects of the experience. She references John Wright Follette (an early Assemblies of God minister and teacher) to this effect when he speaks of God's work as "mystical, intricate, and spiritual" in forming Pentecostal believers. In her approving reading of Follette, Blumhofer states: "More important than energizing [early Pentecostals'] lives for service was the Spirit's role in making them 'overcomers,' in allowing Christ 'to be glorified in them.' Though integrally related to this developing of character, Christian service was not the primary goal of the Pentecostal experience." In her opinion regarding early Pentecostals (including Assemblies of God members), the "enduement with power for service" was secondary to Spirit-baptism's "primary purpose of bringing the believer into a new dimension of constant, conscious fellowship with Christ."[46]

Promising Reassessments: Frank Macchia

Another recent assessment of Spirit-baptism has been offered by one of the most important theologians in the Pentecostal academy, Frank Macchia. In *Baptized in the Spirit*, Macchia recognizes the Lukan and Pauline strands of Spirit-baptism in the New Testament,[47] the former suggesting "power for witness," and the latter involving believers as incorporated into the Christian fold so that they are "in Christ."[48] Sometimes this distinction is considered in terms of service and identity, respectively, and the differentiation has proven important for Pentecostals as they have gone on to stake a claim for their experience among biblical scholars. Macchia is fully aware of these discussions, but his tendency is to synthesize and integrate these accounts so as to render a multi-orbed account that can move forward the discussion surrounding Spirit-baptism.

Macchia offers several statements at the beginning of his work regarding the vision he is entertaining and the outcome he desires: "Perhaps we should speak of a theology of Spirit baptism that is soteriologically and charismatically defined, an event that has more than one

---

46. Blumhofer, *"Pentecost in My Soul,"* 22.

47. In Macchia's work of synthesis, he appropriates a variety of linguistic patterns in the New Testament as "functional equivalents" and brings them together to elaborate a single experience of Spirit-baptism.

48. Macchia is assuming the terrain set forth by Roger Stronstad and Robert Menzies in response to the work of James D. G. Dunn.

dimension because it is eschatological in nature and not wholly defined by notions of Christian initiation." He goes on to propose a correlation between Pentecost and the kingdom of God that lends itself to interpreting Spirit-baptism eschatologically. Macchia declares the following about his project: "Before the book is finished, I will be saying that the highest description possible of the substance of Spirit baptism as an eschatological gift is that it functions as an outpouring of divine love. This is the final integration of the soteriological and the charismatic. No higher or deeper integration is possible."[49]

Before engaging in expanding these notions, Macchia wishes to reclaim Spirit-baptism as the Pentecostal distinctive in light of other proposals that have downplayed it. For Macchia, Spirit-baptism represents a working category, metaphor, doctrine, and experience that cannot be neglected in discussions of what makes Pentecostalism what it is. The ecumenical significance of the theme cannot be put to the side for Macchia, which is partly the reason he is concerned to reclaim it in the contemporary discussion. He cites Steven Land, Harvey Cox, Donald Dayton, and D. William Faupel as those who have engaged Pentecostalism significantly and yet made Spirit-baptism ancillary to their most fundamental contributions. For Macchia, these research agendas have brought important points to light, but the neglect of Spirit-baptism is worrisome. His agenda is largely to broaden the scope of the theme's application and relevance so as to reclaim its central, defining role in Pentecostal life.

Macchia believes Spirit-baptism to be a participatory experience subsequent to regeneration that accounts for the Lukan witness, once it is integrated with the Pauline as its background. He is aware of the theme's crisis dynamic, which hails from American revivalist culture, as well as Pietism generally. He also mentions initial-evidence logic and highlights the way this understanding has varied considerably among Pentecostals. Ultimately, however, Macchia's concern is not so much to engage past proposals in Pentecostal studies as it is to pave a way forward through integration and expansion. For Macchia, Spirit-baptism is a metaphor for life in the Spirit, and this life is constituted and substantiated by nothing less than the love of God. As he notes, "The outpouring of divine love upon us is the ultimate description of Pentecost."[50] Divine love is the essence of

---

49. Frank D. Macchia, *Baptized in the Holy Spirit: A Global Pentecostal Theology* (Grand Rapids: Zondervan, 2006), 16, 17.

50. Macchia, *Baptized in the Spirit*, 91, 257.

Spirit-baptism, and in this light, the latter can account for themes related to both sanctification and charismatic empowerment.

In the opening remarks of Macchia's concluding chapter, he cites *The Cloud of Unknowing*, an anonymous fourteenth-century text of Christian mysticism, as a way of supporting the point that, "even when understanding fails, love keeps us close to the flame of the Spirit." He continues: "This is the great value of the Pentecostal emphasis on speaking in tongues. Tongues are the language of love, not reason."[51] As important as these remarks are, he does not go on to develop them further in this work. In two pivotal articles, however, Macchia does account for these matters in suggestive ways apropos to the present study.

In the inaugural issue of the *Journal of Pentecostal Theology*, Macchia offers a theology of glossolalia, and in this effort, he addresses the difficulties of initial-evidence logic. He states, "Beneath the dogma of tongues-as-evidence was the assumption [by Pentecostals] that tongues symbolized an encounter with God that may be termed 'theophanic,' or as spontaneous, dramatic and marked by signs and wonders." The emphasis on "theophany" is crucial for a number of reasons. First, rather than a phenomenon of human religiosity, Macchia wishes to cast Pentecostal tongues as a feature of divine self-disclosure. The happening, in other words, is theo-logical, or theocentric, to the point that it indicates "God is here" in a context of worship. Second, the emphasis on theophany has a way of situating Acts 2 within a broader dynamic of God's theophanic activity in Scripture. Macchia offers this summary statement, "The description of Pentecost in Acts 2 must be seen in this light. Pentecost was viewed there as an eschatological event that referred back to previous theophanies ... and pointed ahead to the final parousia. Pentecost may be termed an eschatological theophany of God. Tongues were a part of this theophany, as a kairos event that included the transformation of language into a channel of the divine self-disclosure." Third, as noted in the above quote, glossolalia is eschatologically theophanic, and it takes place in event- and tension-laden dynamics. He remarks, "The paradox of encountering the divine reality as present but not yet, as near but still out of reach, as revealed but still veiled is essential to glossolalia as a spoken mystery." In other words, the eschatological dimension helps secure tongues within the mystery of God and God's self-disclosure. As he notes later, "Glossolalia is an unclassifiable, free speech in response to an unclassifiable, free God."

---

51. Macchia, *Baptized in the Spirit*, 257.

This feature adds a fourth dimension to this theophanic understanding of tongues, namely, the way that tongues expose the inadequacy of language to account for the encounter with God. In elaborating specifically how tongues represent a language of the heart, Macchia notes, "Any attempt rationally to communicate the experience [of encountering the divine mystery of God] ends it, for to reflect upon and rationally communicate an experience is to distance oneself from it already. Tongues is a way of expressing the experience without ending it."[52]

In the aforementioned article, Macchia makes a brief reference that tongues as evidence should not be taken to mean that one has the Spirit; rather, it should be taken as a sign that the Spirit has a person and is shaping that person into new creation.[53] This impulse is further developed in a second important article, in which Macchia argues for a sacramental understanding of tongues.[54] The language of sacramentality has traditionally not been widely claimed by Pentecostals, but recently it has become more commonplace in that it has been deemed appropriate for describing latent theological dynamics functional in Pentecostal speech and practice.[55] Macchia sees this possibility on account of the "God is here" dynamic alluded to above: If tongues indicate God's manifest presence, then the language of sacramentality is quite fitting to employ as long as one keeps at bay (as Pentecostals are typically inclined to do) an *ex opere operato* understanding of the sacraments. Macchia sees in the work of Karl Rahner and Edward Schillebeeckx an amenable kind of sacramental theology, one that "views the sacraments primarily as occasions for a personal encounter between God and the believer." Naturally, Macchia admits that glossolalia as sacrament would be different than other sacraments in that it "accents the free, dramatic, and unpredictable move of the Spirit of God,"[56] but this quality is not detrimental to its sacramental quality; quite the contrary, it reinforces the description in that it gives due attention to other aspects of the Spirit's work and presence. Macchia is committed to the recognition of "visible continuities" that exist when the Spirit works

52. Macchia, "Sighs Too Deep for Words: Towards a Theology of Glossolalia," *Journal of Pentecostal Theology* 1 (1992): 48, 53, 59, 61, 62.

53. Macchia, "Sighs Too Deep for Words," 71.

54. Macchia, "Tongues as a Sign: Towards a Sacramental Understanding of Pentecostal Experience," *Pneuma* 15, no. 1 (1993): 61–76.

55. An important study on this topic is Chris E. W. Green, *Toward a Pentecostal Theology of the Lord's Supper: Foretasting the Kingdom* (Cleveland, TN: CPT Press, 2012).

56. Macchia, "Tongues as a Sign," 62, 63.

in corporate worship, whether in Acts, the apostolic testimony, or across the globe. Within this dynamic he sees the warrants for Pentecostalism's emphasis on tongues as evidence, although he is prone to step away from that language, given that it is not biblical, in preference for the language of sign. His account, then, is a qualified appropriation of initial-evidence logic along more sacramental grounds than is typical of portrayals within the Pentecostal fold.

Promising Reassessments: Simon Chan

A final scholar who will be considered for purposes of surveying the pos- sibilities of recasting Spirit-baptism and initial-evidence logic is Simon Chan. Perhaps of the three scholars being mentioned in this survey, Chan is closest to the broad aims of the present work in that he has distinguished himself in Pentecostal academic circles as one who wishes to establish links between Pentecostal theology and the "great spiritual tradition" of Chris- tianity. Therefore, in close proximity with the claims of this work, Chan can state, "When Pentecostals come to see their distinctives as a part of the larger tradition . . . they can preserve them and maintain their integrity." Chan is also aware of the spirituality-theology interface and how it has changed in modernity. And he agrees that a spiritual theology considers reflecting on God and praying to God as closely related (he would say in- distinguishable) acts. He also goes on to note that difficulties in theolog- ical explanation have facilitated impoverished experiences of the Spirit across Pentecostal generations: "Among second-generation Pentecostals Spirit-baptism is received first as a doctrine before it is actualized in per- sonal experience. But when the doctrine is poorly explained, the intended experience does not necessarily follow."[57] In this, Chan is operating out of a sensibility forged in conversation with Lindbeck's cultural-linguistic model of doctrine.[58] Chan also mentions Macchia's theophanic under- standing of Spirit-baptism approvingly and offers his own view of evi- dentialist-logic, which, similarly to Macchia's, is not so much an aban-

57. Simon Chan, *Pentecostal Theology and the Christian Spiritual Tradition*, Journal of Pentecostal Theology Supplement 21 (Sheffield: Sheffield Academic Press, 2000), 7, 12, 10.

58. For an articulation of this sensibility with reference to Pentecostalism, see Joel Shuman, "Toward a Cultural-Linguistic Account of the Pentecostal Doctrine of the Bap- tism of the Holy Spirit," *Pneuma* 19, no. 2 (1997): 207–23.

donment as it is a reconfiguration. He states, "I would like to show that glossolalia which Pentecostals identify as 'the initial evidence' of baptism in the Spirit is a rich theological symbol precisely because it is linked to a reality (Spirit-baptism) which is far bigger than the classical Pentecostal conceptualization of it."[59] At this introductory stage, he also mentions glossolalia as a form of prayer, thereby symbolizing an ascetic dimension to the Christian life that complements the dynamic at work in thinking of tongues as evidence.

Chan develops these last remarks in the second and third chapters of his work. In his opinion, we need to make a case for the "logical relationship between glossolalia and Spirit-baptism." As in Macchia's *Baptized in the Spirit*, Chan sees a broadening of Spirit-baptism as important, and this broadening would involve both charismatic and soteriological dimensions. At the same time, Chan wishes to express "a necessary connection between the physical act of glossolalia and the spiritual reality called Spirit-baptism." This necessity hinges on a scheme of active passivity: glossolalia operates out of an active passivity in that "we speak, yet it is a speech that comes from yieldedness and surrender to the will of God." In light of this understanding, glossolalia mirrors the triune life itself, which is a life "of love and self-giving between the Father and the Son, in which the Father initiates the Son and the Son yields in humble obedience by the power of the Spirit."[60] Therefore, a proper correspondence exists between glossolalia and the experience of the triune God in Spirit-baptism, and this correspondence forms the basis of Chan's understanding of a necessary link or logic existing between the two.

Furthermore, given the uniqueness and strangeness of glossolalia, it can function as a means enabling a person to enter a new spiritual dimension. This enablement, once again, must be cast as passive and receptive at its core so as to avoid anthropological overextension. Chan illustrates the dynamic in the following way: "Tongues are the primordial words . . . that arise spontaneously in response to the invasive coming of the primal Reality to the believers which Pentecostals identify as a Spirit-baptism." More extensively, he draws the comparison with tears and sadness: the former indicates the latter in a connatural, primal, or concomitant way, and the relationship is uniquely important. Analogously, he believes that "glossolalia is not just one of the concomitants of being Spirit-filled, but

---

59. Chan, *Pentecostal Theology and the Christian Spiritual Tradition*, 13.
60. Chan, *Pentecostal Theology and the Christian Spiritual Tradition*, 41, 78, 51, 52.

is the most natural and regular concomitant of Spirit-filling involving an invasive or irruptive manifestation of the Spirit in which one's relationship to Jesus Christ is radically and significantly altered. When one experiences the coming of the Spirit in such a manner, the most natural and spontaneous response is glossolalia."[61]

Interestingly for present purposes, Chan draws connections between his reconfigurations of initial-evidence logic and the Christian mystical tradition. He believes that glossolalia functions similarly among Pentecostal traditions to the way silence does among Christian mystics. Both tongues and silence relate to an intimacy with God; both seem to configure "gracious and powerful affections," with glossolalia doing so in a distinctively Pentecostal way. He also cites the practice of contemplative prayer in the works of Teresa of Ávila to make similar points related to glossolalia's passivity. But he also wants to include active dimensions, which he sees as part of mystical practice. For this point he draws a correlation between the "three crises/blessings" of Wesleyan Pentecostalism (conversion, sanctification, and Spirit-baptism) and the "three ways" of spiritual progress (purgation, illumination, and union). It is especially important in this presentation that Chan readily admits that, despite these correlations, "the mystical tradition has something vital to contribute to Pentecostalism: in the mystical way the devout soul must pass through the dark night of the soul and spirit between illumination and union. But Pentecostals have no place in their schema for the dark night." Chan associates the need for a "dark night" among Pentecostals, given their penchant to inhabit an overrealized eschatology in relationship to their experiences. Only via a dark night can Pentecostals continue to grow in their spiritual pilgrimage, thereby avoiding becoming settled or overreliant on particular moments in their spiritual lives. Also, the introduction of these "ways," including the dark night, would invite an expansion of what conversion is typically taken to mean by Pentecostals. In this matter, Chan believes, Pentecostals are not aided by their evangelical counterparts: "The problem of the Pentecostal doctrine of subsequence arises precisely because they share a faulty doctrine of conversion with their fellow-evangelicals"[62]—one that assumes a crisis-logic. Chan worries that, for many evangelicals, the idea of spiritual progress is impeded by their soteriological commitments, and

---

61. Chan, *Pentecostal Theology and the Christian Spiritual Tradition*, 57, 58.
62. Chan, *Pentecostal Theology and the Christian Spiritual Tradition*, 58–60, 71, 75, 87.

he sees Pentecostalism as potentially improving on this situation if it is more outright in claiming its affinities with the Christian mystical tradition. In this and many other ways, I believe Chan would be sympathetic to the general claims of the present volume.

Conclusion

This chapter covers quite a bit of terrain, some of it painful to consider. The difficult parts involved deconstructing some myths and assumptions that many American Pentecostals, if they describe their Christian experience with an eye to the past, hold quite dearly. But such work is necessary for the ongoing health of the tradition over time. Some Pentecostals may not have found this work worthwhile, but prominent scholars within the Pentecostal academy have occasionally deemed it necessary. Their intuitions and proposals suggest at least the need for expanding the traditional formulations offered by institutional Pentecostalism.

CHAPTER 5

The Spirit-Baptized Life

I n this final chapter, I further develop these thoughts by contemporary Pentecostal scholars in conversation with some prominent figures from the ancient Christian mystical tradition. On the issue of Spirit-baptism, which is so important to Pentecostal identity, I will argue that Pentecostalism must rely on its character as a mystical tradition within the church catholic so as to perpetuate its identity in a lively and relevant fashion.

The modern-day Pentecostal scholars surveyed in the latter part of chapter 4 operate within traditional Pentecostal frameworks, but they also recognize the need to broaden the typically understood implications of these frameworks. These experts assume the biblically constructed trope of Spirit-baptism to account for what they consider to be a, if not *the*, chief Pentecostal distinctive. They affirm that Spirit-baptism is an encounter with the living God typically subsequent to conversion. And as far as I can tell, they allow initial-evidence logic to stand. Nevertheless, they also sense adjustments are necessary to the received formulations of Spirit-baptism, and therefore they introduce alternative framings or at least significant variations to its conventional doctrinal casting. As important as this sensibility is, one wonders, however, whether the reworking of a preexisting formulation in directions not typically promoted is an activity potentially restricted by the formulation itself. In particular, one wonders about the degree to which they can speak about Spirit-baptism in a way that presses beyond the epistemic constraints endemic to that formulation's shape in classical Pentecostalism. The issue at hand could very well be a dilemma of new wineskins versus old wineskins.

In terms of the present argument, this author does not feel obligated to retain initial-evidence logic. Contrary to Chan, I am not compelled to draw a necessary relationship between tongues and Spirit-baptism, for that approach seems to overburden the conceptual task by requiring some kind of generalizing necessity that has to be true for all people and cases. Following Larry Hurtado's catchy title, I am willing to grant the possibility that the link is "normal" but not necessarily "the norm," given the witnesses of the New Testament and of the church throughout time.[1] But then again, if brought out singularly, this line of thought plays into epistemic concerns once more. Plenty of Pentecostals are concerned to establish how one can know if someone is baptized in the Spirit, in turn drawing a correlation between tongues and Spirit-baptism, but this is not necessarily a salutary starting point. I would even argue that it is not a compelling concern at all. More fundamentally, the Pentecostal tradition must wrestle seriously with the ontological and teleological questions surrounding this theme: What is Spirit-baptism, and what is it for? The overemphasis on identifying cases of Spirit-baptism (i.e., the epistemic concern) might be indicative of something more worrisome, namely, that Pentecostals have not given due diligence to the ontology and teleology of Spirit-baptism. But given the importance of Spirit-baptism for Pentecostal identity, its ontological and teleological dynamics should occupy and substantiate a significant part of Pentecostal pneumatological and soteriological efforts. If one knows what something is and its purpose, its identification certainly will be facilitated as a result; identifying something that is not extensively considered or situated within a broader context is premature and of little long-term consequence. The phenomenon of tongues has a place in these discussions to be sure, but when it is front and center epistemically, as it has usually been within initial-evidence logic, one wonders whether this appropriation is perpetuating and masking a more basic lacuna. Generally put, the empirical availability of tongues may have contributed to a theologically impoverished account of Spirit-baptism among classical Pentecostal American denominations.

In Pentecostal perspective, what is Spirit-baptism, and what is its purpose? The interplay between spirituality and theology is crucial here to consider from the onset. As noted already, when Pentecostals speak of Spirit-baptism, they usually indicate both experiential and doctrinal dimensions. This is the case because Spirit-baptism is best considered in mys-

---

1. See Larry W. Hurtado, "Normal, but Not a Norm: 'Initial Evidence' and the New Testament," in *Initial Evidence: Historical and Biblical Perspectives on the Pentecostal Doctrine of Spirit Baptism*, ed. Gary McGee (Peabody, MA: Hendrickson, 1991), 189–201.

tical categories overall. In terms of Christian spirituality, Spirit-baptism is an encounter with the triune God that is powerful, participatory, and transformative; doctrinally, the way this encounter is talked about must reckon with facilitating and illuminating this kind of encounter, as well as extending its ramifications to various domains, both conceptual and practical. In this light, Spirit-baptism for Pentecostals involves both a mystical encounter and a mystical doctrine that support and critique one another. If Spirit-baptism were a mystical encounter but not a mystical doctrine, then dangers of ineffability, privatization, and interiority come to the fore; if it were only a mystical doctrine without a vibrant sense that it is also a mystical encounter, then speculation, abstraction, and excessive conceptualization could be the end result. The ways one apprehends, experiences, speaks, and thinks of Spirit-baptism are all of a piece. Taken together, these ways will influence the corporate and individual embodiment of the theme. And why is embodiment necessary? The simple answer is that without embodiment, the notion of Spirit-baptism is insignificant. Pentecostals need a working sense of what a Spirit-baptized life looks like and what difference this kind of life makes in the world today, especially if Spirit-baptism is called upon to substantiate and characterize the Pentecostal ethos.

Only after gaining some working sense of its identity can Pentecostals go on to ask: What is the purpose of Spirit-baptism? The answer to this question is similar to other mystical domains of the Christian faith: To show an onlooking world that the God of Christian confession is active through a God-seeking community in reconciling and sanctifying all things in the here and now of ordinary life. Admittedly, this is a broad and by no means exhaustive claim, but one wonders whether anything more hopeful could be said. Spirit-baptism from the Pentecostal point of view and from the ethos of the Christian mystical tradition broadly suggests that God makes a tangible and impactful difference on life as we know it.

As one examines this understanding more closely, one should recognize (in the spirit of the current book) that both a mystical encounter and a mystical doctrine must be considered differently from other proposals. For instance, the goal in their elaboration is not necessarily consistency or coherence. The common qualifier between them, "mystical," points to the limits of conceptualization and verbalization, not for the sake of deconstructive aims per se, but so as to show that something more is at stake than conventional ways of speaking and thinking would allow. The generative, self-revealed mystery that is God is the One who drives this work forward, and for this reason, accounting for this One faithfully and fittingly constitutes the stakes at hand. Obviously, theologizing is valuable, but this *theo*-logical admission puts such work in proper perspective.

The edges and limits of past proposals prove especially helpful for delineating a way forward for this kind of work. The concerns raised by Blumhofer, Macchia, and Chan are important in this regard. That they even dare to pursue an agenda that challenges past proposals shows that they have intuited that more is involved with Spirit-baptism than what typically appears in standard classical Pentecostal accounts. However, the restraints they assume so as to be in line with classical Pentecostalism may in some sense keep them from pressing forward into necessary domains—specifically, of reconstructing Spirit-baptism along the lines of the Christian mystical tradition.

In the rest of this concluding chapter, I highlight some of the areas of concern expressed by these writers, with the aim of linking them to proposals within the great heritage of Christian mysticism. This work is more of an invitation and initiatory gesture than a fully developed account; its aim is to begin a conversation in earnest. But it puts forward this call of identifying Pentecostalism as a mystical tradition of the church catholic by granting scaffolding—a workable structure—with particulars on the table so as to display the kind of efforts that are needed to make the identification all the more secure. Not only would this proposal distinguish Pentecostalism from American forms of evangelicalism, but it would also put it in company with forms of Christianity that have readily been dismissed in the West with the dawning of the modern era—ones that nevertheless have seen a resurgence with the rise of charismatic Christianity in the global South.

A Sweet Journey from Glory to Glory

The tension Blumhofer notes of Pentecostal testimonies involving the *attainment* and the *pursuit* of fullness is a critical one. On the one hand, the first point stresses that the experience of Pentecostals is real, authentic, and in some sense satisfying. With Augustine, Pentecostals would claim that their hearts are restless until they find their rest in God, and that when they encounter God in the eschatological happening they deem to be Spirit-baptism, nothing seems sweeter than the "portion of God" they experience. The language of "tasting" and "feasting" is very appropriate on this score, as Blumhofer points out. Gustation is such an important image because it is attentive to human need—humans have to eat in order to nourish their bodies and so survive, but in eating and tasting, humans can also delight in and simply enjoy these acts. Eating is thus a need, but it can also be a joy. Analogously, "being full in God" is not a bland dynamic. Certainly, it is deeply satisfying in that a basic need is addressed. Jesus himself uses this imagery at various points, such as when he remarks, "I am the bread of life. Whoever comes to me will never be hungry, and whoever believes in me will never be thirsty" (John 6:35). But in tasting and seeing that the Lord is good (see Ps. 34:8), there is a delight involved as well. Eschatologically phrased, this would be an "already" dynamic of foretasting God's manifest glory.

But on the other hand, the experience of God in this life is limited by a number of constraints. One limit is simply the nature of human capacities: there is only so much that humans can accommodate before the presence of the living God. The imagery and language of Isaiah's call narrative in Isaiah 6 is helpful on this score. Standing before God exposes our limits, shortcomings, and failures. In a certain sense, we are an unrighteous people who are graced with the presence of a righteous Lord. Another limit worth pointing out is the nature and dynamics of time and the overall topic of human mutability. Given its fleeting nature and the way our bodies are constrained by it, time poses a challenge with the result that our encounters with God (esp. the spectacular ones that Pentecostals wish to celebrate and highlight as integral to Pentecostal identity) are often short-lived and passing. No one can stand in the heights of spiritual ecstasy for the long term. Things settle down, and ordinary life resumes. And we as humans in time change and are changed by our surroundings and circumstances as well. We are prone to forget, misinterpret, lapse, and so on. These and other constraints point to the gap between the Creator and the creature. This gap is potentially misconstrued or ignored when Christians speak excitedly of their encounters with God, but it nevertheless stands and is ignored only to one's peril. Again, to use eschatological language, one can say of this second sense that it is the "not yet" of a creation groaning for its total redemption, healing, and consummation.

The danger of initial-evidence logic in particular and of crisis-orientations toward religious experience in general is that both tend to attainment/already dynamics. "Do you have the baptism in the Holy Spirit?" is a simple enough question, but it is reductive in many ways. On the logic being sustained presently (and it is one that applies to salvation as well), one could also ask, "Are you *being* baptized in the Holy Spirit?" Unfortunately, that latter wording is highly counterintuitive for Pentecostals, and this is precisely the difficulty before us. The way Pentecostals typically think and speak about Spirit-baptism moves in the direction of attainment, or "already" forms, but Blumhofer and others are well aware of the risks involved. As she notes in particular, strategies are needed in testimonies to counteract them. In her case, Blumhofer points to the paradoxical framing of attainment and pursuit.

This wording is important and relevant in discussions related to the spiritual life, for it is quite easy for Christians at one point or another to think in terms of achievement, accomplishment, and—worst of all—"finishing the course." Pentecostals are especially prone to think this way, given that Spirit-baptism is often understood (at least implicitly) to be the summit of Christian experience. But at the end of the day, this way of putting things is simply untrue, since we continue to live, grow, and struggle in the here and now of our lives. We cannot think of "finishing the course" because we are very much still in the middle of it; the race is not over by a long shot. In spite of or in addition to whatever has occurred in our lives, there is always more to experience and consider, given that we live this side of the eschaton. Earnest, God-seeking Christians ought to claim with the apostle Paul: "Not that I have already obtained this or have already reached the goal, but I press on to make it my own, because Christ Jesus has made me his own. Beloved, I do not consider that I have made it my own, but this one thing I do: forgetting what lies behind and straining forward to what lies ahead, I press on toward the goal for the prize of the heavenly call of God in Christ Jesus" (Phil 3:12–14).

The root of the word that the NRSV translates as "straining forward" (*epekteinomai* and its cognates, including *epektasis*) was significantly developed in the thought of Gregory of Nyssa, a Cappadocian Father and one of the most important ancient Christian mystics. In fact, some scholars of Gregory have labeled this concept a significant touchpoint, if not the central theme, for understanding the Cappadocian's thought on the spiritual life.[2] Given its importance, a number of proposals have been made to account for the idea's significance and originating circumstances in

---

2. As noted by Jean Daniélou, "Introduction," in *From Glory to Glory: Texts from Gregory of Nyssa's Mystical Writings* (Crestwood, NY: St. Vladimir's Seminary Press, 1979), 47. A useful resource for this theme is the article *"Epektasis"* by Lucas Francisco Mateo-Seco, in *The Brill Dictionary of Gregory of Nyssa*, ed. Mateo-Seco and Giulio Maspero (Leiden: Brill, 2010), 263–68.

Gregory's usage.[3] My approach toward Gregory of Nyssa here is similar to that developed by Hans Urs von Balthasar in his own work on the Cappadocian; namely, it involves a selective appropriation of an ancient figure's work for its strategic illumination and application in contemporary circumstances.[4] Thus, the use of Gregory here (and the other ancient figures below) would most certainly not be of the kind historians or even historical theologians would necessarily find favorable. The agenda at hand in this present section is to discover how Gregory can be helpful in illuminating this tension detected between attainment and pursuit within Pentecostal speech related to Spirit-baptism. In Gregory's case, his use of the idea of *epektasis* can be of considerable help; to that end, I cite extensively one of his important works, *The Life of Moses*.

Rather than seeing the limits noted above about the "not yet" dimensions of human existence in a negative light, Gregory seems to approach them positively. One of the first steps in reconfiguring this general assessment in a positive direction is to claim the Creator-creation distinction in a basic, nonnegotiable manner. For Gregory, the creature is always preceded and followed by the Creator, both in the here and now and for eternity. This recognition is the bedrock for a worshipful and doxological orientation, for it is a confession that involves God being recognized as incorporeal, incorruptible, and in fact transcending all characteristics. We as creatures, in contrast, have our source and end in God who gives us life. We are dependent, derivative beings who are corporeal, corruptible, and limited. From this conviction, whatever we go on to say about God, fellow creatures, and their interrelationships will be grounded in this category distinction, one that can be spoken of as a differentiation between an infinite and immutable God and a finite and mutable creation.

Complementing this category difference, Gregory tends to speak of God in terms of the transcendentals, including beauty and goodness, and he also reflects on the soul's desire for these. This framing casts a certain

3. For a brief survey of these debates, see Paul M. Blowers, "Maximus the Confessor, Gregory of Nyssa, and the Concept of 'Perpetual Progress,'" *Vigiliae Christianae* 46 (1992): 151–71.

4. See the insightful reasoning on display in the foreword to his *Presence and Thought: An Essay on the Religious Philosophy of Gregory of Nyssa* (San Francisco: Ignatius, 1995). For a discussion of Balthasar's use of ancient sources, see Brian Daley, "Balthasar's Reading of the Church Fathers," in *Cambridge Companion to Hans Urs von Balthasar*, ed. Edward T. Oakes and David Moss (Cambridge: Cambridge University Press, 2004), 187–206.

kind of dynamic, which is illustrated by Gregory's allegorical use of Moses's ascent up the mountain to see God. In a section of *The Life of Moses* that speaks directly to the theme of *epektasis*, Gregory remarks of Moses, "He shone with glory. And although lifted up through such lofty experiences, he is still unsatisfied in his desire for more. He still thirsts for that with which he constantly filled himself to capacity, and he asks to attain as if he had never partaken, beseeching God to appear to him, not according to his capacity to partake, but according to God's true being." Note that here the point of reference is God's true being and the soul's reaction to it, which cannot help but be in some sense affected by the soul's limits before a limitless God. Gregory continues, "Such an experience seems to me to belong to the soul which loves what is beautiful. Hope always draws the soul from the beauty which is seen to what is beyond, always kindles the desire for the hidden through what is constantly perceived. Therefore, the ardent lover of beauty, although receiving what is always visible as an image of what he desires, yet longs to be filled with the very stamp of the archetype." Gregory concludes his line of the thought by saying, "The munificence of God assented to the fulfillment of his desire, but did not promise any cessation or satiety of the desire." Essentially, Gregory conveys a very specific perspective on the attainment-pursuit paradox noted above, one that is grounded in the mystical qualities of divine-human interaction. "What Moses yearned for," Gregory states, "is satisfied by the very things which leave his desire unsatisfied."[5]

What might be difficult for some to accept in Gregory's proposals is that he sees this desire for God as ongoing, both in this life and in the one to come. For Gregory, "True sight of God consists in this: that the one who looks up to God never ceases in that desire." The difficulty in this framing, of course, relates to the assumption that by being perpetual, this yearning of desire is somehow unaccomplished or futile. Some might feel the need for this paradox to be softened or relieved, but we can see that this example clearly shows the need for a mystical understanding. Gregory sets the tone for his work in this direction early on: "We hold the divine nature to be unlimited and infinite. Certainly, whoever pursues true virtue participates in nothing other than God, because he is himself absolute virtue. Since, then, those who know what is good by nature desire participation in it,

---

5. Gregory of Nyssa, *The Life of Moses*, trans. Abraham Malherbe and Everett Ferguson (New York: Paulist Press, 1978), 114–15; Greek: *Gregorii Nysseni Opera*, vol. 7.1: *De Vita Moysis*, ed. Herbertus Musurillo (Leiden: Brill, 1964), 113–15.

and since this good has no limit, the participant's desire itself necessarily has no stopping place but stretches out with the limitless."[6] The challenge here is not to resolve the paradox but to go ever deeper into it.

This claim of perpetual progression should be acknowledged as a joyful and proper orientation at the heart of Christian perfection. When creatures accept and recognize that their growth is an ongoing conformity to God, they can rest in the reality that God is God (and they are not). Once again, the dynamic is worshipful and awe-inducing, since it is based on the fundamental distinction between Creator and creature. The outcome is not a Sisyphysian circularity of perpetual futility and frustration but rather a kind of spiritual growth that is mystical and worshipful at its core. The matter is not that our limits must somehow be overcome by dedicated discipline on our end; rather, it involves the placement of these limits within the more fundamental reality that is God so that these limits can be channels of unforeseen splendor. Every end or arrival (*peras*) of one dynamic serves as the beginning (*archē*) of another.[7] The Christian life is a perpetual ascent toward God made possible by the bridging descent already extended by Christ.

To conclude, the application of Gregory's elaboration of *epektasis* for our present purposes is its resolve to resist the resolution of the paradox of attainment and pursuit out of an intuited sense of the beauty and expansiveness of the Divine. Such is a mystical sensibility because it will allow for the paradox to stand, a paradox that is driven by the splendor of the Trinity and the proper understanding of the human's creaturely limits. Rather than rationalizing away the tension, Gregory's vision of the Christian life allows for the tension to persist as a way to communicate what it means to be a creature who is created and graced by a good and ever-loving God. To put these claims to work in a Pentecostal idiom, one could say that the Spirit-baptized life is one that lives in an ongoing paradox of attainment and pursuit because its ground and end is the triune God of Christian confession. The Spirit-baptized life is epicletic in nature—it is a way of life that is actively receptive. It is driven by a burning desire that tastes and seeks the goodness of God. This dynamic is implicitly at work in Pentecostal testimonies of various kinds, as Blumhofer duly notes, and it is part of the Pentecostal heritage that needs to be maintained practically and conceptually in the face of the many pressures that naturally come to

6. Gregory of Nyssa, *The Life of Moses*, 115, 31; *De Vita Moysis*, 114, 4.
7. Mateo-Seco, "*Epektasis*," 264.

a renewal movement as it strives to understand itself and to promote its identity publicly.

Steadfastness in the Midst of Spiritual Aridity

Moving on to another of our contemporary Pentecostal scholars, we may recall that Chan cites the need for Pentecostalism to go through a dark night in its theologizing. Of course, Chan is not using this language in a technical sense, that is, in a way coinciding thoroughly and consistently with the vision of St. John of the Cross. Chan's broader aim is to use the metaphor of a dark night so as to prompt Pentecostals on to maturity in their spirituality. This maturity he sees as necessary and vital when Pentecostals are overly fixated with the radical inbreaking of God's Spirit. He likens this tendency to the way people fall in love rather than the way mature lovers engage one another. The first kind of interaction, even if enjoyable in a certain sense, is less seasoned and rich than the second. But more crucial here would be accounting for the challenges that life presents. One could say that dark-night imagery propels one toward spiritual maturity by recognizing the challenge, struggle, and pain that come with the vicissitudes of Christian living. Chan remarks in this light: "Here is where Pentecostalism must be open to the challenge of the mystical tradition. It must recognize that trials and spiritual aridity, even spiritual defeat and desolation, are a part of growth even *after* one's baptism in the Holy Spirit."[8]

Chan wishes to expose an overrealized eschatology as the chief culprit at work in the inability of Pentecostals to see trials and difficulties as part of the Christian life. He believes that, when Pentecostals fixate on signs, miracles, and the like, they lose sight of how Christian existence really is. The spiritual life cannot be a movement from one peak to the next; quite the contrary, "progress in the Christian life may involve many dark nights and many re-fillings of the Spirit, each experienced in greater degree of intensity."[9] Pentecostals may not be forthcoming in claiming this dynamic, for typically their tendency is to emphasize the powerful demonstration of

---

8. Simon Chan, *Pentecostal Theology and the Christian Spiritual Tradition*, Journal of Pentecostal Theology Supplement 21 (Sheffield: Sheffield Academic Press, 2000), 76 (emphasis original).

9. Chan, *Pentecostal Theology and the Christian Spiritual Tradition*, 77.

God's power, the victorious battle against sin, and the manifestation of an awe-inspiring miracle. However, if these are the emphases, what happens when their contraries are very much in evidence? What if the sought miracle does not take place? What if the battle against sin is ongoing? What if God appears to be absent or missing? As Paul Alexander has noted of his own experience, an awkward silence typically ensues in such cases, one quickly filled by counterevidence and countertestimonies.[10] The questions are often dismissed, ignored, or reinterpreted; they cannot be left to stand. Nevertheless, these concerns are valid because they are true to experience. They point to the multifaceted nature of life in general and the Christian spiritual life in particular. Chan mentions Balthasar's theology of "Holy Saturday" in this vein; and we could note the Moltmannian "cry of dereliction."

What would a dark night mean specifically for Pentecostals, especially in light of how they configure Spirit-baptism? I think the metaphor can suggest at least two different but interrelated answers. First, a dark night for Pentecostal accounts of Spirit-baptism would mean a reconfiguration of Pentecostal power. As noted previously, historical accounts of Spirit-baptism often emphasized it as an experience of empowerment for witness. Its utility revolved around evangelism and witness. This understanding is not necessarily problematic, but it is perhaps underdeveloped. In particular, a question is worth asking: What understanding of power is being assumed? Again, the tendency here might draw from an overrealized eschatology: The definition of power could revolve around the manifestation of signs and miracles. Again, this approach is not necessarily wrong, but is this the only account of power available in the description of the Christian life? Furthermore, is this account of power the primary way that Christ showed his own power during his earthly life? Certainly we understand power christomorphically in light of the resurrection, but also important is Christ's life of obedience and submission to the Father's will in a way that leads to the cross. In solidarity with those who have died and continue to die presently for the gospel, one must go on to say that Christian power can be manifested through martyrdom. Few Pentecostal resources are available to emphasize this side of the matter, but without due attention to it, we have to admit that Pentecostal spirituality is deficient in its scope and relevance. A vision for the Spirit-baptized life ought

10. See Paul Alexander, *Signs and Wonders: Why Pentecostalism Is the World's Fastest Growing Faith* (San Francisco: Jossey-Bass, 2009), chap. 1.

to be able to account for how one is to face trials and various forms of spiritual aridity. Although this subject is often neglected, Christians do have resources for this kind of vision when they recognize the manner in which Jesus faced his journey toward Calvary, which demonstrated a form of power that was steadfast, faithful, and holy in the face of persecution, injustice, rejection, and suffering.

As a second point, a dark night for Pentecostal conceptions of Spirit-baptism implies a reconstitution of expectation. Why do Pentecostals tend to have an overrealized eschatology in the first place? Most likely a variety of factors can explain this tendency. Many people are attracted to Pentecostalism, not simply because they come to see the gospel therein, but also because of the appeal of leading a kind of "higher life" with God—one of vitality and energy they had not experienced otherwise. Pentecostal forms of Christianity also appeal to people because they often address specific needs people have, whether spiritual, theological, psychological, social, economic, or physical (among others). And other reasons could be offered as well. Again, these appeals are not necessarily mistaken, but they are shortsighted if Pentecostal identity is substantiated only by them. The New Testament repeatedly urges the church to move into ever deeper and more mature levels of existence, not so as to gain greater benefits but in order to honor God all the more faithfully.

A fundamental concern presents itself at this point: Why would Pentecostals not care to think of spiritual progress broadly and deeply—that is, in terms of both spiritual bounty *and* aridity? For a tradition that emphasizes the Spirit-led life, why would this be such a noticeable oversight? What is it about the dispositions of Pentecostals as they enter and live in the Pentecostal fold that makes this very important feature of any Christian spirituality difficult for them to appreciate? Again, a number of proposals could be readily and relevantly offered, but one dynamic that certainly is on the table is the theme of expectation. Given the way the Pentecostal way of life is typically presented, one cannot help but have a very specific expectation-set about what this life should look like and how it should be embodied.[11]

Chan's general call to consider a dark night in Pentecostalism could be

11. On this score, Chan correlates the "three-crises" logic of Pentecostalism with the "three ways" of spiritual progress highlighted above. The difficulty with such a strategy is that it potentially calcifies expectations for a crisis paradigm, thereby perpetuating particular overrealized expectation sets. The irony is that all of this may be precisely what is in need of being purged and purified in a Pentecostal "dark night" dynamic.

applied to these two features of an overrealized eschatology in Pentecostal spirituality—power and expectation. And to sustain this application, it would be helpful to return to St. John of the Cross and his ruminations in *The Dark Night*. Particularly impressive about this work for our purposes is its emphasis on purification and purging. St. John is interested in showing how God moves souls along from a beginner's level to that of a proficient so that they can go on to perfection or union with God. But in this movement, St. John recognizes the need for growth and increase in strength, which he speaks of in terms of "night" imagery. In a remarkable claim, he states that God places "beginners" (*principiantes*) into the realm of "proficients" (*aprovechantes*) and does so precisely by putting them into the dark night.[12] But why would God be the source of spiritual aridity or darkness?

St. John of the Cross recognizes that there is a delight that comes with the practice of spirituality, one that Pentecostals readily understand. He states, "The soul finds its joy, therefore, in spending lengthy periods at prayer, perhaps even entire nights; its penances are pleasures; its fasts, happiness; and the sacraments and spiritual conversations are its consolations."[13] But put bluntly, along with this satisfying quality, Christian spirituality can also be lived out for ends that are self-benefiting. If the latter is the case, then one is participating in a crude and unrefined state. With this in mind, St. John moves quite quickly to talk of motives: "Since their motivation in their spiritual works and exercises is the consolation and satisfaction they experience in them, and since they have not been conditioned by the arduous struggle of practicing virtue, they possess many faults and imperfections in the discharge of their spiritual activities."[14] In a recognition that is hard to hear but all too true, St. John is willing to claim that the spiritual life can be an occasion for the practice of capital *vices* by those who have little formation and training. These vices include pride,

12. See broadly St. John of the Cross, "The Dark Night," in *The Collected Works of St. John of the Cross*, rev. ed. (Washington, DC: ICS Publications, 1991), 361; Spanish: *Obras de San Juan de la Cruz*, vol. 2: *Subida y Noche Oscura*, ed. P. Silverio de Santa Teresa (Burgos, Spain: El Monte Carmelo, 1929), 365.

13. St. John of the Cross, "The Dark Night," 362; Spanish: "Por tanto, su deleite halla en pasarse grandes ratos en oración, y por ventura las noches enteras; sus gustos son las penitencias; sus contentos los ayunos, y sus consuelos usar de los sacramentos y comunicar en las cosas divinas" (366).

14. St. John of the Cross, "The Dark Night," 362; Spanish: "Porque como son movidos a estas cosas y ejercicios espirituales por el consuelo y gusto que allí halla, y como también ellos no están habilitados por ejercicios de fuerte lucha en las virtudes, acerca de estas sus obras espirituales tienen muchas faltas e imperfecciones" (366).

spiritual avarice, spiritual lust, anger, and spiritual gluttony. In elaborating the last sin in terms of prayer, St. John states that spiritual gluttons "think the whole matter of prayer consists in looking for sensory satisfaction and devotion. They strive to procure this by their own efforts, and tire and weary their heads and their faculties. When they do not get this sensible comfort, they become very disconsolate and think they have done nothing."[15] In many of these reflections, St. John is emphasizing the need that believers have to be refined and shaped by God's work. Yes, there is a delight and enjoyment in the things of God, but these do not necessarily lead to growth and maturation. Quite the contrary. In our current state, these can be manipulated and corrupted without a deliberate attentiveness to God's ongoing presence and work, which would include perfection and sanctification.

How do these reflections relate to the themes of power and expectation? It should be clear that Pentecostal ways of understanding the power of the Spirit-baptized life and their expectations surrounding it can easily devolve into the vices St. John speaks of. When Pentecostals talk about Spirit-baptism, they usually think in very concrete, sensory terms (as their preference for the language of evidence clearly shows). In contrast, St. John's reflections note that the sensory part of the soul is the first that needs purification; this process constitutes simply the first stage or the first dark night of a long process of God shaping a holy, maturing people. The movement "from glory to glory" in his vision includes moments and states of dryness, a reconfiguration of appetites, a lack of empirical "evidence," and so on. The vision of St. John of the Cross is one that tries to be honest about the challenges of the spiritual life in ways that Pentecostals might think constitute a betrayal of their hopeful, expectant identity. One senses a very strong tension here. Can a people be hopeful in the midst of a dark night? Can they imagine power in the form of weakness? Can they be expectant and certain without evidence? This is the kind of challenge Chan envisions when he speaks of Pentecostalism requiring a dark night. It is a formidable and yet appropriate challenge: formidable because it runs so contrarily to many ways Pentecostals feel, think, and process matters in the spiritual life, yet appropriate because the spiritual life does in fact entail

15. St. John of the Cross, "The Dark Night," 372–73; Spanish: "Lo mismo tienen éstos en la oración que ejercitan, que piensan que todo el negocio de ella está en hallar gusto y devoción sensible, y procuran sacarle, como dicen, a fuerza de brazos, cansando y fatigando las potencias y la cabeza; y cuando no han hallado el tal gusto, se desconsuelan mucho pensando que no han hecho nada" (382–83).

moments in which an overrealized eschatology is ultimately not helpful and may be even burdensome to the practice of faithfulness across time.

Ignorance as a Dynamic of Grace

Although taken out of order from our original presentation in chapter 4, the last of the contemporary Pentecostal scholars surveyed here is Frank Macchia. For his part, Macchia's attempts to claim Spirit-baptism generally and tongues in particular as a theophanic sign or sacrament are exceptionally noteworthy. In these proposals, Macchia is trying to broaden the Pentecostal imagination by casting Spirit-baptism and tongues as more than simply phenomena inherent to an ideal Pentecostal worship service. In Macchia's proposals, when people experience Spirit-baptism, they can claim with holy confidence that they have been touched by God. When people speak in tongues, they are not practicing an inherent anthropological capacity but are showing by their very bodies that God is present and at work. Such an event is not fittingly examined in a laboratory; it should not be flippantly considered or talked about. It is a holy event that pushes participants to another domain of awareness and consciousness in relation to God's self-manifestation.

Of course, talk of "God working" or of "God revealing Godself" is difficult in a certain sense. Many rightfully worry about the presumption that can come with such conventions. Some may level this critique at Macchia himself. "How is it possible," the critic may ask, "to use the language of theophany in Pentecostal worship? Is this language not best reserved for those biblical moments that are unique and nonrepeatable, such as Moses's interactions with God at Sinai or Jesus's experience on the Mount of Transfiguration?" As I read Macchia, the use of this language is not presumptive so much as it is constructive so as to communicate faithfully what Pentecostals genuinely believe is at work in their spirituality. Naturally, the language must be guarded for its overreaching or overexhausting effects, but Christians of varying stripes have done so to good effect via a number of strategies, including the dynamic of mediation. Pentecostals may be prone to say they have a direct experience of God, but the preference Macchia demonstrates for the language of sign and sacrament as opposed to evidence indicates that Macchia is implicitly trying to account for mystical dynamics in his theology of Spirit-baptism and glossolalia similar to how other traditions might speak of the Eucharist, baptism, the preached sermon, and other doxological happenings.

How does one guard the language of theophany, sacrament, and sign so that it is not overreaching or overexhausting in relation to the divine presence? With this task in mind, I wish to examine the following claim of Macchia's theology of glossolalia, namely, that the transformation of language can be a channel of divine self-disclosure. How can one conceptualize this dynamic as it relates to the Christian spiritual life and to Spirit-baptism in particular? How can language be used by God in God's self-revelation without somehow the language itself rendering an unfaithful constraint upon God's very self? In some ways, we are back to the question of logo-centricity, which was mentioned as a repeated challenge for evangelicals. Although the critique of logo-centricity has been significantly developed and sustained for centuries, we look briefly for help from one of the towering figures in the background of these debates, the revered and challenging Christian mystic known as Pseudo-Dionysius.

Pseudo-Dionysius is often appealed to for a number of reasons in the current intellectual climate, particularly as it relates to the limits of language and signification. Although these uses are important, they often neglect other themes from the *Corpus Areopagiticum*, which in turn could lead to a misrepresentation or mischaracterization of this sixth-century Syrian figure. For instance, given his reputation, one may be surprised to read this line from the beginning of *The Divine Names*: "Let us therefore look as far upward as the light of sacred scripture will allow, and, in our reverent awe of what is divine, let us be drawn together toward the divine splendor." In this line alone, this author alludes to both a faithfulness to the scriptural testimony in whatever is said of the divine names, as well as a kind of mystical beholding of God's self-revealed glory. These claims should qualify and substantiate what Dionysius is most usually known for, namely, a running sense of how God is beyond our cognitive and perceptual grasp. Just a few lines below this quote, he adds, "Just as the senses can neither grasp nor perceive the things of the mind, just as representation and shape cannot take in the simple and shapeless, just as corporal form cannot lay hold of the intangible and incorporeal, by the same standard of truth beings are surpassed by the infinity beyond being, intelligences by that oneness which is beyond intelligence. Indeed the inscrutable One is out of the reach of every rational process. Nor can any words come up to the inexpressible Good, this One, this Source of all unity, this supra-existent Being."[16]

16. Pseudo-Dionysius, "The Divine Names," in *Pseudo-Dionysius: The Complete*

What is clear in Dionysius that sometimes does not come through in popular presentations of his views is his wish to emphasize a paradox of his own, one that accounts for God's infinity and creaturely limits, and the latter in turn affecting how one goes about speaking and thinking of this dynamic. Indeed, Dionysius argues that, on scriptural grounds, God should be spoken of as invisible, incomprehensible, unsearchable, and inscrutable, but this remark does not mean that a real connection cannot be made between God and creatures. On the contrary, "The Good is not absolutely incommunicable to everything. By itself it generously reveals a firm, transcendent beam, granting enlightenments proportionate to each being, and thereby draws sacred minds upward to its permitted contemplation, to participation and to the state of becoming like it."[17] The goal in this kind of work is not to stress the gap between God and creatures for its own sake; rather, it is to emphasize this gap so that a proper ordering of the relationship can ensue, one that utilizes language while exposing the limits of language all in one continuous movement.[18] Those who embark on this process "are raised firmly and unswervingly upward in the direction of the ray which enlightens them. With a love matching the illuminations granted them, they take flight, reverently, wisely, in all holiness."[19]

It should be noted that Pseudo-Dionysius also works from an implicit eschatology that anticipates union with God. He speaks of a "time to come, when we are incorruptible and immortal, when we have come at last to the blessed inheritance of being like Christ," and he goes on to speculate as to how that situation will be. But in light of this time to come, he also admits of the realities surrounding the present moment. "But as for now," he remarks, "what happens is this. We use whatever appropriate symbols we can for the things of God. With these analogies we are raised upward toward the truth of the mind's vision, a truth which is simple and one."

Works (New York: Paulist Press, 1987), 49–50; Greek: *Corpus Dionysiacum*, vol. 1: *De Divinis Nominibus*, ed. Beate Regina Suchla (Berlin: Walter de Gruyter, 1990), 109.

17. Pseudo-Dionysus, "The Divine Names," 50; *De Divinis Nominibus*, 110.

18. This quality of "negative theology"—that the negation and the affirmation are interpenetrating—is a hermeneutical position required so as to appreciate apophaticism in our current context. I came to appreciate this sensibility via the work of Denys Turner. See, for instance, "The Art of Unknowing: Negative Theology in Late Medieval Mysticism," *Modern Theology* 14, no. 4 (1998): 473–88, and "The Darkness of God and the Light of Christ: Negative Theology and Eucharistic Presence," *Modern Theology* 15, no. 2 (1999): 143–58.

19. Pseudo-Dionysius, "The Divine Names," 50; *De Divinis Nominibus*, 110–11.

The vision Dionysius entertains is one that anticipates union with God as the goal of God-knowledge, and given this goal, one must, on his reading, recognize the limits and shortcomings of speech and representation.

> Truly and supernaturally enlightened after this blessed union, [divinized minds] discover that although it is the cause of everything, it is not a thing since it transcends all things in a manner beyond being. Hence, with regard to the supra-essential being of God—transcendent Goodness transcendently there—no lover of the truth which is above all truth will seek to praise it as word or power or mind or life or being. No. It is a total remove from every condition, movement, life, imagination, conjecture, name, discourse, thought, conception, being, rest, dwelling, unity, limit, infinity, the totality of existence.[20]

What Dionysius does in *The Divine Names* is to critique logo-centricity in a very particular—and I would add, helpful—way.[21] With a guiding vision of how God is both beyond our limits and available within them, he stresses in this work both the fittingness and the shortcomings of divine attribution. In doing so, Dionysius opens the door for apophatic considerations, but these are cast *within* the Christian pilgrimage as it moves alongside the cataphatic. The point of apophaticism in this framing is a reverent beholding of the superabundant, infinite God of Christian confession.[22] Denial and its accompanying ignorance in this vein, therefore, are theologically productive in a certain sense. The recognition that we cannot do justice to God with our words *is itself* a fitting form of worship that is part and parcel to theological speech. Put another way, not just the proximity but the gap in the Creator-creation interface is theologically significant—both are needed, both feed and work off each other, and one without the other represents a move toward idolatry.

I would argue that the unknown quality of glossolalic tongues—those tongues often associated with Spirit-baptism among classical Pentecostals today—points precisely in the direction of this gap. Whereas known tongues (xenolalia) might move closer to the proximity dynamic, glosso-

---

20. Pseudo-Dionysius, "The Divine Names," 52–54; *De Divinis Nominibus*, 114–17.

21. I have purposefully limited myself to *The Divine Names* and not to *The Mystical Theology* (despite its titular connection with the current project) because I find the former to be more nuanced and elaborate in comparison to the latter's brevity and ambiguity.

22. See Pseudo-Dionysius, "The Divine Names," 60; *De Divinis Nominibus*, 125.

lalia moves toward that of distance. All in all, proximity and distance are both needed in talk of Spirit-baptism. Such is also fitting with talk of the-ophany, sacrament, and sign. In all these cases, there needs to be a sense of excess, of superabundance, of an overwhelming dynamic in which God is simply beyond the constraints utilized to make sense of what is taking place. And such is not only fitting but very much needed in accounts of the Spirit-baptized life.

Put directly, Pentecostals need to wrestle with the claim that igno-rance in the spiritual life generally and Spirit-baptism in particular can be a dynamic of grace because the ignorance in question is not vacuous but distance-creating or space-accommodating for the possibility of be-holding uniquely the divine splendor. The Spirit-baptized life trades in holy mysteries. When Pentecostals speak in glossolalic tongues, they do not know what they are saying, and that is very much an appropriate epistemic space to occupy. In some sense, *they do not need to know* what they are saying because what is happening at such moments resists and defies description beyond the surface, since the One at work is infinite, transcendent, and thus beyond words. Pentecostals at various moments implicitly sense this dynamic in their spirituality. For instance, we have already alluded to how Smith speaks of testimonies that have a "I know that I know that I know" quality—they operate out of a certainty principle that runs deeper than conventional forms of cognitive or linguistic affir-mation.[23] But then again, when Pentecostals move from their spirituality to the theological task, the temptation to register their intuitions in a kind of totalizing and corrupting discourse persists. As a case in point, some Pentecostals suggest that these tongues are spiritually edifying, that they encourage the believer, and so on. The danger of such comments is that they signify a benefits orientation toward the Christian life that is in need of a dark-night purging of its own. On the contrary, and first and foremost, glossolalia stands as a phenomenon that points to the superabundance of the God Pentecostals believe they experience in their worship settings. This effulgence, this glory, this radiance simply defies logo-centric pa-rameters. Glossolalia points in this direction, and Pentecostals and others have continually sensed this.

I believe evangelicals of various kinds, in noticing this defiance of logo-centricity within Pentecostalism, have repeatedly been repulsed or

23. James K. A. Smith, *Thinking in Tongues* (Grand Rapids: Eerdmans, 2010), chap. 3.

threatened by it. Pentecostals have been characterized in many unflattering ways by those claimed as kin by some Pentecostals, and those sobriquets have often been in relation to this implicit feature of Pentecostal spirituality. They have been called fanatical, excessive, and innovative. Their spirituality is often deemed incoherent and unruly. Ultimately, all these characterizations, besides being reactive, rest on certain plausibility structures—ones that assume for themselves their own exquisite adequacy for trading in the things of God. Pentecostals, on the contrary, often keep company with what may appear as destabilizing and chaotic happenings, but they do so because of a more basic conviction—one that eludes logocentrists in particular.

The basic conviction is this: when the Spirit of God is witnessed as being poured out on all flesh, this Spirit breaks through the confinements and barriers that are safe in one sense but potentially exclusive, diminishing, and detestable in another. This is a linguistic dynamic to be sure, as pointed out in the phenomenon that is tongues. It is an intellectual dynamic—some things "make sense" to Pentecostals in ways that evangelicals cannot understand (and this ignorance occasions the unflattering characterizations). But it is also a social dynamic. When *in this context* African-Americans and other nonmajority racial and ethnic groups are sometimes used powerfully in a society dominated by Anglo-Saxon privilege or when *in this context* women sometimes manifest gifts of Christian leadership within a society dominated by patriarchy, the eccentricity, the unconventionality, or the distance is celebrated by some quarters today (and detested by others) but, all the same, rarely fully appreciated. These occurrences have taken place, and continue to take place, from time to time in Pentecostal history not because Pentecostals have somehow been ahead of their times. To be sure, they sometimes fail, stumble, and transgress along the way in relation to this intuition. But their desire for a destabilizing God, a God who self-reveals in terms of proximity and distance, sometimes registers itself in other kinds of destabilizations—whether linguistic, intellectual, social, or otherwise. And this destabilization process is nothing short of a fanning of eternal (i.e., godly) desire. The desire for God is what makes Pentecostalism vital and relevant in Christian and non-Christian contexts, past and present. Furthermore, in a generalizing way, this desire involves the many subthemes of this text; it is fundamentally what makes Pentecostalism a Christian mystical tradition within the church catholic.

Postscript

This book stands as a working proposal. Its aim has been to facilitate a theological exercise of rethinking Pentecostalism in light of mystical categories for the sake of deepening the connections of this movement within wider Christianity and also as a way of differentiating it from forms of reasoning typically associated with American evangelicalism. Given the sweeping scope of this aim, I am sure there will be significant resistance to the thesis from a number of quarters and a variety of standpoints. At some level, the debate is warranted. All proposals should be evaluated, critiqued, and assessed. My concern at this stage is whether the arguments presented in the volume will be seen in their context, on their own terms.

I say this in part because I have repeatedly mentioned theological methodology and epistemology as themselves needing a kind of recalibration if they are to be helpful in the present effort, and in my work as an educator, I have readily seen that recalibrating *these domains* is nearly impossible for those already invested in the theological task. Emphasizing the spirituality-theology interface, calling into question the viability of something called systematic theology, rehabilitating the language of mysticism from its unhelpful religious-studies accoutrements to be something more theologically rigorous, stressing the limits of logo-centricity, emphasizing the reductive nature of initial-evidence logic—each of these themes, as well as others in the book, could find an unhappy reception simply because they fly against so much of what passes as conventional and accepted in Pentecostal theological efforts and beyond.

So why dare undertake the task in the first place? First and foremost, the effort stems out of a love for a tradition—one that nourished and shaped me. In fact, my sense of calling as a theologian has always arisen from and returned to this movement. I have tried here to engage the tradition lovingly yet critically for its own well-being. The critiques and reassessments I have offered stem from a genuine concern to see this movement thrive and move forward faithfully across time. This kind of effort represents an activity best termed tradition-negotiation. Anyone who deeply cares about a tradition will undertake such work for the sake of seeing the tradition thrive into the future. This is my most basic orientation in presenting this volume.

Of course, some may find that nothing needs repairing. They might believe that the Pentecostal movement as represented in American Pentecostal denominationalism is fine just as it is. The proposals in this work might therefore seem to such readers as unnecessary, unwarranted, and maybe even excessive and threatening. I admit that, for the arguments in this book to be compelling, there must be some underlying sense on the part of readers that something is askew within the tradition as it has aged—not that the "golden years" have passed per se but that capitulations have been made and opportunities missed, and that, on the whole, these have not been adequately accounted for in a thoroughly theological way within the Pentecostal fold.

Others may say that the Pentecostal movement is so unique and different that it cannot be subsumed into the broader category of Christian mysticism. Interestingly, both insiders and outsiders to the movement could say as much for different reasons. The overall tone of the present book is precisely its experimental character in questioning the assumptions at work that make such an identification difficult or impossible. Are there important characteristics and qualities surrounding Pentecostalism that would make its alignment with the Christian mystical tradition difficult? Of course there are. Christian mysticism, however, is not a uniform tradition—there are unity and diversity in this strand of Christian embodiment, as with any other. I believe there are sufficient confluences between it and Pentecostalism broadly to make a case for their connection, and I have tried to show the warrants for this relationship in the book. Naturally, I am open to counterproposals of varying kinds, but I believe something significant is at stake for making *this particular* connection. The stakes do not simply revolve around Pentecostalism's inner discussions about its own character, but they also concern the way Christianity is narrated as it thrives across the globe in both unexpected and traditional ways. One of the challenges for classical Pentecostals, or "first-wavers," is to see how God has gone on to work in similar yet different ways among established churches, new movements, and indigenous groups. The challenge can be seen as a positive or negative, but I prefer to speak in terms of hope and joy. Why? Because both before and after Pentecost on up to the present day, God's Spirit has been at work in the world. And this is truly a remarkable claim.

Bibliography

Albrecht, Daniel. *Rites in the Spirit: A Ritual Approach to Pentecostal/Charismatic Spirituality.* Journal of Pentecostal Theology Supplement 17. Sheffield: Sheffield Academic Press, 1999.

Alexander, Paul. *Signs and Wonders: Why Pentecostalism Is the World's Fastest Growing Faith.* San Francisco: Jossey-Bass, 2009.

Anderson, Allan H. *An Introduction to Pentecostalism.* 2nd ed. Cambridge: Cambridge University Press, 2014.

Anselm of Canterbury. *The Major Works.* Edited by Brian Davies and G. R. Evans. Oxford: Oxford University Press, 1998. Latin version: *S. Anselmi Cantuariensis Archiepiscopi Opera Omnia.* Edited by Franciscus Salesius Schmitt. 6 vols. Edinburgh: Thomas Nelson & Sons, 1946.

Archer, Kenneth J. *A Pentecostal Hermeneutic: Spirit, Scripture, and Community.* Cleveland, TN: CPT Press, 2009.

Arrington, French L. *Christian Doctrine: A Pentecostal Perspective.* 3 vols. Cleveland, TN: Pathway Press, 1992–94.

Balthasar, Hans Urs von. *Explorations in Theology.* Vol. 1, *The Word Made Flesh.* San Francisco: Ignatius Press, 1989.

———. *Presence and Thought: An Essay on the Religious Philosophy of Gregory of Nyssa.* San Francisco: Ignatius Press, 1995.

Barrett, David, and Todd Johnson. "Global Statistics." In *New International Dictionary of Pentecostal and Charismatic Movements*, edited by Stanley M. Burgess, rev. and exp. ed., 284–302. Grand Rapids: Zondervan, 2003.

Barth, Karl. *Anselm: Fides Quaerens Intellectum.* London: SCM Press, 1960.

———. *Dogmatics in Outline.* New York: Harper & Row, 1959.

———. *Prayer.* 50th anniversary ed. Louisville: Westminster John Knox, 2002.

Bebbington, David W. *Evangelicalism in Modern Britain: A History from the 1730s to the 1980s*. London: Unwin Hyman, 1989.

Blowers, Paul M. "Maximus the Confessor, Gregory of Nyssa, and the Concept of 'Perpetual Progress.'" *Vigiliae Christianae* 46 (1992): 151–71.

Blumhofer, Edith. *"Pentecost in My Soul": Explorations in the Meaning of Pentecostal Experience in the Assemblies of God*. Springfield, MO: Gospel Publishing House, 1989.

Boersma, Hans. *Heavenly Participation: The Weaving of a Sacramental Tapestry*. Grand Rapids: Eerdmans, 2011.

———. *Nouvelle Théologie and Sacramental Ontology: A Return to Mystery*. Oxford: Oxford University Press, 2013.

Boethius. *The Theological Tractates and the Consolation of Philosophy*. Translated by H. F. Stewart, E. K. Rand, and S. J. Tester. Loeb Classical Library 74. Cambridge, MA: Harvard University Press, 1973.

Boyer, Steven D., and Christopher A. Hall. *The Mystery of God: Theology for Knowing the Unknowable*. Grand Rapids: Baker Academic, 2012.

Bozeman, Theodore Dwight. *Protestants in an Age of Science: The Baconian Ideal and Antebellum American Religious Thought*. Chapel Hill: University of North Carolina Press, 1977.

Brumback, Carl. *Suddenly . . . from Heaven: A History of the Assemblies of God*. Springfield, MO: Gospel Publishing House, 1961.

Buber, Martin. *I and Thou*. New York: Touchstone, 1970.

Buckley, James J., and David S. Yeago, eds. *Knowing the Triune God: The Work of the Spirit in the Practices of the Church*. Grand Rapids: Eerdmans, 2001.

Burgess, Stanley. "Evidence of the Spirit: The Ancient and Eastern Churches." In *Initial Evidence: Historical and Biblical Perspectives on the Pentecostal Doctrine of Spirit Baptism*, edited by Gary B. McGee, 3–19. Peabody, MA: Hendrickson, 1991.

Cartledge, Mark J., ed. *Speaking in Tongues: Multi-Disciplinary Perspectives*. Milton Keynes, UK: Paternoster, 2006.

Castelo, Daniel. "An Apologia for Divine Impassibility: Toward Pentecostal Prolegomena." *Journal of Pentecostal Theology* 19, no. 1 (2010): 118–26.

———. *Pneumatology: A Guide for the Perplexed*. London: Bloomsbury T&T Clark, 2015.

———. *Revisioning Pentecostal Ethics—the Epicletic Community*. Cleveland, TN: CPT Press, 2012.

Chan, Simon. *Pentecostal Theology and the Christian Spiritual Tradition*. Journal of Pentecostal Theology Supplement 21. Sheffield: Sheffield Academic Press, 2000.

Charry, Ellen T. *By the Renewing of Your Minds: The Pastoral Function of Christian Doctrine*. Oxford: Oxford University Press, 1997.

Coakley, Sarah. *God, Sexuality, and the Self: An Essay "On the Trinity."* Cambridge: Cambridge University Press, 2013.

Copleston, Frederick. *A History of Philosophy.* Vol. 2, *Medieval Philosophy.* New York: Image Doubleday, 1993.

Coulter, Dale. "What Meaneth This? Pentecostals and Theological Inquiry." *Journal of Pentecostal Theology* 10, no. 1 (2001): 38–64.

Cox, Harvey. *Fire from Heaven: The Rise of Pentecostal Spirituality and the Reshaping of Religion in the Twenty-First Century.* Reading, MA: Addison-Wesley, 1995.

Cross, Terry L. "Can There Be a Pentecostal Systematic Theology? An Essay on Theological Method in a Postmodern World." Paper presented at the Thirtieth Annual Meeting of the Society for Pentecostal Studies, 2011; pagination (145–66) from the collected papers of the conference.

———. "The Rich Feast of Theology: Can Pentecostals Bring the Main Course or Only the Relish?" *Journal of Pentecostal Theology* 8, no. 16 (2000): 27–47.

Dabney, D. Lyle. "Otherwise Engaged in the Spirit: A First Theology for a Twenty-First Century." In *The Future of Theology: Essays in Honor of Jürgen Moltmann*, edited by Miroslav Volf, Carmen Krieg, and Thomas Kucharz, 154–63. Grand Rapids: Eerdmans, 1996.

———. "Why Should the Last Be First? The Priority of Pneumatology in Recent Theological Discussion." In *Advents of the Spirit: An Introduction to the Current Study of Pneumatology*, edited by Bradford E. Hinze and D. Lyle Dabney, 240–61. Milwaukee, WI: Marquette University Press, 2001.

Daley, Brian. "Balthasar's Reading of the Church Fathers." In *Cambridge Companion to Hans Urs von Balthasar*, edited by Edward T. Oakes and David Moss, 187–206. Cambridge: Cambridge University Press, 2004.

Dawson, David. *Literary Theory: Guides to Theological Inquiry.* Minneapolis: Fortress, 1995.

Dayton, Donald. "The Limits of Evangelicalism: The Pentecostal Tradition." In *The Variety of American Evangelicalism*, edited by Donald W. Dayton and Robert K. Johnston, 36–56. Downers Grove, IL: InterVarsity, 1991.

———. *Theological Roots of Pentecostalism.* Peabody, MA: Hendrickson, 1987.

Deere, Jack S. *Surprised by the Power of the Spirit.* Grand Rapids: Zondervan, 1993.

Ellington, Scott. "Pentecostalism and the Authority of Scripture." *Journal of Pentecostal Theology* 4, no. 9 (1996): 16–38.

Ervin, Howard M. "Hermeneutics: A Pentecostal Option." *Pneuma* 3, no. 2 (1981): 11–25.

Evagrius. *On Prayer.* In *The Philokalia*, edited and translated by G. E. H. Palmer, Philip Sherrard, and Kallistos Ware, 1:55–71. New York: Faber & Faber, 1979.

Ewart, Frank J. *The Phenomenon of Pentecost.* Houston: Herald Publishing, 1947.

Fee, Gordon. *Gospel and Spirit: Issues in New Testament Hermeneutics*. Peabody, MA: Hendrickson, 1991.

———. "Hermeneutics and Historical Precedent—a Major Problem in Pentecostal Hermeneutics." In *Perspectives on the New Pentecostalism*, edited by Russell P. Spittler, 118–32. Grand Rapids: Baker, 1976.

Florovsky, Georges. *Bible, Church, Tradition: An Eastern Orthodox View*. Belmont, MA: Nordland Publishing, 1972.

Ford, David F., and Graham Stanton, eds. *Reading Texts, Seeking Wisdom*. Grand Rapids: Eerdmans, 2003.

Friesen, Aaron T. *Norming the Abnormal: The Development and Function of the Doctrine of Initial Evidence in Classical Pentecostalism*. Eugene, OR: Pickwick Publications, 2013.

Gadamer, Hans-Georg. *Truth and Method*. 2nd rev. ed. London: Continuum, 1989.

Gilson, Etienne. *History of Christian Philosophy in the Middle Ages*. New York: Random House, 1955.

Goff, James R., Jr. *Fields White unto Harvest*. Fayetteville: University of Arkansas Press, 1988.

Goldberg, Michael. *Theology and Narrative*. Nashville: Abingdon, 1982.

Green, Chris E. W. *Toward a Pentecostal Theology of the Lord's Supper: Foretasting the Kingdom*. Cleveland, TN: CPT Press, 2012.

Green, Joel. *Practicing Theological Interpretation: Engaging Biblical Texts for Faith and Formation*. Grand Rapids: Baker Academic, 2011.

Gregory of Nyssa. *From Glory to Glory: Texts from Gregory of Nyssa's Mystical Writings*. Crestwood, NY: St. Vladimir's Seminary Press, 1979.

———. *The Life of Moses*. Translated by Abraham Malherbe and Everett Ferguson. New York: Paulist Press, 1978. Greek: *Gregorii Nysseni Opera*. Vol. 7.1, *De Vita Moysis*. Edited by Herbertus Musurillo. Leiden: Brill, 1964.

Grenz, Stanley. *Renewing the Center: Evangelical Theology in a Post-Theological Era*. 2nd ed. Grand Rapids: Baker Academic, 2006.

———. *Revisioning Evangelical Theology: A Fresh Agenda for the Twenty-First Century*. Downers Grove, IL: InterVarsity, 1993.

———. *Theology for the Community of God*. Grand Rapids: Eerdmans, 2000.

Grenz, Stanley, and John R. Franke. *Beyond Foundationalism: Shaping Theology in a Postmodern Context*. Louisville: Westminster John Knox, 2001.

Grudem, Wayne. *Systematic Theology: An Introduction to Biblical Doctrine*. Grand Rapids: Zondervan, 1994.

Gunton, Colin. "A Rose by Any Other Name? From 'Christian Doctrine' to 'Systematic Theology.'" *International Journal of Systematic Theology* 1, no. 1 (1999): 4–23.

Guyon, Madame. *Jeanne Guyon: Selected Writings*. Edited by Dianne Guenin-Lelle and Ronney Mourad. New York: Paulist Press, 2012. French: *Les Opuscules Spirituels de Madame J. M. B. de la Mothe-Guyon*. New ed. Paris: Libraires Associés, 1790.

Hart, Larry D. *Truth Aflame: Theology for the Church in Renewal*. Grand Rapids: Zondervan, 2005.

Henry, Carl F. H. *God, Revelation, and Authority*. Vol. 1. Waco, TX: Word, 1976.

———. *The Uneasy Conscience of Modern Fundamentalism*. Grand Rapids: Eerdmans, 1947.

Hodge, A. A., and B. B. Warfield. "Inspiration." *Presbyterian Review* 2, no. 6 (1881): 225–60.

Hodge, Charles. *Systematic Theology*. 3 vols. Peabody, MA: Hendrickson, 2003.

Hollenweger, Walter. "The Critical Tradition of Pentecostalism." *Journal of Pentecostal Theology* 1 (1992): 7–17.

———. "Pentecostals and the Charismatic Movement." In *The Study of Spirituality*, edited by Cheslyn Jones, Geoffrey Wainwright, and Edward Yarnold, 549–54. Oxford: Oxford University Press, 1986.

Horton, Stanley M. *Systematic Theology: A Pentecostal Perspective*. Springfield, KY: Logion, 1995.

Hurtado, Larry W. "Normal, but Not a Norm: 'Initial Evidence' and the New Testament." In *Initial Evidence: Historical and Biblical Perspectives on the Pentecostal Doctrine of Spirit Baptism*, edited by Gary B. McGee, 189–201. Peabody, MA: Hendrickson, 1991.

Hütter, Reinhard. *Suffering Divine Things: Theology as Church Practice*. Grand Rapids: Eerdmans, 2000.

Irenaeus of Lyons, St. *On the Apostolic Preaching*. Translated by John Behr. Crestwood, NY: St. Vladimir's Seminary Press, 1997.

Jacobsen, Douglas. *Thinking in the Spirit: Theologies of the Early Pentecostal Movement*. Bloomington: Indiana University Press, 2003.

Jenkins, Philip. *The Next Christendom: The Coming of Global Christianity*. Rev. and exp. ed. Oxford: Oxford University Press, 2007.

John of the Cross. *The Collected Works of St. John of the Cross*. Rev. ed. Washington, DC: ICS Publications, 1991. Spanish: *Obras de San Juan de la Cruz*. Edited by P. Silverio de Santa Teresa. Burgos, Spain: El Monte Carmelo, 1929.

Johns, Cheryl Bridges. "The Adolescence of Pentecostalism: In Search of a Legitimate Sectarian Identity." *Pneuma* 17, no. 1 (1995): 3–17.

———. "Partners in Scandal: Wesleyan and Pentecostal Scholarship." *Pneuma* 21 (1999): 183–97.

Johns, Jackie David. "Pentecostalism and the Postmodern Worldview." *Journal of Pentecostal Theology* 3, no. 7 (1995): 73–96.

Johns, Jackie David, and Cheryl Bridges Johns. "Yielding to the Spirit: A Pentecostal Approach to Group Bible Study." *Journal of Pentecostal Theology* 1 (1992): 109–34.

Jones, Cheslyn, Geoffrey Wainwright, and Edward Yarnold, eds. *The Study of Spirituality*. Oxford: Oxford University Press, 1986.

Kärkkäinen, Veli-Matti. *Toward a Pneumatological Theology: Pentecostal and Ecumenical Perspectives on Ecclesiology, Soteriology, and Theology of Mission*. Edited by Amos Yong. Lanham, MD: University Press of America, 2002.

Kendrick, Klaude. *The Promise Fulfilled: A History of the Modern Pentecostal Movement*. Springfield, MO: Gospel Publishing House, 1961.

Kerr, D. W. "The Bible Evidence of the Baptism with the Holy Ghost." *Pentecostal Evangel*, August 11, 1923, 2–3.

Knight, Henry H., III. "The Wesleyan, Holiness, and Pentecostal Family." In *From Aldersgate to Azusa Street: Wesleyan, Holiness, and Pentecostal Visions of the New Creation*, edited by Henry H. Knight III, 1–9. Eugene, OR: Pickwick Publications, 2010.

Laird, Martin. "'Whereof We Speak': Gregory of Nyssa, Jean-Luc Marion, and the Current Apophatic Rage." *Heythrop Journal* 42 (2001): 1–12.

Land, Steven J. *Pentecostal Spirituality: A Passion for the Kingdom*. Journal of Pentecostal Theology Supplement 1. Sheffield: Sheffield Academic Press, 1993.

Lindbeck, George. *The Nature of Doctrine*. Philadelphia: Westminster, 1984.

Lindsell, Harold. *The Battle for the Bible*. Grand Rapids: Zondervan, 1976.

———. *The Bible in the Balance*. Grand Rapids: Zondervan, 1979.

Lossky, Vladimir. *The Mystical Theology of the Eastern Church*. Crestwood, NY: St. Vladimir's Seminary Press, 2002.

Louth, Andrew. *The Origins of the Christian Mystical Tradition: From Plato to Denys*. Oxford: Clarendon, 1981.

———. *Theology and Spirituality*. Oxford: SLG Press, 1978.

Lyotard, Jean-François. *The Postmodern Condition: A Report on Knowledge*. Minneapolis: University of Minnesota Press, 1984.

Macchia, Frank D. *Baptized in the Spirit: A Global Pentecostal Theology*. Grand Rapids: Zondervan, 2006.

———. "Sighs Too Deep for Words: Towards a Theology of Glossolalia." *Journal of Pentecostal Theology* 1 (1992): 47–73.

———. "Tongues as a Sign: Towards a Sacramental Understanding of Pentecostal Experience." *Pneuma* 15, no. 1 (1993): 61–76.

Marsden, George. "From Fundamentalism to Evangelicalism: A Historical Analysis." In *The Evangelicals: What They Believe, Who They Are, Where They Are*

Changing, edited by David F. Wells and John D. Woodbridge, rev. ed., 142–62. Grand Rapids: Baker, 1977.

———. *Fundamentalism and American Culture*. 2nd ed. Oxford: Oxford University Press, 2006.

———. *Reforming Fundamentalism: Fuller Seminary and the New Evangelicalism*. Grand Rapids: Eerdmans, 1987.

———. *Understanding Fundamentalism and Evangelicalism*. Grand Rapids: Eerdmans, 1991.

———, ed. *Evangelicalism and Modern America*. Grand Rapids: Eerdmans, 1984.

Martin, David. *Pentecostalism: The World Their Parish*. Oxford: Blackwell, 2002.

Mateo-Seco, Lucas Francisco. "*Epektasis.*" In *The Brill Dictionary of Gregory of Nyssa*, edited by Lucas Francisco Mateo-Seco and Giulio Maspero, 263–68. Leiden: Brill, 2010.

May, Henry F. *The Enlightenment in America*. New York: Oxford University Press, 1976.

McCabe, Herbert. *God and Evil in the Theology of St. Thomas Aquinas*. New York: Continuum, 2010.

McFarland, Ian A. *From Nothing: A Theology of Creation*. Louisville: Westminster John Knox, 2014.

McGee, Gary, ed. *Initial Evidence: Historical and Biblical Perspectives on the Pentecostal Doctrine of Spirit Baptism*. Peabody, MA: Hendrickson, 1991.

McGinn, Bernard. *The Foundations of Mysticism: Origins to the Fifth Century*. New York: Crossroad, 1991.

McIntosh, Mark A. *Mystical Theology*. Malden, MA: Blackwell, 1998.

McKay, John. "When the Veil Is Taken Away: The Impact of Prophetic Experience on Biblical Interpretation." *Journal of Pentecostal Theology* 2, no. 5 (1994): 17–40.

Migliore, Daniel. *Faith Seeking Understanding: An Introduction to Christian Theology*. Grand Rapids: Eerdmans, 1991.

Mills, Watson E., ed. *Speaking in Tongues: A Guide to Research on Glossolalia*. Grand Rapids: Eerdmans, 1986.

Moore, Rickie D. "A Pentecostal Approach to Scripture." In *Pentecostal Hermeneutics: A Reader*, edited by Lee Roy Martin, 11–13. Leiden: Brill, 2013.

Myland, D. Wesley. *The Latter Rain Covenant and Pentecostal Power*. Reprinted in *Three Early Pentecostal Tracts*. New York: Garland, 1985.

Nichol, John Thomas. *Pentecostalism*. New York: Harper & Row, 1966.

Noll, Mark A. *Jesus Christ and the Life of the Mind*. Grand Rapids: Eerdmans, 2011.

———. *The Scandal of the Evangelical Mind*. Grand Rapids: Eerdmans, 1994.

———, ed. *The Princeton Theology, 1812–1921*. Grand Rapids: Baker, 1983.

Oliverio, L. William, Jr. *Theological Hermeneutics in the Classical Pentecostal Tradition: A Typological Account.* Leiden: Brill, 2012.

Origen. *On First Principles.* In *Ante-Nicene Fathers,* vol. 4. Peabody, MA: Hendrickson, 2004.

Otto, Rudolf. *Mysticism East and West: A Comparative Analysis of the Nature of Mysticism.* Wheaton, IL: Theosophical Publishing House, 1987.

Parham, Charles. *The Everlasting Gospel.* Pentecostal Books.com, 2013. Orig. pub. 1911.

Parham, Sarah E. *The Life of Charles Parham: Founder of the Apostolic Faith Movement.* Reprinted New York: Garland, 1985.

Pearlman, Myer. *Knowing the Doctrines of the Bible.* Springfield, MO: Gospel Publishing House, 1937.

Pieper, Josef. *Scholasticism: Personalities and Problems of Medieval Philosophy.* New York: McGraw Hill, 1964.

Pinnock, Clark H. "Divine Relationality: A Pentecostal Contribution to the Doctrine of God." *Journal of Pentecostal Theology* 8, no. 16 (2000): 3–26.

———. *Flame of Love: A Theology of the Holy Spirit.* Downers Grove, IL: InterVarsity, 1996.

———. *Tracking the Maze: Finding Our Way through Modern Theology from an Evangelical Perspective.* San Francisco: Harper & Row, 1990.

Plüss, Jean-Daniel. "Azusa and Other Myths: The Long and Winding Road from Experience to Stated Belief and Back Again." *Pneuma* 15, no. 2 (1993): 189–201.

Poloma, Margaret M. *Main Street Mystics: The Toronto Blessing and Reviving Pentecostalism.* Lanham, MD: Altamira Press, 2003.

Pseudo-Dionysius. *Pseudo-Dionysius: The Complete Works.* New York: Paulist Press, 1987. Greek: *Corpus Dionysiacum.* Vol. 1, *De Divinis Nominibus.* Edited by Beate Regina Suchla. Berlin: Walter de Gruyter, 1990.

Quebedeaux, Richard. *The Young Evangelicals: The Story of the Emergence of a New Generation of Evangelicals.* San Francisco: Harper & Row, 1974.

Rae, Murray. *Kierkegaard's Vision of the Incarnation.* Oxford: Clarendon, 1997.

Ramm, Bernard L. *The Evangelical Heritage.* Waco, TX: Word Books, 1973.

Rescher, Nicholas. *Cognitive Systematization: A Systems-Theoretic Approach to a Coherentist Theory of Knowledge.* Totowa, NJ: Rowman & Littlefield, 1979.

Saliers, Don. *Worship as Theology: Foretaste of Glory Divine.* Nashville: Abingdon, 1994.

Sandeen, Ernest R. *The Roots of Fundamentalism: British and American Millenarianism, 1800–1930.* Grand Rapids: Baker, 1978.

Shuman, Joel. "Toward a Cultural-Linguistic Account of the Pentecostal Doctrine of the Baptism of the Holy Spirit." *Pneuma* 19, no. 2 (1997): 207–23.

Sloan, Douglas. *The Scottish Enlightenment and the American College Ideal.* New York: Teachers College Press, 1971.

Smith, James K. A. "The Closing of the Book: Pentecostals, Evangelicals, and the Sacred Writings." *Journal of Pentecostal Theology* 5, no. 11 (1997): 49–71.

———. *Desiring the Kingdom: Worship, Worldview, and Cultural Formation.* Grand Rapids: Baker Academic, 2009.

———. "Scandalizing Theology: A Pentecostal Response to Noll's Scandal." *Pneuma* 19 (1997): 225–38.

———. *Speech and Theology: Language and the Logic of Incarnation.* London: Routledge, 2002.

———. *Thinking in Tongues: Pentecostal Contributions to Christian Philosophy.* Grand Rapids: Eerdmans, 2010.

———. *Who's Afraid of Postmodernism? Taking Derrida, Lyotard, and Foucault to Church.* Grand Rapids: Baker Academic, 2006.

Springstead, Eric O. "Theology and Spirituality; or, Why Theology Is Not Critical Reflection on Religious Experience." In *Spirituality and Theology: Essays in Honor of Diogenes Allen,* edited by Eric O. Springstead, 49–62. Louisville: Westminster John Knox, 1998.

Stephenson, Christopher A. *Types of Pentecostal Theology: Method, System, Spirit.* Oxford: Oxford University Press, 2013.

Stolz, A. "Zur Theologie Anselms im *Proslogion.*" *Catholica* 2 (1933): 1–24.

Surin, Kenneth. "'A Politics of Speech': Religious Pluralism in the Age of the McDonald's Hamburger." In *Christian Uniqueness Reconsidered: The Myth of a Pluralistic Theology of Religions,* edited by Gavin D'Costa, 192–212. Maryknoll, NY: Orbis Books, 1990.

Synan, Vinson. *The Holiness-Pentecostal Tradition: Charismatic Movements in the Twentieth Century.* Grand Rapids: Eerdmans, 1997.

Tanner, Kathryn. *God and Creation in Christian Theology.* Minneapolis: Fortress, 1988.

Taylor, G. F. *The Spirit and the Bride.* No location, 1907. Reprinted in *Three Early Pentecostal Tracts.* New York: Garland, 1985.

Teresa of Ávila. *The Life of Teresa of Jesus: The Autobiography of Teresa of Avila.* Translated and edited by E. Allison Peers. Garden City, NY: Doubleday Image Books, 1960. Spanish: *Obras de Sta Teresa de Jesús.* Edited by P. Silverio de Santa Teresa. Burgos, Spain: Monte Carmelo, 1915.

Thomas, John Christopher. "Editorial." *Journal of Pentecostal Theology* 18, no. 1 (2009): 2–3.

———. "Pentecostal Theology in the Twenty-First Century." *Pneuma* 20 (1998): 3–19.

Tomlinson, Dave. *The Post-Evangelical*. Rev. North American ed. Grand Rapids: Zondervan, 2003.

Torrey, R. A. *The Baptism with the Holy Spirit*. New York: Fleming H. Revell, 1897.

———. *The Holy Spirit: Who He Is and What He Does*. Old Tappan, NJ: Fleming H. Revell, 1927.

Turner, Denys. "The Art of Unknowing: Negative Theology in Late Medieval Mysticism." *Modern Theology* 14, no. 4 (1998): 473–88.

———. "The Darkness of God and the Light of Christ: Negative Theology and Eucharistic Presence." *Modern Theology* 15, no. 2 (1999): 143–58.

Volf, Miroslav, and Dorothy Bass, eds. *Practicing Theology: Beliefs and Practices in Christian Life*. Grand Rapids: Eerdmans, 2002.

Wacker, Grant. *Heaven Below: Early Pentecostals and American Culture*. Cambridge, MA: Harvard University Press, 2001.

Wariboko, Nimi. "*Fire from Heaven*: Pentecostals in the Secular City." *Pneuma* 33, no. 3 (2011): 391–408.

Warrington, Keith. *Pentecostal Theology: A Theology of Encounter*. London: T&T Clark, 2008.

Webber, Robert E. *The Younger Evangelicals*. Grand Rapids: Baker, 2002.

Weber, Timothy P. "Fundamentalism Twice Removed: The Emergence and Shape of Progressive Evangelicalism." In *New Dimensions in American Religious History*, edited by Jay P. Dolan and James P. Wind, 261–87. Grand Rapids: Eerdmans, 1993.

Williams, Ernest S. *Systematic Theology*. 3 vols. Springfield, MO: Gospel Publishing House, 1953.

Williams, J. Rodman. *Renewal Theology: Systematic Theology from a Charismatic Perspective*. 3 vols. Grand Rapids: Zondervan, 1996.

Williams, Rowan. *The Wound of Knowledge: Christian Spirituality from the New Testament to Saint John of the Cross*. Rev. ed. London: Darton, Longman, & Todd, 1990.

Wirzba, Norman. "The Art of Creaturely Life: A Question of Human Propriety." *Pro Ecclesia* 22, no. 1 (2013): 7–28.

Yong, Amos. *Renewing Christian Theology: Systematics for a Global Christianity*. Waco, TX: Baylor University Press, 2014.

———. *Spirit-Word-Community*. Eugene, OR: Wipf & Stock, 2002.

———. "Whither Systematic Theology? A Systematician Chimes In on a Scandalous Conversation." *Pneuma* 20 (1998): 85–93.

Index

Printed in the USA
CPSIA information can be obtained
at www.ICGtesting.com
LVHW091054191223
766888LV00007B/75